HUMAN RESOURCE DEVELOPMENT AND INFORMATION TECHNOLOGY
Making Global Connections

Sponsored by

OPERATIONS RESEARCH/COMPUTER SCIENCE INTERFACES SERIES

Series Editors

Professor Ramesh Sharda
Oklahoma State University

Prof. Dr. Stefan Voß
Technische Universität Braunschweig

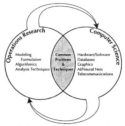

Other published titles in the series:

Greenberg, Harvey J. / *A Computer-Assisted Analysis System for Mathematical Programming Models and Solutions: A User's Guide for ANALYZE*

Greenberg, Harvey J. / *Modeling by Object-Driven Linear Elemental Relations: A Users Guide for MODLER*

Brown, Donald/Scherer, William T. / *Intelligent Scheduling Systems*

Nash, Stephen G./Sofer, Ariela / *The Impact of Emerging Technologies on Computer Science & Operations Research*

Barth, Peter / *Logic-Based 0-1 Constraint Programming*

Jones, Christopher V. / *Visualization and Optimization*

Barr, Richard S./ Helgason, Richard V./ Kennington, Jeffery L. / *Interfaces in Computer Science & Operations Research: Advances in Metaheuristics, Optimization, and Stochastic Modeling Technologies*

Ellacott, Stephen W./ Mason, John C./ Anderson, Iain J. / *Mathematics of Neural Networks: Models, Algorithms & Applications*

Woodruff, David L. / *Advances in Computational & Stochastic Optimization, Logic Programming, and Heuristic Search*

Klein, Robert / *Scheduling of Resource-Constrained Projects*

Bierwirth, Christian / *Adaptive Search and the Management of Logistics Systems*

Laguna, Manuel / González-Velarde, José Luis / *Computing Tools for Modeling, Optimization and Simulation*

Stilman, Boris / *Linguistic Geometry: From Search to Construction*

Sakawa, Masatoshi / *Genetic Algorithms and Fuzzy Multiobjective Optimization*

Ribeiro, Celso C./ Hansen, Pierre / *Essays and Surveys in Metaheuristics*

Holsapple, Clyde/ Jacob, Varghese / Rao, H. R. / *BUSINESS MODELLING: Multidisciplinary Approaches — Economics, Operational and Information Systems Perspectives*

HUMAN RESOURCE DEVELOPMENT AND INFORMATION TECHNOLOGY
Making Global Connections

Edited By

Catherine M. SLEEZER
Oklahoma State University,
Stillwater, Oklahoma, USA

Tim L. WENTLING
University of Illinois
Champaign, Illinois, USA

Roger L. CUDE
McLeodUSA
Cedar Rapids, Iowa, USA

SLEEZER, CM C

KLUWER ACADEMIC PUBLISHERS
Boston/Dordrecht/London

Distributors for North, Central and South America:
Kluwer Academic Publishers
101 Philip Drive
Assinippi Park
Norwell, Massachusetts 02061 USA
Telephone (781) 871-6600
Fax (781) 871-6528
E-Mail <kluwer@wkap.com>

Distributors for all other countries:
Kluwer Academic Publishers Group
Distribution Centre
Post Office Box 322
3300 AH Dordrecht, THE NETHERLANDS
Telephone 31 78 6392 392
Fax 31 78 6546 474
     E-Mail <orderdept@wkap.nl>

 Electronic Services <http://www.wkap.nl>

Library of Congress Cataloging-in-Publication Data

A C.I.P. Catalogue record for this book is available from
the Library of Congress.

Printed on acid-free paper.

Printed in the United States of America

Contents

Technology Pre-Conference Committee

Loretta L. Donovan	Chair
Catherine Sleezer	Pre-conference co-chair
Tim L. Wentling	Pre-conference co-chair
Roger Cude	Pre-conference co-chair
Larry Dooley	Board representative
Claudia C. Hill	
Arthur Johnson	
James Kirk	
Ramesh Sharda	
Brenda Solomon	

Technology Pre-Conference Participants

Sue Abbey	Nicholas Romano
Daniel Alexander	Darlene Russ-Eft
Carson R. Arnett	Barry K. Sanford
Ross E. Azevedo	George Scheets
John W. Bing	Kimberly Shaw
Rose Bonjour	Susan Stansberry
Mike A Boyle	Kathryn Statham
Hsin-Chih Chen	Mark Van Buren
Jason Greer	William R. Venable
Ruth King	Anders Vind
James J. Kirk	Minjuan Wang
Diane Knights	Pei-ru Wang
Peni Mungania	Debbie A. Watson
Carolyn Rude Parkins	Saundra Wall Williams
Jennifer Peacock	Chris Woodard
Marie Phillips	Sheryl Zumwalt
Nicholas Romano	

PREFACE

Technology, people, e-workplaces. In today's fast-paced environment, people race to meet changing customer and market requirements by using technology to invent new business processes, to re-align organizational structures, and to institute contemporary management practices. Moreover, in a global information economy where gaining access to capital, finding ways to pay for technologies, and purchasing physical assets have lost much of their importance as sources of competitive advantage, human talent is fast becoming *the* primary scarce resource that distinguishes market leaders from everyone else. Countries, communities, and organizations are all suddenly very interested in developing the human capacities that will allow them to compete in a networked world. It is not surprising that decision-makers have moved the development of information technology and human resources front and center. Further, the advances in technology that have galvanized

> *Decision-makers have moved the development of information technology and human resources front and center.*

the laser-like focus on human talent are the same advances that are being used to create new strategies for assessing, developing, and managing a workforce that meets the new workplace requirements.

To be most effective in the e-workplace, decision makers and human resource professionals must grasp the pertinent aspects of both people and technology issues. These issues occur at the intersection of such disciplines as computer science, operation research, and human resource development. Because these issues are complex, we, the book editors, believe they can best be understood through cross-disciplinary collaboration among experts who approach them from a range of perspectives. Their collaboration can produce useful views and potential solutions. The intent of this book is to present the results of just such a collaborative effort.

Our approach involved several key activities:

Identify leaders in various fields

1. Host a pre-conference as part of the Academy of Human Resource Development (AHRD) Annual Conference
2. Engage in dialogue on the issues, the research, and the ideas
3. Coordinate the writing of a range of papers
4. Encourage an exchange of timely and useful commentary on the papers
1. Publish the papers for widespread distribution

We invited experts and leaders from various fields to join us in examining HRD in a Networked World. We asked them to share recent research and their latest thinking on the topic. Those who accepted our invitation represented a broad range of perspectives: scholars from such academic disciplines as human resource development, management, computer science, adult learning, education technology, and management information systems; leaders in such professional associations as the Academy of Human Resource Development, the National Alliance of Business, and the American Society of Training and Development (ASTD); practitioners from business, government, and education; consultants with major firms; and a writer of best-selling fiction. Those who accepted had expertise that they had gained from studying the data, facts and information of using IT to change an aspect of how people accomplish work. They also had expertise they had gained from putting their "know about" knowledge to use through practice. They had "know how" expertise.

We hosted the 2001 Technology Pre-Conference of the Academy of Human Resource Development at Williams Learning Center, a woodland retreat near Tulsa, Oklahoma. We had a relatively ambiguous road map to guide the event and wondered what adventures we would have.

No need to wonder. The first presenter had us hanging on his words. We took notes, and interacted by asking insightful questions and receiving

The final presenter captured the energy and spirit of this successful event by taking us on a safari.

equally insightful answers. During the many outstanding presentations and discussions, we experienced the learning that comes from genuine dialogue. The final presenter captured the energy and spirit of this successful event by taking us on a safari.

Following the pre-conference, we gathered the ideas and the pre-conference papers. We requested additional papers from other experts to fill voids or complement existing papers. We also facilitated an exchange of papers, feedback, and comments among chapter authors and other referees, which generated further discussion and produced additional insights. All the papers were refereed extensively. The result is this book, which meets our goal of sharing the adventure with you.

In Swahili, the word *safari* means journey. Going on a safari conjures exotic images of traveling with interesting people through dense jungles, over vast deserts, and down winding rivers to see new and wondrous sites. Think of this book as a collection of expert snapshots from our safari through the networked world. Just as individual photographs capture the spectacular landscapes, the speed of the gazelle, and the majesty of the lion, every chapter in the book offers a unique and compelling image of the e-workplace. You can expect to gain the greatest value by reading the entire

We invite you to engage in dialogue with each chapter.

book and examining the various perspectives on HRD in a networked world. However, each chapter stands on its own. We invite you to start anywhere in the book. We hope you find these chapters to be similar to those special photographs that invite you into the scene, so we bid you to engage in our dialogue, which we partially captured in each chapter.

Section 1 contains aerial snapshots of the terrain. "The Foundation of HRD in a Networked World" provides a brief history of the disciplines of human resource development and information technology. "Building a Competitive Workforce for the New Economy" identifies current and future workforce shortages and skill misalignments. The authors propose a model of workforce development that recognizes employee mobility, competitive pressures, globalization, and the demanding pace of skill development that are required in today's workplace. "HR to the Power of e: Internet-Powered Transformation of Human Resources" describes human resource departments use technology to better connect with their stakeholders. The final chapter in this section, "Information Technology Changes in the Workplace: A Systems Perspective," applies a systems perspective to examine workplace changes that resulted from applications of new technologies in ten organizations.

In Section 2, we zoom in to take a close-up of knowledge management. "The Role of Human Resource Development in Transitioning from Technology-Focused to People-Centered Knowledge Management" argues that knowledge management is not exclusively about databases. The author describes communities of practice, a metaphor for integrating the human, social, and organizational capital of an organization. "Making Knowledge Count: Knowledge Management Systems and the Human Element" describes research by ASTD to define and measure knowledge management.

In Section 3, we zoom in on learning. "Web-Based Leadership Training: Determining Success Factors and Effectiveness" compares the process, the success factors, and the initial outcomes of a leadership training program delivered in two types of locations: on line and classroom. "An Exploration of Engagement and Mentoring in On-line Problem Solving" examines the emotional and the engagement aspects of communications and problem solving for on-line learners. The last two chapters in this section focus on using technology to support remote learning in collaborative laboratory programs that generally require hands-on interaction with the equipment and collaboration among the learners. "A Conceptual Framework for Computer Supported Collaborative Learning Requiring Immediate Presence (CSCLIP)" presents a framework for integrating learning theory, learning processes, interactive technologies, and human-computer interaction principles that will make it possible for learners to take a laboratory course without having to be physically present in the laboratory. "Implementing a Remote and Collaborative 'Hands-On' Learning Environment" brings the framework to life by providing a behind-the-scenes look at the ongoing implementation of such a laboratory environment. The authors describe the application of current and emerging technologies, the development of new software and equipment, and the implementation strategies that enable remote learners to gain a laboratory experience they can later apply in actual situations.

Section 4 contains photographic exhibits on the societal effects of technology "Using Adult Learning to Bridge the Digital Divide" describes the Digital Divide as a powerful force that threatens to divide the world into "haves" and "have nots" based upon technology. The author studied the users of eBay's auction process to identify who participated and how they engaged in self-directed learning. "Touch & Technology: The Look of Sensory Contact in the New Millennium" points out the paradoxes that develop when new technologies enter our workplaces. The author argues that we need the "touch" of communities. He describes "Eight Habits of the Heart" for building meaningful communities. The concluding chapter in this section, "Reflecting on our Journey through HRD in the e-workplace" captures the learning from our adventure together. It integrates the perspectives from all the chapters, captures the insights and the discontinuities, and presents topics for future research.

Just as technology needs the human component of touch, so did our efforts in developing and hosting the pre-conference and publishing this book. We received a great deal of support from the project sponsors, the Academy of Human Resource Development, the Williams Companies, and the Center for Research in Information and Telecommunications Technology at Oklahoma State University. AHRD Board members provided encouragement and created an environment where it was safe to take risks for learning and where research could be exciting and fun. Board members Gary McLean, Gene Roth, and Larry Dooley provided additional support for this effort. The Academy's technology committee, especially Loretta

Donavon, the committee chair, contributed substantially to the conceptualization and implementation of the pre-conference. Debra Vloedman and Brenda Solomon, conference coordinators, provided logistics, administrative and budgeting support, and humor. Graduate students from Oklahoma State University's Human Resource/Adult Education Program facilitated on-site conference logistics. Lisa Korner, Williams Executive

We hope you enjoy the results of our efforts and that you get a sense of the Safari by which we found adventure, friendships, and community.

Director of HR Strategy, provided troubleshooting support. Graduate students from Oklahoma State University's Human Resource/Adult Education Program facilitated on-site conference logistics. Graduate students from the University of Illinois National Center for Supercomputing Applications, Knowledge and Learning Systems Group created the web page that the authors used for sharing papers.

During the pre-conference, all participants took risks as they challenged prevailing patterns of thinking, provided new insights, and created an atmosphere for enjoyable learning. The staff at Williams Learning Center provided an ideal learning environment. The Oklahoma State University College of Education, The University of Illinois National Center for Supercomputing Applications, Knowledge and Learning Systems Group, and McLeodUSA supported the writing of this book. Deane Gradous, an experienced copy editor, retired management professor, and current executive coach reviewed the manuscripts for grammar and flow and, more important, challenged our assumptions. Maite Mijares prepared manuscripts through all phases of this effort. Carolyn Ford at Kluwer Publishing guided the publication process. Our families listened to the many retellings of our adventure, read the papers, asked penetrating questions, and encouraged us throughout. The book reflects all of these contributions.

We hope you enjoy the results of our efforts and that you get a sense of the Safari by which we found adventure, friendships, and community. Most important, we survived, we learned, and we feel empowered to take action in this exciting arena!

THE FOUNDATION OF HRD IN A NETWORKED WORLD

Tim L.Wentling
Department of Human Resource Education and
National Center for Supercomputing Applications
University of Illinois

Consuelo Luisa Waight
University of Illinois

Ruth C. King
University of Illinois

Abstract

The recent histories of information technology (IT) and human resource development (HRD) reveal parallel developments in their transitions from tangential activities to strategic thrusts. After defining terms and concepts, we describe five stages of parallel development within IT and HRD. We conclude by projecting HRD and IT advances as organizations move to the next stage.

The recent histories of information technology (IT) and human resource development (HRD) reveal that the evolution and revolution of both have included struggles and challenges. They also reveal parallel developments in the transition from tangential activities to strategic thrusts. Comparing IT and HRD allows us to view how they evolved over time and offers us a glimpse of their futures. Executives who set the vision for the organization and its intellectual capital in this information age; organization decision makers who implement strategic projects that rely on IT and HRD; HRD professionals who help employees deal with technology; and IT developers who need to know the human aspects of their projects could benefit by such a perspective.

In this introductory chapter we provide a foundation for the chapters that follow. We define terms and concepts, and we identify the parallel developments within IT and HRD that have occurred since 1951.

Definitions

Networks permeate almost every dimension of personal and business lives—from historical experiences with postal networks, telegraph networks, telephone networks, and television networks to more recent experiences with the Internet, intranets, wireless networks, and cellular networks (Harasim, Hiltz, Teles & Turoff, 1996). These networks, which were initially supposed to enhance communication and computation, have instead changed how we work, play, learn, and interact.

IT is an umbrella term that encompasses many forms of hardware, software, and services used for collecting, storing, retrieving, and communicating information. The scope of and the rapid growth of IT underscore its importance. In the U.S. alone, IT grew from an estimated $371 billion industry in 1992, accounting for 5.9 percent of the economy's gross domestic income, to an estimated $815 billion industry in 2000, accounting for 8.3 percent (U. S. Census Bureau, 2000).

And the growth in IT is expected to continue. The global IT market alone is expected to exceed $584 billion in 2004 (Fraser, 2000). A recent survey of 894 global companies (25 countries, 4 continents) reported that 75 percent intend to increase their IT expenditures in 2001 (InformationWeek, 2001). Similarly, Gartner, Inc.'s worldwide survey of IT expenditures for 2001 and 2002 projected increases in IT spending of 10.1 percent in 2001 and 6.1 percent in 2002 (Cowley, 2001). Although recent economic developments indicate that such projections may have been overly optimistic, IT expenditures will continue to grow as developing countries expand their economies.

HRD is rooted in training, organizational development, industrial psychology, and education. McLagan (1989) defined HRD as the integrated use of training and development, organization development, and career development to improve individual, group, and organizational effectiveness (p.52). Since that time, the availability and the multiple uses of information technology have changed the function, role, and form of HRD (Commission on Technology and Adult Learning, 2001; Rosenberg, 2001). For example, HRD professionals have recently become broadly interested in regional and national workforce development.

We acknowledge that HRD's historical and worldwide roots include, but are not limited to, training in the Greek and Roman Empires (Swanson & Torraco, 1995), apprenticeship training in the Middle Ages in Europe (Steinmetz, 1976; Swanson & Torraco, 1995; Anderson & Rampp, 1993), the Tavistock Sociotechnical Systems approach that began in England (Rothwell, Sullivan, and McLean, 1995), and in recent eras professional practices that are devoted to developing the skills of large numbers of employees. HRD has throughout its history concentrated on achieving strategic organizational objectives through people (Pace, Smith, Mills, 1991, Nadler & Nadler, 1989, Steinmetz, 1976). In this chapter, we trace the recent history of HRD as it relates to IT from 1951 to the present.

Parallel advances of IT and HRD

Interesting parallels can be drawn between the evolution of IT and HRD. In fact, the comparisons are quite remarkable. IT advances in organizations can be roughly divided into five stages, based on the major innovations, developments, and applications that significantly shifted management practices (Hayes, 1999; DeSanctis, Dickson, and Price 2000). For each stage, we describe the technological advances, the business applications, and the state of IT and HRD functions. (See Table 1.)

Stage one: Early adopters and primitive tools (1951–1962)

The first stage of IT was marked by the installation of the UNIVAC I computer in the Census Bureau in 1951 and 3 years later in General Electric (McLeod, 1998). Other large organizations began to adopt the use of computers. At this time, computers were large, mainframe machines powered by vacuum tubes. They produced information that was stored on punch cards or magnetic tapes. Using mainframe computers required knowing code-based languages that were machine specific and difficult to learn (Oz, 2000).

Senior managers did not understand computer operations or their capabilities. They saw computers as complex, data-processing tools for accountants, scientists, and engineers (Groe, Pyle, Jamrog, 1996). In most organizations, computers supported such routine accounting activities as payroll and general ledgers. No strategic visions or plans to adopt, use, or fully integrate computers into other business functions were evident. Because each machine was one of a kind, maintaining and expanding its

Table 1. Five Stages of Evolution of IT and HRD

	Computing technology	Business applications	State of IT in organizations	State of HRD in organizations
Stage one (1951–1962)	Mainframe. Programs languages are machine-specific. Structured programming languages are developed.	Computers provide data processing for scientific, engineering, and accounting functions.	IT applications are narrowly focused. Top managers do not understand computer operations or capabilities.	HRD is invisible or is a one-person approach in the organization. Specialists have expert knowledge. Information is controlled. Training is narrowly focused on specific skills
Stage two (1963–1974)	Mini-Computer. IBM 360 Series. DASD. Data can be transmitted beyond the computer room. More affordable and flexible computer technology is available.	Automation of additional business processes is possible. Computer use expands to include inventory control.	Increased requests for computer applications. Application backlogs grow. User expectations are unmet. DP managers are pushed to justify IT costs and benefits.	The term, human resource development gains prominence. OD emerges. The emphasis on training increases. Training focuses on routinizing tasks and the knowledge and skills to do the work. HRD is not aligned with the organizational goals and strategies.
Stage three (1975–1984)	Stand alone PCs are available. Vendors develop customized software and service	User-specified applications are customized. Computers are used in most business functions. Computers are used in manufacturing robots.	End users gain control of IT. Department applications flourish. Information is used to support decision making. Failed and fragmented IT efforts lead to corporate oversight.	Retraining is emphasized. HRD function is responsible for training. Training analysis becomes more sophisticated in determining specific needs. Computer-based training emerges. Performance is isolated.

Stage				
Stage four (1985–1995)	Windows environment. Personal Productivity software. Local area networks. Wide area networks. Client/Server Computing. User friendly browsers.	User-friendly Desktop applications. Groupware. Enterprise Resource Planning Systems. Real-time information. Distance communication.	Management of multiple communication media. Customized IT busines applications. IT-enables streamlining of organization processes. IT is viewed as a strategic resources.	HRD is integrated into the organization. Training is customized and emphasis is placed on measuring training impact. HRD moves from an activity to a results-driven focus. Organizational and individual performance become significant. HRD strategy and business strategy are aligned. HRD takes on the internal consultant, philosophy.
Stage five (1996–Present)	Personal Digital Assistants (PDA). Mobile and wireless technologies to interact with Internet.	Electronic commerce systems. Anytime, anyplace data retrieval and updating, professional development. Rapid growth of e-learning.	Flexibility and dynamic operations are key. Inter-organizational strategic alliances facilitated by IT.	Human resource development is aligned with business strategies. HRD partners with business units. Training is a core value. New HRD issues (e.g., core vs. contingent "contract" employees, the learning organization, intellectual capital, knowledge sharing and management, and just-in-time learning anywhere, anytime). Knowledge management has become important.

applications was a daunting task. However, several structured programming languages were developed, including Fortran in 1957, COBOL in 1959, and BASIC in 1962 (McLeod, 1998). These programming languages provided fertile ground for the later development and automation of many business functions.

HRD at this stage focused on training activities. The function was almost invisible to senior management and was usually limited to a one-person department. Training was viewed as a support function that provided individuals with necessary knowledge, skills, and attitudes. The use of training was consistent with the then prevalent management view that work should be distributed among employees and scientifically managed (Fredrick Taylor, 1911). Work in process was passed from one department of specialists to another, with each department making its contribution to the product. The resulting departmental silos and narrow management visions supported organizational cultures bent on controlling and hoarding information. The purposes of training were to control employees and change individual employee behaviors. Training was viewed as an overhead expense, and employee learning was viewed as a depreciable asset (Hackett, 1997). HRD activities were not aligned to business goals (Gilley & Maycunich, 1998). However, in many organizations, these initial training efforts grew over time. They first became training departments and later HRD departments.

In summary, three parallel developments in IT and HRD were evident at stage one. First, the capabilities of the functions were neither fully understood nor valued by senior managers. Second, IT and HRD activities were narrowly focused on specific parts of the organization. Third, the foundations that developed at this stage led to increased use of IT and HRD at later stages.

Stage two: Regulated environment and frustrated users (1963–1974)

Stage two began in 1963 with the introduction of the first minicomputer, the DEC PDP-5. In 1964 IBM delivered its Systems 360 series of computers (Jessup & Valacich, 1999). These computers were more affordable because applications could be upgraded, expanded, and integrated without incurring tremendous learning curves, costs, and time delays. The direct-access storage device (DASD), which replaced magnetic tapes and punch cards (Dickson and DeSanctis, 2001), enabled users to retrieve ad hoc information with greater speed. Additional IT advances allowed data to be transmitted beyond the computer room to peripheral devices (e.g., terminals located at remote sites). Transistors replaced vacuum tubes, which drastically reduced power consumption and maintenance costs and set the stage for the development of smaller, more powerful computers.

As computers became flexible and more affordable, managers of organizational functions (e.g., purchasing, production, shipping and receiving) were eager to automate their processes. However, developing, maintaining, and operating computer applications at the time required the technical skills of experts, who generally resided in data processing (DP) departments. DP departments quickly became overwhelmed. Filling users' requests for changes in computer systems could be delayed for two to three years. In the interim, the technology often became obsolete, or user specifications changed. Concerned managers demanded that DP departments justify their costs and show organizational benefits.

During stage two, the concept of *human resources* gained acceptance (Nadler & Nadler, 1989; Nadler, 1980). In the 1960s, organization development (OD), which focused on helping groups initiate and manage change, emerged. In the early 1970s, the term, *human resource development*, became prominent (Nadler, 1980). Also in the 1970s, organization development's impact on organizational capabilities was recognized (Cummings & Worley, 1997; Nadler & Nadler, 1989). Training received more emphasis, and a few organizations hired training managers. Training departments focused on routinizing tasks and training people accordingly. Most training was delivered in instructor-led classrooms that targeted mass audiences. Little thought was given to using computer applications to automate training processes. Training departments delivered courses on management and technical skills, but not on computer skills. Computer training was considered too highly technical for the average training department; therefore, it resided with the computer manufacturer (Swanson & Torraco, 1995). The major HRD uses of IT at this stage were limited to

IT and HRD experience increased importance, capability, and momentum.

creating and showing the videos that trainers used to deliver course content (Nadler and Nadler, 1989). HRD had gained momentum, but it was still invisible within most organizations. And when it was visible, it enjoyed little credibility (Gilley & Maycunich, 1998). Furthermore, HRD was not aligned with the strategic and performance goals of the organization.

In summary, both IT and HRD experienced increased importance, capability, and momentum. However, neither function was well integrated with business functions, goals, and strategies. Both functional areas were engaged in a lot of activity, but senior managers did not see tangible results that were linked to business objectives. As a consequence, neither function provided optimum contributions to the organization.

Stage three: End user computing and decentralization (1975 -1984)

Stage three began in 1975 with the development of the first personal computer (PC), the Altair 8800, and Microsoft's microcomputer version of BASIC. In 1976 Apple began producing computers, and in 1981 IBM announced the development of a personal computer (Jessup and Valacich, 1999). Equally important to the development of the PC was the creation of ARPANET in 1979. ARPAnet, the grandfather of today's Internet (Deitel, Deitel, and Steinbuhler, 2001), used high-speed communication lines to network major computers and to facilitate the exchange of information among research universities and military organizations. Another important advance was the development, mostly by vendors, of software and services. These developments included customisable software packages and services for business functions and departments, database concepts and software that improved data consistency and integrity (Kroenke, 1983), and sophisticated educational and communication tools for the ARPAnet (Harasim, Hiltz, Teles & Turoff, 1996).

IT developments at this stage fundamentally changed the way computers were used (Ives and Olson, 1984). With support from software vendors and easy-to-use technology at their sides, users took control of computing and data management. IT development, operation, and maintenance quickly became decentralized. Computers were used by almost every function to improve business processes. For example, manufacturing used them to program robots, especially in the automobile industry (Nadler & Nadler, 1989). Soon, issues of cost effectiveness emerged. Many IT efforts failed to deliver on their promises because the end users lacked training and experience. IT efforts often were compromised by the use of diverse computer platforms, incompatible applications, and inconsistent organization policies and procedures. Although end users seemed satisfied with their new capabilities and their strong involvement in IT development, senior managers recognized the need to provide corporate-level oversight for cross-functional IT efforts and to standardize IT hardware, software, and processes. Top managers' demands that IT developments meet organization goals helped to build the foundation for a new vision of IT as a corporate strategic resource (King, 1978).

The use of the computers in every business function created new avenues of working and training that effected HRD. (Swanson & Torraco, 1995; Nadler & Nadler, 1989). For example, computers made it possible for information about work to be documented and shared. In contrast to the scientific management approach, where employees had in-depth expertise in one area, the new avenues of work often required employees to have broader knowledge and skills in technical product areas, team building, and, of course, the operation of computer applications. HRD professionals often facilitated the process of change from individual work to teamwork, and they also managed the training and retraining efforts. The HRD function gradually assumed responsibility for most training efforts, including that provided by vendors. As a consequence, HRD gained a significant role in the organization (Hackett, 1997). Then computer-based training became

*As IT and HRD facilitated affordable
new ways of working, their importance and visibility
within the organization increased.*

possible. Despite these changes, HRD continued, for the most part, to remain unaligned with organizational goals. Performance was still isolated as vendor-driven training came into play (Gilley & Maycunich, 1998). HRD needed a new approach, a new mindset, a new vision.

In summary, as IT and HRD facilitated affordable new ways of working, their importance and visibility within the organization increased. While they provided greater value at departmental levels, their services were fragmented and did not effectively build the overall capabilities of the organization. In other words, IT and HRD became skilled in treating symptoms of problems, but they remained ineffective in implementing systemic change across the organization.

Stage four: IT as competitive strength (1985 - 1995)

In stage four, PC hardware and software companies continuously introduced better products. Examples include the graphical user interface (GUI), which is common to point-and-click applications, and personal productive software (e.g., spreadsheet, word processing and presentation packages). These products allowed users to manage and share data. In the 1980s, new computing architectures were developed, including the local area network (LAN), the wide area network (WAN), and client/server computing. PCs could communicate via networks with other computers throughout the world (Harasim, Hiltz, Teles & Turoff, 1996). In 1993, NCSA Mosaic, the first user-friendly browser was released. In 1995 the World Wide Web consortium was formed. The consortium supported user-friendly browsers that turned the Internet into a commercial sensation.

Organizations began using IT to achieve competitive advantages (Wiseman, 1988). During this stage, IT was an engine of organizational change and learning. Stories of customized IT-driven business applications abounded in the business press. The stories focused on using new desktop and groupware applications, gathering real-time information from geographically dispersed locations, and developing electronic linkages with suppliers. The stories also focused on using IT to manage multiple communication media and to streamline internal and external business operations. The espoused advantages of IT included cost cutting, market expansion, and product differentiation. As this stage came to an end, organizations turned to using enterprise resource planning (ERP) systems to update and integrate their legacy IT systems. Implementing these large, complex, and costly ERP systems proved extremely challenging and genuinely risky to many organizations. Managers finally started to accept IT as a strategic resource. The need to align IT with corporate strategy became evident (Bakos & Treacy, 1986; Henderson & Sifonis, 1988). Soon, many IT managers were elevated to the role of chief information officer, in which capacity they reported directly to chief executive officers.

IT drove organizational change and learning, and HRD became more strategic, as improving organizational and individual performance became more critical. HRD replaced its traditional activity-driven focus with a results-driven focus and emphasis was placed on measuring training impact. Training again increased in value (Hackett, 1997), and OD became a daily activity in many organizations (Larsson, Lowstedt, & Shani, 2001; Miller & Clardy, 2000). HRD professionals produced customized, decentralized programs and adopted the role of internal consultant (Gilley & Maycunich, 1998; Rothwell & Kazanas, 1994; Torraco & Swanson, 1997). At the same

IT and HRD empowered individual employees to meet organizational goals.

time that HRD experienced new credibility, many managers realized the value of encouraging self-management practices among their employees. The need to develop the interpersonal and behavioral skills of employees became essential (Townsend, DeMarie, & Hendrickson, 1998).

In summary, the information infrastructure that developed during this stage fundamentally changed IT and HRD. Both functions grew in importance, and both empowered individual employees to meet organizational goals. IT and HRD were beginning to have more strategic impact (as we witnessed increases in the numbers of chief information officers and chief learning officers). Moreover, IT and HRD were on the brink of a strategic and integrated alliance through which to deliver knowledge management, distance learning and other breakthrough ideas that added significant value to organizations.

Stage five: E-business and anywhere-anytime computing (1996–present)

Recent IT advances have enabled electronic commerce, a new form of strategic competition. In e-commerce, the Internet is used for communicating with customers and buying and selling products. The mobile and wireless technologies and personal digital assistants that are used for data retrieval may be updated anywhere at any time. Similarly, advances in e-learning enable professional development anywhere at any time. Inter-organizational strategic alliances facilitated by IT are common.

With the advent of e-commerce, traditional well-established firms suddenly had to compete with new Internet companies. Existing brick-and-mortar enterprises had to rethink their business models and realign their strategic partners. Huseman and Goodman (1999) related that today's companies need to be faster than ever in product development, speedier to market, and quicker to change. They need to be tied to their customers, and most of all, they need to manage their only resource for sustainable competitive advantage: knowledge (p. 58). Flexible and dynamic operations by IT and the continuous updating of employee skill sets by HRD are key to organization success.

HRD has become strategically integrated in the organization (Gilley & Maycunich, 1998). Training has become a core value for organizations (Hackett, 1997), and managers view employee education, training, and development as critical to organizational success.

Simultaneously, the rapid change of organizations has created new challenges for HRD. In response, HRD has become a proactive function that anticipates human resource issues. A few of these issues are core versus contract employees, the learning organization, intellectual capital, knowledge sharing and management, open systems, the balance between life and work, self-directed learners, free agents, skills gaps, the aging workforce, and continuous learning. To address these issues, HRD has begun moving beyond its traditional focus on training and development, career development, and organization development to become a more global, open and inclusive HRD function and concept. HRD, for example, is strategically involved in deploying learning and development at a distance.. Today's personal digital assistants (PDAs), mobile phones, and wireless connections enable accessibility and connectivity among workers across geographies. Workplace learning is no longer bound to one physical location.

Global knowledge repositories, virtual communities, and teleconferencing technologies allow employees to learn anywhere at anytime. For example, e-learning and classroom-based training can be blended (Rosenberg, 2001).

In summary, both IT and HRD are strategically important to organizations. Flexibility in addressing customer needs, knowledge-management capabilities, and employee learning is important to both functions. Moreover, the processes and the technologies of IT and HRD have broken through the walls of organizations, where individuals now use the latest technologies to gather information and learn anywhere, anytime. Computer literacy and a focus on life-long learning have created an environment where individuals are in control of both.

The future: What will it be like?

As organizations move to the next stage, the alignment of IT strategy, HRD strategy, and corporate strategy will remain a management priority for many years to come. IT and HRD will continue to respond proactively to the changing economic, educational, technological, and political trends that affect organizations and nations. To be proactive, however, HRD and IT professionals need to take a look at the future. Hodgins (2000) noted that the future isn't just happening to us any more, "We make decisions every day that determine what decisions we will be able to make tomorrow. As we stand at the inflection point of the new learning economy, we realize that it will be shaped as we choose to shape it; it will be as rewarding and humane as we make it: the decisions we reach will determine what the world will be like for all of us" (p.1). This section looks into some futuristic aspects of HRD and IT.

The lines between HR and HRD will become blurred

Traditionally, the human resource (HR) function has been responsible for hiring, compensation, and accounting. As of late these processes are being automated or outsourced. (See Christie's chapter, "HR to the Power of ^{e}: Internet-Powered Transformation of Human Resources" for information on this topic.) Simultaneously, the role and importance of HRD are expanding, and HR and HRD will merge or ally their efforts to champion innovative ideas and practices and promote the sharing of knowledge across the organization (Walker, Reif, Gratton, Swiercz, & Michael, 1999; Ulrich, 1998). As employees increasingly become responsible for their own development, HR and HRD will be called on to lead change at all levels.

Walker et al. (1999) stated that HR professionals will be consultants to managers, will facilitate organizational change, and will focus on aligning organizational capabilities with business strategy. They will design and implement HR processes and initiatives that address important people-related business issues. Together HR and HRD face the challenge of ensuring that the workforce will be able to perform no matter what internal or external trends dictate.

E-learning will continue and advances in technology will revolutionize the way training is delivered

The Web-Based Education Commission (2000) reported that between 1998 and 2008 more than 2 million skilled IT workers will be needed to fill newly created jobs and to replace workers leaving the field. (See Meeder and Cude's chapter, "Building a Competitive Workforce for the New Economy" for additional information on workplace demographics.) The increased demand for a skilled workforce, the anticipated shortage of skilled workers, the need for continuous training, the shift to a blended approach of Web-based training and classroom training for workers, and the increasing number of corporate universities will influence workforce training in the information economy.

The corporate e-learning market in the United States, for example, is expected to jump from $1.1 billion to $11.4 billion by 2003 (Commission on Technology and Adult Learning, 2001). According to the Commission on Technology and Adult Learning the development of common technical standards, open design, and the widespread sharing of information across states and sectors about successful and innovative approaches will contribute to a continued rise in the e-learning market.

The Knowledge and Learning Systems Group (KLSG) at the National Center for Supercomputing Applications provides insight into how e-learning changes the traditional training and development function. KLSG defines e-learning as

> the acquisition and use of knowledge distributed and facilitated primarily by electronic means. This form of learning currently depends on networks and computers but will likely evolve into systems consisting of a variety of channels (e.g., wireless, satellite), and technologies (e.g., cellular phones, PDA's) as they are developed and adopted. E-learning can take the form of courses as well as modules and smaller learning objects. E-Learning may incorporate synchronous or asynchronous access and may be distributed geographically with varied limits of time (Wentling, Waight & Kanfer, 2000).

Tapscott (1996) in his book, *The Digital Economy*, listed six themes of new learning that add to KLSG's definition of e-learning:

1. Increasingly, work and learning are becoming the same thing.
2. Learning is becoming a lifelong challenge.
3. Learning is shifting away from formal schools and universities.
4. Some educational institutions are working hard to reinvent themselves for relevance, but progress is slow.
5. Organizational consciousness is required to create a learning organization.
6. The new media can transform education, creating a working-learning infrastructure for the digital economy.

In the future, e-learning will be wireless, highly intelligent, interactive, integrative, accessible, easy to use, and of benefit to business and education globally (Close, Humphreys, Ruttenbur 2000; Web-Based Education Commission, 2000). E-learning will allow continuous processes of inquiry and improvement that keep pace with the speed of change in business and society (Commission on Technology and Adult Learning, 2001). It will also allow humanized, virtual-learning environments. On-line teams will be able to see and hear each other in real time on large, high-resolution computer screens. E-Learning will become so 'matter of fact' and so much a part of what we do that the lines between doing and learning will become blurred. An e-learning infrastructure will be responsive to learners, no matter their age, nationality, ethnicity, educational background, intelligence levels, learning styles, language or learners' needs (Wentling & Waight, 2000).

Corporate users and institutions of higher education are actively engaging e-learning within their learning environments. Organizations view cost savings and wide-area access as major reasons for e-learning (Chute, Thompson & Hancock, 1999). Organizations with distributed workforces view e-learning as an economical way to reach employees around the world. Of course, not all learning needs can be met through e-learning; it is not a universal training solution. Thus we will see a blending of e-learning and classroom training. Studies conducted by ASTD, the National Association of Governors, and the Web-Based Congressional Commission, all point to the growth of e-learning among academic, government, private, and public organizations.

Knowledge management will be a core organizational activity

Rosenberg (2001) defines knowledge management as a means to support creating, archiving, and sharing valued information, expertise, and insight within and across communities of people and organizations with similar interests and needs (p.66). HRD and IT will be the cornerstones for realizing knowledge management as Rosenberg describes it.

Knowledge demands will continue to increase. First, knowledge is growing faster as the half-life of human skills and knowledge grows shorter and shorter. Lifelong learning is and will continue to be the norm, as risk, uncertainty, and constant change are the rule, rather than the exception (Urdan & Weggen, 2000; Hodgins, 2000). Second, the aging workforce means many knowledgeable people will retire. Third, the intense competition for employees among organizations has led to greater-than-usual turnover among valued employees. And finally, as organizations become more global, with widely distributed workforces, the need to share knowledge across great distances has become more difficult. Technological advances, however, will facilitate the growth of knowledge sharing and knowledge management. The Internet, for example, enables knowledge to be stored centrally and accessed by individuals regardless of their physical location. Additionally, it enables professionals to be linked electronically for problem solving and expertise sharing. The combination of asynchronous and synchronous knowledge management activities will lead to competitive advantage.

The workforce will be significantly more educated and more diverse

The workforce will be self-directed, will operate on flextime, will be technologically savvy, will have high collaborative fluency, and will be intrinsically motivated to pursue lifelong learning (Wentling & Waight, 2000). The report of the Commission on Technology and Adult Learning (2001) stated that the percentage of post-secondary students enrolled in distance education is expected to triple from just 5 percent in 1998 to 15 percent in 2002. The Web-Based Commission (2000) reported that 84 percent of two- and four-year colleges in the United States expect to offer distance-learning courses in 2002. This figure represents a 26 percent rise from 1998. The Commission on Technology and Adult Learning (2001) also reported that 90 million Americans have low levels of literacy and that from a social perspective e-learning could bridge skill education and income gaps by making high-quality learning experiences more widely available and by tailoring them to individual workers' needs (p.12).

Human resource and technology will continue to fuel an organizations' competitive advantage

To remain competitive, organizations will need to know how to operate, perform and change effectively and efficiently. As organizations continue to expand geographically, HRD professionals will become more salient because the human aspect will underline every aspect of a global organization. HRD professionals will be challenged to position their organizations within the knowledge economy, while helping to keep them sustainable and profitable. The transformational use of IT will proactively continue to support employee development, and HRD professionals will capitalize on this potential. Thus, to remain effective, HRD professionals must continually update their IT competencies.

Enhanced communication and collaboration tools will continue to surprise us

IT will continue to help people connect within the work environment, regardless of time and place. It will fuel the potential for increased productivity and creativity. The Internet and corporate intranets, for example, will continue to provide mechanisms that allow people to work together on important projects and to share their ideas, words, documents, images—anything—digitally. Scientists and businesses around the globe will continue to collaborate 24 hours a day. One commonly cited example is

Technologies are expected to converge to become multi-modal, transparent, and embedded, creating new work environments.

the software-development team that passes off its work at the end of its working day to a team in a distant time zone at the beginning of its working day—from California to London to Hyberbad to Tokyo to San Francisco—a full, continuous, and diverse cycle of creativity and productivity.

Thus, teamwork will continue virtually and face-to-face. As people share knowledge, skills, and resources and work cooperatively in the manufacture of their products, new forms of teamwork will develop (Casey, 1995). IT will continue to facilitate team activities and extend working relationships. Expected IT developments include improvements in network security, infrastructure and bandwidth, and the appearance of cheaper wireless technologies. Technologies are expected to converge to become multi-modal, transparent, and embedded, creating new work environments. In turn, employees will need to learn new behaviors and skills for new work environments (Web-Based Education Commission, 2000; Hodgins, 2000). HRD professionals, who will be needed at the forefront of these opportunities, must have the skills and competencies to collaborate with IT to produce work designs, work environments, and the skilled employees that can favorably impact organization performance. Knoll (1995), for example, offered a series of practical suggestions related to virtual socialization skills and virtual collaboration skills that will be crucial for a competent workforce. Knoll suggested that for virtual socialization, for example, one should use phrases to include everyone in the team and ask permission before using risky humor. For virtual collaboration, Knoll suggested that addressing the issues on the table and agreeing on activities, and assigning, scheduling and monitoring the status of activities are important. Overall, HRD professionals will play important roles in restructuring work and in speeding technology-driven organizations to success in the global market.

Conclusion

The historical parallels of IT and HRD offer a shiny pool for reflection. Over the five stages, HRD and IT developed from narrowly-focused efforts that were generally not understood to strategically-focused, integrated efforts that facilitate new ways of doing work. At each stage, strategic alignment, employee learning, and credibility have contributed to the success and growth of both HRD and IT. Understanding the struggles and challenges of these recent histories provides a foundation for considering future HRD and IT contributions to human enterprise.

References

Anderson, C., & Rampp, L. C. (1993). *Vocational education in the 1990x, II: A sourcebook for strategies, methods and materials*. Ann Arbor, MI: Prakken Publications, Inc.

Bakos, J. Y., & Treacy, M. E. (1986). Information technology and corporate strategy: A research perspective, *MIS Quarterly,10*(2), 107-119.

Casey, C. (1995). *Work, self and society after industrialization*. London: Routledge.

Chute, A. G., Thompson, M. M., & Hancock, B W. (1999). The McGraw-Hill handbook of distance learning. New York: McGraw-Hill.

Close, R. C., Humphreys, B., Ruttenbur, B. W. (2000). *E-learning & knowledge technology: Technology & the Internet are changing the way we learn*. SunTrust Equitable Securities.

Commission on Technology and Adult Learning (2001). *A vision of e-learning for America's workforce*. Washington, DC: Government Printing Office.

Cowley, S. (2001). Gartner: IT spending still rising. *ITWorld.com*. Available: http://www.itworld.com/Man/4215/IDG010717gartner/

Cummings, T. T., & Worley C. D. (1997). *Organization development and change* (6th ed.). Cincinnati, Ohio: South-Western College Publishing.

Deitel, H.M., Deitel, P.J., & Steinbuhler, K. (2001). *E-business and e-commerce for managers*. Upper Saddle River, NJ: Prentice Hall.

DeSanctis, G., Dickson, G. W., & Price, R. (2001). Information technology management: Perspective, focus and change in the twenty-first century. In Dickson, G. W. & DeSanctis, G. *Information technology and the future enterprise*. Upper Saddle River, NJ: Prentice Hall.

Dickson G.W. & DeSanctis, G. (2001). *Information technology and the future enterprise*. Upper Saddle River, NJ: Prentice Hall.

Fraser, S. (2000). Global IT services: Double-digit growth. *e-Services Advisor*. Available: http://www.advisor.com/Articles.nsf/aidp/Frass325.

Gilley, J. W., & Maycunich, A. (1998). *Strategically integrated HRD: Partnering to maximize organizational performance*. Reading, MA: Addison-Wesley.

Greengard, S. (1994). Database and software integration: Allowing HR to work more efficiently. *Personnel Journal 73*(3), p. 45.

Groe, G. M., Pyle, W., Jamrog, J. J. (1996). Information technology and HR. *Human Resource Planning, 19*(1). 56-61.

Hackett, B. (1997). *The value of training in the era of intellectual capital: A research report*. The Conference Board: Report #1199-97-RR.

Harasim, L., Hiltz, S. R., Teles, L., & Turoff, M. (1996). A field guide to teaching and learning guide: *Learning Networks*. Cambridge, MA: MIT Press.

Hayes, F. (1999, April 5). 100 years of IT. *Computerworld, 33*(14), 74-78.

Henderson, J.C., & Sifonis, J.G. (1988). The value of strategic IS planning: Understanding consistency, validity and IS markets. *MIS Quarterly, 12*(2), 186-200.

Hodgins, H. W. (2000). *Into the future: A vision paper for American Society for Training and Development*. National Governors' Association. Commission on Technology and Adult Learning.

Huseman, R. C., & Goodman, J. P. (1999). *Leading with knowledge: The nature of competition in the 21st century*. Thousand Oaks, CA: SAGE

InformationWeek (2001). Global IT Strategies.

Ives, B., & Olson, M. H. (1984). User involvement and MIS success: A review of research, *Management Science, 30*, 586-603.

Jessup, L. M and Valacich, J. S.(1999). *Information Systems Foundations*. Indianapolis, IN: Macmillan Publishing.

King, W. R. (1978). Strategic planning for management information systems, *MIS Quarterly, 2*(1), 27-37.

Knoll, K. (1995) Practical advice for global virtual teamwork. Available: http://www.cs.tcd.ie/courses/ism/sism/resource/papers/knoll/advice.htm.

Kroenke, D. (1983). *Database processing: Fundamentals, modeling applications*. Science Research Associates, Inc.

Larsson, P., & Lowstedt, J. S. (2001). IT and the learning organization: Exploring myths of change. *Organization Development, 73*(1), 73-91.

McLagan, P. (1989). *Models for HRD practice*. Alexandria, VA: ASTD Press.

McLeod R. (1998). *Management Information Systems*. Upper Saddle River, N.J: Prentice Hall.

Miller, J. S., & Clardy, R. L. (2000). *Journal of Labor Research, 21*(3). 447-461.

Nadler, L. (1980). *Corporate human resource development: A management tool.* Madison, WI: Van Nostrand Reinhold Company.

Nadler, L., & Nadler, Z.(1989). *Developing human resources.* San Francisco: Jossey-Bass, Inc.

Nonaka, I. (1998). The knowledge creating company. In *Harvard Business Review on Knowledge Management.* Boston, MA: Harvard Business School Publishing.

Oz, E. (2000). *Management information systems, course technology.* Cambridge, MA.

Pace, W. R., Smith, P. C., & Mills, G. E. (1991). *Human resource development: The field.* Englewood Cliffs, NJ: Prentice-Hall, Inc.

Rothwell, W. J., & Kazanas, H. C. (1994). *Human resource development: A strategic approach.* HRD Press Inc: Amherst, Massachusetts.

Rothwell, W. J., Sullivan, R. & McLean, G. N. (1995). Introduction. In W. J. Rothwell, R. Sullivan, G. N. McLean (Eds.). *Practicing organization development: A guide for consultants.* San Francisco: Jossey-Bass

Rosenberg, M. J. (2001). *E-learning: Strategies for delivering knowledge in the digital age.* New York: McGraw Hill.

Steinmetz, C. S. (1976). The history of training. In Craig, R. L. (1976). *Training and development handbook.* New York: McGraw-Hill, Inc.

Swanson, R. A., & Torraco, R. J. (1995). The history of technical training. In Kelly, L. (Ed). *Technical and skills training handbook of the American society for training and development* (pp. 1 – 29). New York: McGraw-Hill.

Tapscott, D. (1996). *The digital economy: Promise and peril in the age of the networked intelligence.* New York: McGraw Hill.

Taylor, F. W. (1911). *The principles of Scientific Management.* New York: Norton.

Torraco, R. J., & Swanson, R. A. (1997). The strategic roles of human resource development. *Human Resource Planning, 18*(4), 11 –21.

Townsend, A., DeMarie, S. M., & Hendrickson, A. R. (1998). Virtual teams: Technology and the workplace of the future. *Academy of Management Executive, 12*(3), 13 pages.

Ulrich, D. (1998). A new mandate for human resources. *Harvard Business Review, 76*(1), 124 -134.

Urdan, T. A., & Weggen C. C. (2000). *Corporate e-Learning: Exploring a new frontier.* WR Hambrecht + Co.

U.S. Census Bureau (2000). Statistical Abstracts of the United States. Available: http://www.census.gov/prod/www/statistical-abstract-us.html.

Walker, J. W., Reif, Gratton, W.E., Swiercz, L., & Michael, P. (1999). Human resource leaders: Capability strengths and gaps. *Human Resource Planning, 22*(4), 21 – 32.

Web-Based Education Commission (2000, December). *The power of the Internet for learning: Moving from promise to practice.* Washington, DC.

Wentling, T., Waight, C. L, & Kanfer, A. (2000). *E-learning: A review of literature.* Available: http://learning.ncsa.uiuc.edu.

Wentling, T., & Waight, C. L. (2000). *The future of e-Learning: A corporate and academic perspective*. Knowledge and Learning Systems Group, National Center for Supercomputing Applications. Available: http://learning.ncsa.uiuc.edu

Wiseman, C. (1988). Strategic information systems: Trends and challenges over the next decade. *Information Management Review, 4*(1).

BUILDING A COMPETITIVE WORKFORCE FOR THE NEW ECONOMY[1]

Hans Meeder
National Alliance of Business

Roger L. Cude
McLeodU.S.A, Inc.

Abstract

Current and future workforce shortages and skill misalignments pose significant challenges for long-term economic viability and growth. Projections of population growth, job growth, education patterns, and demographics have profound implications for decision-makers in organizations and human resource professionals. In response to economic and societal changes, more individuals are taking advantage of postsecondary education and lifelong learning opportunities. The demise of post World War II-based assumptions of long-term attachment between employers and employees, requires a new model of workforce development that recognizes employee mobility, competitive pressures, globalization, and the pace of change in valuable technologies and skills. The Knowledge Development Network (KDN) is presented as an emerging model of collaboration among business, education, employee organizations, and policy makers. The KDN addresses the need for ongoing education and training for workforce preparation and development.

> *Learning is what most adults will do for a living in the 21st century.*
> *—Perelman*

Today's economy creates workplace opportunities and challenges. To better understand the issues, we discuss the implications of demographic and

---

[1] The authors acknowledge the valuable research contributions of Robert Harmon, Staff Economist, National Alliance of Business.

macro-economic factors on our collective ability to ensure that qualified workers are available to fill the jobs created by economic growth. After all, people provide the foundation for competing in the world marketplace. Our discussion begins with U.S. factors because of that country's great impact on the world economy, and because U.S. data were more accessible. We then compare world economic and demographic projections. To address the need for a current and future workforce development model, we propose a Knowledge Development Network (KDN) model for accelerating the collaborative efforts that are required to build the workforce of the future. The term *network* is defined here as a strategic alliance of stakeholders in knowledge development. Decision-makers in business, education, and HRD can use the KDN model to implement effective strategies to develop workers who are prepared for the requirements of the new economy.

U.S. jobs and growth: The old deficit

Many of us recall personal experiences or stories of lean times in the United States when jobs were scarce and economic development was flat. However, during the past 17 years, with the exception of an 8-month period during 1990–1991, the U.S. has experienced the longest sustained period of economic growth in its history. Since the early 1980s, the U.S. economy has created 40 million new jobs at an average rate of 2 million jobs per year. And nearly every expert projection tells us that job growth can be expected to accelerate (Employment Policy Foundation, 2000, p.8).

We also know that the rate of growth of qualified workers will not keep pace (see Figure 1).

But the gap is not widening as quickly as one could expect. As the Baby Boom generation moves through the workforce, the average age of workers climbs (see Figure 2). Individual workers are healthier than ever before and more likely to remain in the workforce for longer periods of time. Given the Baby Boomers' vast knowledge and experience, their extended involvement in the U.S. workforce is certainly good news. But this generation of workers is beginning to leave the workforce. Furthermore, they will not be completely replaced by the U.S. workers in subsequent generations or by current immigration levels. The projected annual growth rate of the workforce is expected to range from 1 percent per year in the years 1998-2015 to nearly 0 percent per year in the years 2015-2025 (Porter, 2001).

In addition to the expected increase in jobs and decrease in qualified workers, jobs in the U.S. economy will continue to shift dramatically from manufacturing to information work. Nearly 93 million American workers (holding approximately 80 percent of all jobs) do not spend their workdays

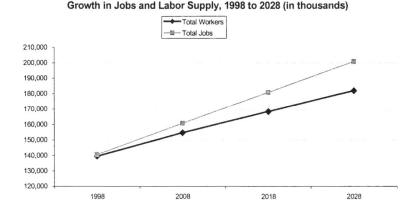

Figure 1. Growth in jobs and labor supply

making or growing goods. Instead, they move products, process or generate information, or provide services to people (Atkinson, Court, and Ward, 1999). In combination with rapid advances in technology, globalization, and consumer demands, the knowledge and skills needed to perform these jobs are dramatically changing. The challenge is to build a workforce equipped with the requisite abilities to perform.

Highly qualified knowledge workers: The new deficit

The Hudson Institute forecasts that 60 percent of all new jobs created in the early 21st Century will require skills possessed by only 20 percent of the current U.S. workforce (Judy & D'Amico, 1997). Moreover, the State New Economy Index (Atkinson, Court, and Ward, 1999) found that "knowledge-based jobs (those requiring postsecondary, vocational, or higher education) grew from approximately 27 percent of total employment in the U.S. in 1983 to 31 percent in 1993 and are expected to grow to about 33 percent in 2006" (p.16). Clearly, large segments of the U.S. workforce will require rapid development in knowledge and skills. To meet the demands of the new economy we must develop new ways of constructing and implementing

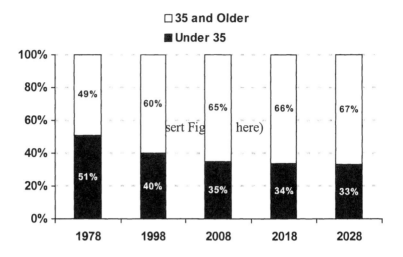

Source: U.S. Census Bureau and National Alliance of Business

Figure 2. The aging workforce

workforce development initiatives. If we do not, many potential workers will be left behind at a time when all are needed to sustain the competitiveness that fuels economic growth in the U.S.

A sign that we recently spotted outside a restaurant may be truer than we care to admit. It read, "Got a pulse? Apply inside!" However, many of the jobs being created demand a complex set of technical, problem solving, teamwork, and critical thinking competencies—and of course, "a pulse."

In specific disciplines, the growth in worker needs and the educational requirements of jobs will be dramatic. For example, the Bureau of Labor Statistics estimates that by 2006, the need for workers in certain technical fields (e.g. science, engineering, skilled manufacturing, computer science) will increase by more than 20 percent (Bureau of Labor Statistics, 2001). The Information Technology Association of America (ITAA) estimates that for want of qualified applicants half of the jobs posted for information technology (IT) workers (in IT companies and in IT-reliant companies) will go unfilled in coming years (ITAA, 2000). Overall estimates of job growth in IT occupations have dropped since early 2000 when the high-technology sector began to slow. However, the mismatch between available jobs and available workers with the right skills continues to challenge business organizations in the U.S. and in most industrialized nations. The recent high-technology slowdown only temporarily allows us to catch our collective breath. Organizations in industries that rely on high technology, such as the financial services industry, are continuously creating jobs to enable their efficient and innovative business practices. So how are workers in these and other sectors reacting to the scarcity of qualified labor?

How is the workforce responding?

Jobs are becoming more intellectually challenging and are creating demands for workers with postsecondary education. In 1973, only 28 percent of U.S. workers had education beyond a high school diploma. By 1998, 57 percent of workers had some college education and more (Carnevale & Desrochers, 2001, p. 50).

Today's workers are engaged in much more lifelong learning after they obtain an initial experience of postsecondary education up to and including a "terminal degree." Figure 3 indicates that between 1991 and 1999 the participation rate of adults who had already received at least some postsecondary education in continuing education increased by 10 percentage points, from 47 to 57 percent. Figure 3 also indicates that individuals with higher levels of terminal degrees participated in continuing education at higher rates. Higher learning begets the need for more learning.

In addition to the continuing education offered by colleges and universities, corporations have increased their educational opportunities. Employers are spending increasing amounts on training the current workforce. According to surveys conducted by Training Magazine (October 2000), expenditures for employer resources dedicated to all forms of training were estimated to be $54 billion.

Adults access learning opportunities in a wide variety of settings. Of the 5 million non-degree seeking students enrolled in community colleges in the U.S., 30 percent already have bachelor's degrees or postgraduate coursework. These adult learners are enrolled in school to upgrade their current skills, take career-specific courses, and earn certifications (Philippe & Valiga, 2000). In an environment where accelerated job creation is marked by a concomitant change in required competencies, the demand for systematic workforce development continues unabated. We have seen workforce-development models change from focusing on traditional education providers to offering increased flexibility to learners. For example, the chapter titled, "Using Adult Learning to Bridge the Digital Divide," by Ghost Bear and Conti shows how adults engage in self-directed learning on the Internet. Moreover, adults are starting to engage in smaller and more specialized learning units. They then stack or sequence these units to meet the changing requirements of their jobs and professional disciplines.

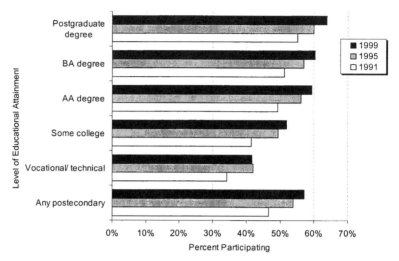

U.S. Department of Education, National Center for Education Statistics. Digest of Education Statistics, Various Years

Figure 3. Percentage of adults participating in continuing education

Workforce development globally

Economic growth, job creation, and demographics in developed countries follow patterns similar to the U.S. For example, Turpin (2000) states that thousands of companies in Britain are affected by major shortages of skilled staff and that many companies may soon cast their recruitment efforts worldwide under a new government plan to fast-track workers through the immigration process. Moreover, a recent article in the Wall Street Journal (Zachary, 2000) reported that German workers were angry that efforts to protect their jobs from foreign workers were breaking down. The Federal Institute of Labor blames corporate Germany for the shortage of skilled technicians. Compare this to a plan recently implemented in the U.S. to ease immigration requirements for computer programmers from India and other countries that have developed the ability to provide highly trained technology workers quickly.

Table 1 shows the projected population growth and job growth worldwide. A quick look at the population and job projections worldwide shows similarities between the U.S. and worldwide data.

Similar to U.S. projections, these worldwide job and population growth projections support the need for new workforce development models. Factors that could especially impact non-U.S. countries and drive the need for new workforce development models include the spread of free markets, improved international labor conditions and workers' rights (U.S. Department of Labor, 2001), and the emergence of powerful economic alliances among countries.

Table 1. Population, Labour Force and Labour Force Growth, 1950-2025

Region	Population (millions)				Labor force (millions)			
	1950	1985	2000	2025	1950	1985	2000	2025
World	2,516	4,837	6,122	8,206	1,189	2,164	2,753	3,649
Industrialized Countries	832	1,174	277	1,397	387	568	615	636
Developing Countries	1.684	3.663	4.845	6.809	802	1.596	2.138	3.013
Africa	224	555	872	1.617	99	214	318	650
Eastern Africa	63	166	272	537	32	75	111	228
Middle Africa	27	60	92	170	13	24	33	69
Western Africa	65	169	277	558	31	68	101	219

Region	Labor force growth (millions			Average annual labor force growth rate (%)		
	1950-1985	1985-2000	2000-25	1950-1985	1985-2000	2000-25
World	975	589	896	1.73	1.62	1.13
Industrialized Countries	181	47	21	1.10	0.53	0.14
Developing Countries	794	542	875	1.98	1.97	1.38
Africa	115	104	331	2.22	2.69	2.89
Eastern Africa	43	36	117	2.45	2.67	2.92
Middle Africa	11	10	35	1.66	2.26	2.92
Western Africa	37	33	119	2.29	2.67	3.17

From: "Demographic, employment, and development trends: The need for integrated planning" by G. M Farooq and F. L. MacKellar, 1990, *International Labour Review*, *129*(3), p. 301-305.

Knowledge Development Networks

We propose integrating new workforce development efforts into a model for collaboration, the Knowledge Development Network (KDN). The network is fashioned after the concept of supply chain management (Chopra & Meindl, 2000). We speak of "knowledge chain management" that will help to create the workforce required in today's and tomorrow's competitive world. The model allows us to observe and include the many effective workforce initiatives that occur in various geographic areas and industrial sectors. After we define the KDN model, we will explore three aspects of implementing such a network: consortia, competency models, and non-linear learning.

A new workforce development model is needed because the post World War II assumptions about the long-term attachment between employers and employees have been bypassed (Osterman, 1999). The two dominant employment models of the post-War era, IBM and the auto industry, although they were different in many respects, shared an inherent assumption that employees would remain attached to a single employer for a long period of time. In that relationship, employees entered employment with a basic set of educational or skill credentials, and additional learning would occur through company-directed efforts.

For the most part, assumptions of long-term attachment are a relic of the past. The new model of employee development is a loose hybrid of company-facilitated training and individual efforts to upgrade skills and knowledge. Drucker (1998) states,

> The knowledge society will inevitably be far more competitive than any society we have known—for the simple reason that with knowledge being universally accessible, there will be no excuses for nonperformance. There will be no 'poor' countries. There will only be ignorant countries. And the same will be true for companies, industries and organizations of all kinds (p. 545).

Calls for new approaches that are more flexible and responsive to changing market forces are emerging.

The KDN attempts to capture the energy and the flexibility necessary for today's fast-paced, global economy. Modeled after the concept of supply chain management, it is intended to spur collaboration and enable faster and higher quality workforce development efforts in communities, industries, and market segments. Futurist Joel Barker (1993) suggests that many breakthrough innovations involve borrowing ideas and concepts from one discipline and applying them in another one. In supply chain management, organizations with specific core competencies work closely together in complex, interactive sets of relationships. They form an integrated network, often under the direction of a single company that provides the ultimate consumer product or service. For example, employers, insurance companies, health care providers, pharmaceutical companies, and others form an integrated network to provide routine healthcare to employees and their families. The entire set of organizations involved in producing or assembling a product or providing a service may be considered a supply chain. Recently, however, a new term, *supply network,* has replaced the older term. It better represents the spirit of the highly interactive relationships that form among organizations that actively seek mutual advantage in collectively providing customer products and services. Moreover, integrated supply networks have

> *We apply fundamental aspects of supply chain management to workforce development.*

adopted state-of-the-art technology solutions (e.g., B2B, extranets) to increase the speed and the effectiveness of end-to-end processes. In the KDN model, we apply some of the fundamental aspects of supply chain management to workforce development.

Atkinson, Court, and Ward (1999) proposed a similar idea in their State New Economy Index. These authors contended,

> In the new economy, states' economic success will be increasingly determined by how effectively they can spur technological innovation, entrepreneurship, education, specialized skills, and the transition of all organizations, public and private, *from bureaucratic hierarchies to learning networks*" (p. 4; emphasis added).

Consortia, competencies and non-linear learning: Implementing the Knowledge Development Network

KDNs involve strategic alliances of community partners that must work together by building a deeper and broader set of learning alternatives. A KDN is comprised of a complex, interactive, adaptive system of relationships between employers, education and training organizations, employee organizations, community organizations, public policymakers, and the individuals who seek employable skills. Although new technology is currently being used in some areas of KDNs, we believe there are significant opportunities to increase the use of technology in developing consortia, competencies, and non-linear learning.

Consortia are the foundation of KDNs

We have found several cases where efforts are underway that embody some or all of the principles embedded in the KDN to successfully educate the workforce in the U.S. (a few examples are highlighted later in the chapter). In these cases, a handful of educators, policy makers, concerned parents, and business people in the local community launched integrated development efforts. They developed a shared vision, secured minimal funding, and implemented programs. But these organizers would be the first to admit that such programs are not easy to create. For example, when a roomful of educators, policy makers, business people and parents ask the question "who is the customer?" the concept of mutual interests immediately starts to break down. The educators claim students are the customers. They believe education is for the students. The parents claim they are the customers because they are responsible for preparing their children for life. The policy makers claim taxpayers are the customers because they fund the programs.

The network challenge begins with gathering together the many customers of workforce education efforts.

The business people claim they are the customers because they need qualified workers to fill jobs and create economic growth within the community. Finally, the adult learners claim they are the customers because they should be able to choose the learning options that fit their career goals. All are correct.

The network challenge begins with gathering together the many customers of workforce education efforts. One of the authors participated in such an organizing process in a local community. The members of the organizing group, who were committed to finding common ground, worked through their differences in several long sessions. They finished with a shared vision of creating sustained competitive advantage for several stakeholders:

- Local businesses need to create a competitive advantage in the war for talent by building a local labor market with high skills and the right skills.
- Students need to have an advantage in the competition for good jobs.
- Policy makers need to build competitive advantage in attracting new development and growth to the community based on an excellent educational infrastructure.

Their shared vision allowed all stakeholders to embrace the initiatives and programs because they clearly understood their shared interests. Once a vision is established, the leaders of the KDN must address at least three strategic issues: the demand for knowledge and skills, alignment, and communication.

The demand for knowledge and skills

A KDN must establish processes to accurately measure and report the knowledge and skills needed by the labor market at two levels. At the macro level, the network must develop a shared understanding of the occupations that are currently in demand and the trends that will influence future needs for skilled employees. Businesses contribute by sharing their high-level workforce plans. Policy makers contribute by communicating their high-level economic development plans. And, educators contribute by sharing their best practices and the latest techniques for assessing and developing skills in essential occupations.

At the micro level, individual jobs and occupational clusters will be analyzed to understand the strategic mix of academic, workplace, and technical skills that reside in current and future jobs and tasks.

With a deep understanding of demands for knowledge and skills and labor market trends, the KDN will share this information with all educational and training partners, including high schools, 2-year and 4-year postsecondary institutions, private for-profit training companies, publicly funded workforce-development programs, adult literacy organizations, and community-based organizations. As all members of the consortia take advantage of their access to common information about essential workforce knowledge and skills, they can appropriately align their education and training programs.

When consortia members align programs around specific human capital development, adult learners in the area of the network can access a broad and expanding array of educational and training opportunities that are made available to them by the education and training partners. Moreover, these educational programs can be made available through traditional classroom learning and through Web-based, self-paced on-line learning or any combination in between. A KDN becomes most effective when all educational opportunities are aligned around the career goals and the learning needs of the students and the goals and the workforce needs of business and policy makers.

Aligning resources

Over the next thirty years, tens of millions of adults already in the workforce will need to engage in learning activities at postsecondary levels. Within a purely competitive paradigm, educational organizations will be reluctant to align their programs for fear of losing their students. In the past, many institutions tried to be all things to all people. For two reasons, we advocate their taking a more specialized approach to workforce education to achieve the vision of a local KDN. First, policy makers and businesses generally work to create a local "critical mass" in one or more industry sectors. The existence of an integrated "supply network" that can provide qualified workers is fundamental to the sustainability of competitive advantage of local businesses in industry sectors. Second, opportunities to market educational products to other local geographies will arise as other communities attempt to build human competencies and organization capacities in the same industry sectors. Using technology and distance learning, local organizations will be prepared to export their educational products and services. The chapter titled, "Implementing a Remote and Collaborative Hands-On Learning Environment," is an excellent example of exporting best practices for work-force education in telecommunications.

Educational consortia that are aligned to achieve shared goals are bound to create the ease of entry and enhanced flexibility that will appeal to potential learners. As a result, much larger numbers of youth and adults will grasp opportunities to become lifelong learners. Thus, rather than trying to get their proverbial "bigger piece of the pie," most learning organizations in a KDN will work together in an open-source system that will "grow the pie."

One definition of insanity, often attributed to Albert Einstein, is doing the same thing over and over and expecting a different result. Businesses, policy makers, and education providers have often worked together in the past. Since the early 1980s, businesses have been urged to get involved with education. *A Nation at Risk* (National Commission on Excellence in Education, 1983), the landmark report that called for systemic reforms to improve the quality of the American education system, caused many businesses to eagerly form school-by-school partnerships. In addition, businesses developed relationships with specific institutions to create educational programs designed to relieve narrowly targeted, site-specific skill shortages. However, given the future marketplace trends and extensive challenges outlined in the beginning of this chapter, all stakeholders in a KDN will need to collaborate in meaningful ways. Some serious "heavy lifting" is required for the strategic work of developing a KDN.

Using communication to build community

Communication is at the heart of maintaining alignment in any consortium. Multiple stakeholders in a KDN will need to assess continuously their progress toward established goals and periodically evaluate the changing needs of competitive business organizations for skilled, technologically prepared workers. Continuous interaction among all stakeholders in a KDN contributes to building a thriving community that is focused on meeting the challenges and the opportunities of building sustained competitive advantage. In addition, frequent interactions among stakeholders are vital for creating effectiveness and efficiency within a well-integrated network. When

Some serious "heavy lifting" is required
for the strategic work of developing KDNs.

discussing these multiple stakeholders, Drucker (1998) states that together these organizations are the community and both the public and private sectors must share in the work.

Effective communication requires a common language. A major challenge in developing an effective consortium is that businesses find it difficult to articulate their needs to the educational community and educational institutions find it difficult to communicate their learning outcomes to the business community. This issue can come closer to resolution when all stakeholders in a KDN employ the language of competencies in articulating job requirements and workforce knowledge and skills. In addition, network participants can benefit from building community by applying the *Habits of the Heart* that Taulbert describes the chapter titled, "Touch and Technology."

Competencies

An effective KDN allows employers to articulate the knowledge, skills and competencies that the labor market is and will be demanding. First, employers can specify the skills and knowledge that are needed for various occupations. Job-task analyses are helpful in defining competencies that are required nationally, internationally, and by industry. Job-task analyses also identify the general academic preparation, the workplace skills, and the technological fluencies that all workers need. Further, they articulate the job-specific competencies that are needed within similar clusters of job occupations. In the chapter titled, "HR to the Power of [e]: Internet-Powered Transformation of Human Resources," the author outlines how human resource professionals in businesses are using technology to create competency-based management systems. A natural extension of the KDN model is to begin exploring real-time sharing of non-proprietary information. The KDN will measure and forecast new directions in the job market in order to understand the extent to which certain sets of knowledge and skills will be needed in the future. Such information about the labor market will be valuable to all stakeholders in many different ways. Real-time knowledge sharing at this level benefits all KDN stakeholders because they can beat the competition in responding quickly to market needs.

Having access to macro-level information about job and skill trends enables individual workers to make well-informed decisions about their education and skill-building efforts. In many cases, individuals will begin to see a bright line between education and training and personal career

Effective KDNs allow employers to articulate the knowledge, skills and competencies that the labor market is and will be demanding.

opportunities. Although many individuals are internally motivated to be lifelong learners, others may need incentives, such as greater confidence in the specific competencies that are valued by the regional labor market.

Information about the macro and micro labor markets and occupational job-task analyses can inform the planning efforts of education and training institutions., They can focus their resources on areas that represent significant job growth and the need for skills. Educational organizations that better understand the current and future work environments of their learners can more effectively provide curricula that are aligned with the required learning outcomes. Of course, the educational organizations will not be required to reduce their curricula to achieving only these outcomes, but they will be better prepared to ensure that their programs provide just-in-time as well as just-in case content Further, educational organizations may develop or adopt specific learner assessments and offer credentials that better communicate to the business community the competencies their graduates. This phenomenon is already evidenced by the explosive increase in the number of workers who obtain certificates in specialized areas. Of course, some institutions clearly benefit from offering courses leading to professions that are not in high demand or for which the cost of training outweighs the financial benefits to the student (e.g., cosmetology, outdoor recreation, low-skilled technologies). These and other preparatory courses may be in high demand because students perceive them to lead to good jobs or, at least, attainable ones. Since consumers are willing to pay tuition for such courses, it is certainly not in the institution's immediate financial interest to curtail their offerings of courses that are in high demand. Furthermore, although local job opportunities may not exist, if students are willing to relocate, it may make sense for them to obtain certain skills and knowledge.

In some instances, public policymakers have chosen to limit public expenditures on courses for which little local demand exists. In some ways, this makes sense, especially when institutions seem to take advantage of a student's ignorance and the bill for education is footed almost entirely by taxpayers.

But draconian efforts to curtail educational choices could backfire by creating a bureaucratic bottleneck that puts significant educational decisions in the hands of a few decision makers, further limiting schools' abilities to respond to changing educational needs. We suggest that the best policy for a KDN is develop a strong customer information system that will give consumers direct access to information, formatted in an easy-to-understand way, about job trends and the level of education and training needed for various types of jobs.

Finally, the information developed by KDNs makes it easier for complementary and competing institutions to align their efforts. They can collaborate to help learners navigate through multiple learning options and at the same time avoid unnecessary duplication of content. High schools can create outcome standards and curricula that will encourage lifelong learning and outcomes that are aligned with the entrance standards of postsecondary organizations. Alignment reduces the need for remediation and allows students to matriculate in the programs of multiple learning providers as their learning needs and situations change.

Non-linear learning

Cross (1981) describes a particular social norm found in most industrialized nations, "the linear life plan." This plan dictates that education is for the youth, work is for the middle-aged, and leisure is for the elderly. While many expectations of this norm have eroded, they still seem to be embedded in the "DNA" of many industrialized nations. Best and Stern (1976) argue that such expectations damage our society because they inhibit career change (mostly because of the need for additional education that accompanies career change) and because they have constrained lifelong learning goals for adults. The belief that education is key to finding new career opportunities, when it is accompanied by the belief that education should be completed early in life, presents a dilemma.

The focus on career learning has been further complicated by the changing assumptions of the relationship between employer and employee. Traditionally, U.S. companies managed career learning on behalf of their employees. New technologies were introduced to employees in classroom instruction and on-the-job training, or managed through the employee union. Training was offered on the job. Individuals were not required to assess their own career paths and to make choices about their training. Although many Americans are not happy about it, for the most part, long-term employer-employee relationships are a thing of the past. While companies still invest considerable sums in training their current workforce, they typically provide training to those who are able to benefit immediately from the training and to implement these new skills on the job—essentially this amounts to relatively incremental training.

By contrast, when a company dramatically re-directions its business strategy, it may lay off lower-skilled workers and simultaneously hire higher skilled workers. The onus for remaining employable—for maintaining and developing a set of skills and knowledge that employers find valuable—is now placed on the individual, not the company.

The KDN works to break down this cultural norm by providing information to individuals about new career opportunities and the specific competencies needed to take advantage of them. In time, individuals will gradually abandon the linear life plan paradigm and accept that a non-linear life plan is best for career advancement and for meeting the opportunities that will arise during their lifetimes. Carl Rogers has stated, "I have come to feel that the only learning which significantly influences behavior is self-discovered, self-appropriated." Adults are becoming "free agents" in career learning and job choice.

A brief analogy will clarify what we mean by non-linear learning. The technology of video editing in the early 1980s required the editor to cut video clips in the sequence in which they were to be shown. If the video editor wished to insert a clip in the middle of a finished product, all the clips that followed the insertion had to be re-edited to maintain the appropriate sequence. A similar situation prevailed in education. Often, students who completed a few courses at a junior college and then transferred to a university had to re-take several courses. This requirement held even when the content of the courses was essentially the same and the students had demonstrated proficiency in the subject matter. In the 1990s video editors adopted non-linear digital editing technology. Today they can insert any form of media into any section of a finished video product at any time. The insertion is instantly integrated into the finished product, and the sequence is maintained. Likewise, it is feasible to create a career-development process and an educational system where adults can insert formal and informal learning into their repertoire of competencies at any time. However, before adult learners strive to develop proficiency in specific competencies, they ought to know the value that employers place on those competencies. Moreover, adult learners ought to know which educational resources will most efficiently and effectively help them develop specific competencies.

A question arises about our capacity to develop the competencies that will be required by business, non-profit, and government organizations. There are 9600 learning organizations for adults in the U.S. These include large public universities, tiny private liberal arts colleges, 1600 2-year colleges, 650 local Workforce Investment Boards that manage federal training resources, and over 5000 private-education vendors of training that serve a relatively small populations. In addition, incentives are provided by state subsidies to public institutions. State funding is targeted to encourage technology learning. Massive federal and state funding is provided for disadvantaged students to participate in college. And an array of miscellaneous tax credits is given to individuals and their families and companies to encourage continuous learning. We have no shortage of providers or funding mechanisms. The U.S. educational system has the capacity to fill the need. It is the means by which nearly all current and future employees will prepare for work. Other countries are either building similar capacity or relying on the U.S. and other industrialized countries to provide educational resources, particularly at postsecondary levels. Moreover, distance-learning technology is removing geographic barriers to participating in the best education and workforce-development resources in the world. Thus, we are not suggesting a need for additional funding for education through the KDN model. We are suggesting a way to optimize the resources already in place.

The emergence of KDNs

As we conceptualize the Knowledge Development Network, many regional efforts are underway that embody some or all of the principles embedded in the model. In this section, we briefly profile these efforts.

Pierce County Careers Consortium

The Pierce County Careers Consortium, located in Pierce County, Washington, is a successful partnership of Pierce College District, Bates Technical College, Clover Park Technical College, Tacoma Community College, and numerous business, labor, government, and community-based partners. The mission of the consortium is to provide model Information Technology (IT) programs that will educate and train a highly skilled workforce in response to Pierce County's explosive gain of more than 100 technology companies in the last two years. To address this large-scale demand, colleges are committed to working together to develop IT curricula that correspond with Working Connections II (a Washington state initiative) program goals.

In two years, the consortium partners implemented a number of worker re-training projects, and collaborated on the development and integration of industry verified IT skill standards. The specific plan articulated "2+2+2" agreements where learners begin in high school, move to a 2-year college, and then to a 4-year university. The large number of educational institutions in Pierce County necessitates a coordinated effort for initiating and maintaining articulation agreements among the 31 high schools, four community and technical colleges, and five universities.

Houston Gulf Coast Board: Addressing nursing shortages

The WorkSource, a regional partnership of business, education, labor, and community organizations, is committed to providing the education, training, and labor market services that will make employers and residents more competitive in the global economy.

The WorkSource system covers a 13-county region in Southeast Texas, which includes Houston, the nation's fourth largest city. The system is available to the more than 90,000 businesses and the 4.5 million residents in the area.

When the Gulf Coast Workforce Board identified the health care industry as one of the 10 industries in the Gulf Coast Region most in need of current and future employment assistance, it decided to find a way to help and to make a difference. It asked the Greater Houston Partnership to join it in the effort by approaching CEO's of the region's hospitals to learn which of the many positions in their service systems were in the most critical condition. The answer was registered nurses.

A partnership was formed between the two organizations and the Health Service Steering Committee. Together with the hospital CEOs and their representatives, the partnership has been working since the latter part of last year to meet the challenge. A low estimate of the current shortage of registered nurses in the Workforce Board's 13-county service area is approximately 1,000 vacancies for hospital and non-hospital positions.

To approach the problem from different directions, the Steering Committee divided into four action subcommittees. They are

- Marketing Career Opportunities in Health Care. This group is charged with developing an ongoing, region-wide marketing campaign 1) to change the image of nursing in a hospital setting and 2) to develop and implement an industry-based outreach and recruitment effort. Target markets include students K-12, minorities, and employees who currently work in health professions and who want to become registered nurses.
- Enhancing Educational Capacity and Increasing Access to Career Opportunities. This group is working with community colleges in the region to determine how current nurse training and degree programs can be expanded to allow more educational and associate degree program

opportunities. Opportunities to increase funding for faculty, scholarships, loans and other incentives for registered nurses to earn advanced degrees are being employed, as well as The group is also exploring employer/education partnerships and distance learning via the Internet.

- Addressing the Internal Challenge, the Work Environment in Hospitals. This group is exploring ways to attract and retain registered nurses from the inside out. Issues under investigation include salaries, transportation, national recognition, increased control over work environment, and attitude change towards the profession.
- Making Government a Facilitating Partner. This group is charged with determining how government strategies could correspond with that of the Texas Nurses Association and the Texas Hospital Association. Specific areas of support are in the areas of increasing nursing school capacities and faculty salaries, addressing in-state tuition and fees for non-state residents, and similar issues.

Work on the Health Services Steering Committee is ongoing. Once goals are met for the registered nurse crisis, other health care occupations will be approached in a similar manner.

Pittsburgh Technology Council and Southwestern Pennsylvania Industrial Resource Center (SPIRC)

The Pittsburgh Technology Council located in Pittsburgh, Pennsylvania, is one of the largest regional technology trade associations in the U.S. and has a special emphasis in the Advanced Manufacturing, Biotechnology, and IT clusters. The Southwestern Pennsylvania Industrial Resource Center (SPIRC), the Council's sister organization, helps small and medium-sized manufacturing companies improve their competitive performance and enhance the 13-county region's ability to sustain manufacturing growth. Two initiatives are:

- Manufacturing Pathway Initiative, sponsored by the Council's Advanced Manufacturing Network. This initiative uses the Ford Academy of Manufacturing Sciences (FAMS) curriculum, which integrates work skills into an academic curriculum, as its core. The curriculum teaches students basic skills that can be integrated into a number of careers, including information systems, statistics, and communications, and reinforces these concepts through such employer and community-based support services as internships, job shadowing, and mentoring during the summer and the school year.

- Technology Literacy Initiative. This initiative recognizes that technology literacy has become part of the menu of basic skills required for all learners and all workers. It utilizes the IT Pathway/Pipeline model developed by the Techforce Initiative, a partnership of the Education Development Center, the Information Technology Association of

The Technology Literacy Initiative recognizes that technology literacy has become part of the menu of basic skills required for all learners and workers.

America, and the National Alliance of Business. The model focuses on: 1) providing technical assistance to school districts to assess curriculum, 2) strategically integrating IT skill standards into all K-12 classrooms, 3) developing community and business partnerships to support students, teachers, administrators, and school directors, and 4) engaging students in meaningful industry partnerships. Initial activities included the formation of partnerships with school districts, awareness building among employers, and crosschecking the technology literacy skill matrix with Pennsylvania's Science and Technology Academic Standards.

Future plans include establishing a Web-based clearinghouse for employer involvement in school and community programs to serve as a one-stop information exchange between business and education.

Conclusion

Paul Osterman (1999) observes,

> The rules of the postwar labor market—its institutional structure—fitted together in a logical way and constituted a coherent map of behavior for employers and for workers. This map has been erased, and this erasure explains why—even in the face of some good economic news—the sense of unease is so widespread. The erosion of the old rules also helps explain why some outcomes we dislike are becoming increasingly common.

A major part of the angst surrounding this transition from a set of old assumptions to new revolves around the need to develop a sustainable model for

- Helping individuals gain knowledge and skills to remain employable
- Helping companies obtain the talent they need to remain competitive
- Helping regions develop the base of successful companies and aligned talent to remain prosperous and able to promote general civic health

The KDN model, recognizes and adapts to the mobility of today's workforce, the enormous competitive pressure placed upon businesses, and the fast-changing nature of technology and related work-place competencies.

We see strong evidence across regions and localities that KDNs are emerging in various stages of maturity. Business, educators, employee organizations and policymakers must recognize that old relationships and assumptions have vanished, and no amount of yearning for the past can turn back the clock. Rather, these partners should aggressively and creatively work to develop new organizational structures, new public policies, and new ways of thinking about developing human resources that can capitalize on this period of significant change.

We hope that the ideas and information presented in this chapter will help partners see the opportunity before them so they can adopt a positive approach to change in building a series of effective Knowledge Development Networks.

References

Atkinson, R.D., Court, R.H., and Ward, J.M. (1999). *The state new economy index.* Washington, DC: Progressive Policy Institute. Available: www.neweconomyindex.org

Barker, J.A. (1993). *Paradigms: The business of discovering the future.* New York: Harper Business Press.

Best, F., and Stern, B., (1976). *Lifetime distribution of education, work and leisure.* Washington, DC: Institute for Educational Leadership, Postsecondary Convening Authority.

Carnevale, A., Descrochers, (2001). *Help wanted...Credentials required. Community colleges in the knowledge economy.* Annapolis Junction, MD: Community College Press.

Chopra, S., and Meindl, P., (2000). *Supply chain management: Strategy, planning and operations.* New Jersey: Prentice Hall.

Cross, K.P., (1981). *Adults as learners.* San Francisco: Jossey-Bass Publishers.

Judy, R,. & D'Amico, C, (1997). *Workforce 2020: Work and workers in the 21st century,* Indianapolis: Hudson Institute.

Drucker, P.F., (1998). The Age of Social Transformation. In G.R. Hickman (Ed.), *Leading organizations: Perspectives for a new era.* Thousand Oaks, CA: Sage Publications.

Employment Policy Foundation. (2000). *Workplace policy for the new economy,"* p.8, Washington, DC. Available: www.pef.org.

Farooq, G. M. & MacKellar, F. L. (1986). Demographic, employment and development trends: The need for integrated planning, *International Labour Review, 129*(3), 301-315.

Information Technology Association of America (ITAA). (April 2000). *Bridging the gap: Information technology skills for a new millennium,* Rosslyn, VA

National Commission on Excellence in Education. (1983). *A nation at risk,* Washington, DC: U.S. Department of Education. Available: http://www.ed.gov/pubs/NatAtRisk/index.html

Osterman, P., (1999), *Securing prosperity. The American labor market: How it has changed and what to do about it*, (A Century Foundation Book). Princeton, NJ: Princeton University Press.

Phillippe, K.A, Valiga, M. J. (2000, April). *Faces of the future*, Washington, DC: American Association of Community Colleges.

Porter, M.E. (2001). *U.S. Competitiveness 2001: Strengths, vulnerabilities, and long-term priorities*, Washington, DC: Council on Competitiveness.

Training Magazine, (2000, October). Industry report 2000, *Training Magazine, 37*(10). Available: http://www.trainingsupersite.com

Turpin, A., (2000). *Moving in for the skill*. London: Director.

Zachary, G.P., (2000, January 17) Hire wall: As high tech jobs go begging, Germany is loath to import talent. *Wall Street Journal*.

HR TO THE POWER OF ^{e}

Internet-Powered Transformation of Human Resources

Mike Christie
Hewitt Associates, LLC

Abstract

For the past decade, the Human Resources (HR) profession has been undergoing a fundamental shift—from performing as a tactical administrative function to performing as a strategic and consultative business-planning group. While this shift has been underway for some time, it has suddenly accelerated because HR is using a whole new set of solutions made possible by Internet technologies. Early experiences with Internet-powered HR transformations have illuminated the possibilities of "*e*HR" for transforming not only the human resources function, but also the organization's relationship with its workforce—one employee at a time.

What's driving the "eTransformation" of HR?

HR transformation efforts in organizations have produced process efficiencies and have shifted administrative work into shared services or outsourced service centers. But in most cases, the fundamental nature of the work itself has not changed. Companies have changed where the work gets done and who does it, but they have not changed *what* work gets done. Today, the vast majority of HR's time and resources continue to be dedicated to administrative activities—whether this work is done in a centralized processing group or is distributed among the field HR staff. For example, we recently conducted an activity analysis of a client's HR function[1]. Our study revealed that more than 74 percent of HR staff time and money was spent on administrative activities, such as data entry, process coordination, and re-work. Only 14 percent was spent on consultation-related activities, such as workforce planning, job design, and performance planning. And only 12 percent was spent on strategic activities, such as compensation, benefits design, succession planning, and special projects. Studies of other organizations with blue-collar and white-collar workers, have shown similar results. We concluded from these studies that HR transformation efforts may have created efficiencies by centralizing and streamlining administrative activities, but they have not yet accomplished the ultimate outcome of creating an entirely new strategic business role for HR.

Many HR executives recognize that the Internet can positively impact their organizations. It offers a new set of solutions that can help HR change the fundamental nature of its work. Table 1 shows how three distinctly different companies plan to use Internet solutions within HR, as stated in their strategic planning documents. Company A is a global technology and engineering organization with a mix of highly technical employees, a well-educated managerial staff, and manufacturing workers. Company B is a leading printing and publishing company with long-tenured manufacturing workers. Company C is a retail company with short-tenured, high-turnover service employees.

Although these three companies are engaged in different businesses, their objectives for deploying HR Internet solutions are similar. They hope to change the role of HR, and they all seek outcomes that they are not viewing through a purely technical or operational lens. They hope to get the following fundamentals right: increased operational efficiency, lower costs, and better service to the end users of HR information and processes. The specific solutions these companies design and deploy are—and will continue to be—tailored to suit the demands of their businesses. These companies speak of HR Internet initiatives in terms consistent with the eTransformation of HR.

Note that the companies described above are neither the youngest nor the most technologically advanced organizations in the world. They have

---

[1] This chapter presents the perspectives and knowledge of Hewitt consultants, based on their work and study in the area of HR effectiveness. Hewitt Associates LLC is a global management consulting firm specializing in human resource solutions, with more than 11,000 associates working in 37 countries worldwide. Hewitt is the largest multi-service HR delivery provider in the world. Its client roster includes more than two-thirds of the *Fortune 500* and more than a third of the *Global 500*. The information included in this chapter is not intended to profile Hewitt's client engagements. It does include references to HR projects (such as Dell and Cisco) that did not involve Hewitt consultants.

Table 1. In Their Own Words: Company Objectives for HR eTransformation

Company A	Company B	Company C
Global technology and engineering company	Printing and publishing company	Major U.S. retailer
1. Make HR more strategic	9. Focus on high visibility/immediate impact solutions	13. Drive speed, efficiency, productivity, consistency, and accessibility
2. Reduce process cycle times	10. Reduce HR administrative burden and make HR more strategic	14. Increase associate satisfaction/reduce frustration
3. Reduce transaction costs		
4. Increase satisfaction with HR services	11. Increase satisfaction with HR services	15. Reduce HR administrative work and forge a more strategic role for HR
5. Improve accuracy, consistency, and currency of information	12. Create savings and process improvements	16. Heighten our attractiveness to job seekers
6. Drive manager and employee effectiveness		
7. Enhance company image with current and potential employees		
8. Drive the "Web mentality"		

several decades (in one case, almost a century and a half) of history baked into their cultures and processes. Technology and the Internet are not coded into their organizational DNA—at least not yet. Rather, the three companies, and many others like them, are large, traditional, complex organizations that are focused on using the Internet to catalyze and accelerate the transformation of HR by leveraging two dimensions of eTransformation:

- Empowering HR customers. Internet technologies make it possible for organizations to automate HR processes and allow end users to own their HR information and outcomes so that the need for intervention by HR staff is significantly reduced or eliminated.
- Enabling the (*new*) HR professional. The Internet can deliver new tools and accurate, timely information to HR professionals and can help them succeed in their new role as consultants to the business.

Empowering HR customers

Customer empowerment is giving employees, managers, employee candidates, and other customers of HR services direct access to and ownership of information and outcomes. It begins with providing access to decision-support content and personal data, expands to the execution of transactions and processes, and eventually transforms relationships in the organization.

The self-service misnomer

Customer empowerment is not merely about self-service, a concept that is often used to describe the activities and solutions associated with putting HR services on the Web. HR eTransformation efforts have been most successful in situations where organizations have looked beyond the concept of self-service.

Dell Computer, for example, calls its eTransformed HR model "HR Direct." By extending to internal customers the "Be Direct" brand message that the company espouses with its external customers, Dell's HR eTransformation efforts have given employees and managers direct ownership of HR information. The concept seems simple enough. But when this philosophy is implemented in the context of HR processes, managers have direct, on-line access to a broad range of information about employees, and they can act on that information. At Dell, managers can hire, transfer, promote, and change pay for individual employees—all on-line, all on their own. Controls, for the most part, are built into the system, rather than into the HR staff.

Dell's HR Direct team did not conceive of its Internet-related HR efforts as self-service solutions. In fact, in internal and external communications about these efforts, references to self-service are plastered with a bold red

Customer empowerment
is not merely about self-service.

"X." The message is clear: Dell's Web-enabled solutions are about empowering HR customers to take ownership, obtain the information they need, and achieve the outcomes they desire in order to be effective. These solutions are not an effort to get others to do the work of HR. The HR Direct team has insisted that this distinction was a critical ingredient to the project's success (Dell "HR Direct" Presentation, March 2001).

The self-service concept fails, from an HR customer perspective, to capture the power of the Internet. To the HR customer, self-service is a lot like pumping gas—something most of us are not excited about doing and would prefer to have someone else do it for us. The eTransformation of HR creates opportunities for customers to access information they never had before and to get results fast. From a strictly process view, the Internet allows HR to put existing transactions and processes on-line, as-is. From the eTransformation view, on the other hand, the Internet allows HR to eliminate unnecessary steps; to remove degrees of separation between users, information, and outcomes; and essentially to strip out a lot of the excess junk that accumulates around processes over time.

It may appear that the distinctions drawn here between self-service and eTransformation are merely semantic. But the shift in mindset is critical. If the focus were merely to let employees and managers fill out forms on-line instead of on paper, HR would miss opportunities for cost savings *and* for strategic change in HR's role in the organization. Customer empowerment is about a real change in ownership and control in the organization. It is about getting HR out of the middle and enabling employees, managers, and others to be self-sufficient.

The evolution of HR customer empowerment solutions

With this distinction between self-service and HR customer empowerment in mind, we use the framework below to discuss, with clients, the three stages of HR customer empowerment solutions: information, automation, and transformation.

Most organizations have implemented, or are in the process of implementing, solutions at various points along this evolutionary path. But many organizations have found it helpful to think directionally about their position and progression on this path and where they should be focusing their energies.

Information

In the past, most organizations used the Internet purely as a communication medium. It was another channel through which to disseminate, gather, and share information. In the early 1990s, many organizations began to develop externally facing Internet sites that included such static content as the mission statement, descriptions of products and services, profiles of senior managers, and contact information for customers, suppliers, investors, job seekers, and the press. Alongside their externally facing Websites, they quickly began to develop internally facing intranet sites. Their HR groups immediately saw an opportunity to leverage this internal channel as a means to distribute information more quickly, and they began to develop static, content-based Websites. The promises of content-based Websites were

- Reduced costs for developing, disseminating, and maintaining communication
- Easy access to targeted, timely, and accurate information for employees, managers and other HR customers

The HR group used to produce and distribute thousands (in large organizations, millions) of booklets, newsletters, forms, etc. Every change in policy or plans required HR to update, re-produce, and re-distribute its publications. In addition, HR could never be sure that employees, managers, and others had on hand the most current version of the relevant publication when a need for information arose. Even if employees and managers possessed the most accurate version of the information, they would have to navigate a large volume of if-then statements to find the nugget of policy information that applied. HR's costs of communication in a large organization were overwhelming, and the effectiveness of their efforts was questionable at best.

The Internet promised to resolve these issues by delivering the right information to the right user at the right time and to maintain all the information in one place—on-line. Based on the promises of lower costs and greater accuracy of information, many organizations developed HR intranet sites. Some even developed disparate Websites within HR, one for benefits

Customer empowerment is about a real change in ownership and control in the organization.

and compensation, another for training, and so on. In most cases, these sites were not well organized from a customer's perspective, and they were not well connected to each other—from either a content or a usability standpoint. The sites consisted primarily of static content that employees, managers, and others could find in printed materials.

As organizations gained experience with their Internet and intranet sites, it became clear that if they were to achieve the promise of reduced communication costs and better end-user access to current information, they would need to manage their on-line environment more effectively. HR began to consolidate on-line information and organize it according to the ways users accessed it. Soon, they began to deliver truly personalized information. For example, where an employee once could navigate only static pages of reference material on the rules of the 401(k) plan, she now could access her personal account balance and her contribution rate. Today, companies are developing personalized portals that offer targeted, role-based access to all the information and transactions employees need—from static policy reference materials to the advanced applications described in the "Automation" and "Transformation" sections below.

For example, groups at AlliedSignal have been developing Websites since 1997. These Websites focused on benefits, diversity, learning, and other areas. Recently, the company (the former AlliedSignal, post-merger with Honeywell) worked with Yahoo! to deliver a single, integrated portal that enables users to customize their own Web pages according to their specific, individual needs and preferences. This portal integrates external content (world and local news, sports, and weather) with internal corporate content (company news and policies) and personal information (benefits and compensation). But all these changes did not happen overnight. The current company portal is three or four generations beyond the disparate collection of static Websites that once constituted its intranet (Wilky, 2000) In addition to personalizing the delivery of content through portal interfaces, content-management solutions are making the information stage of customer empowerment more effective and more efficient. They help to streamline efforts to author and publish information, and they help to deliver targeted and personalized information to users. Content-management software packages, such as Interwoven and Vignette, allow content owners to author and publish information with a Web browser, rather than having to learn and manipulate HTML code. Some software packages, such as Authoria, offer a wealth of pre-developed, configurable HR content. These software solutions essentially manage content and permit creating rules about which content should be presented to which users under which circumstances. This means HR's customers will see only the information that is relevant to them. For example, an employee in a lab in Seattle could not see policy information about security at the headquarters building in New York. The concept is simple, and the advantages to users are tremendous.

While the information stage is not the most exciting stage along the evolutionary path in Figure 1, it is absolutely fundamental, and many organizations still do not have it entirely right. Many HR staffs continue to publish content on-line without developing standards for quality and consistency and without assigning accountability for ongoing maintenance. In these organizations, developing and maintaining most HR content still requires the attention of technical experts to make changes in HTML pages. Nevertheless, getting the information base right and creating a meaningful gateway for users is the foundation to the more advanced stages.

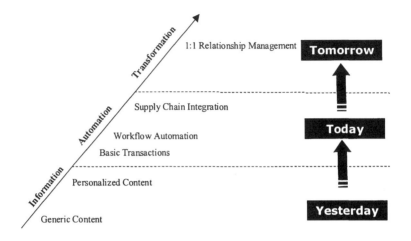

Figure 1. Three stages of HR eTransformation evolution

Automation

The continuing advancement of Internet technology and HR's increasing experience with applications have led to using the Web for many more functions than distributing information. From permitting the isolated execution of basic transactions, to automating complex processes, to wiring external suppliers into company processes, the Internet allows HR to change how and where its work is done. The automation stage is where most of the energy, attention, and funds are being invested today. Over the past two years in particular, a flood of activities has driven HR processes to the Web.

Automating HR processes begins with basic transactions and builds on the foundation laid in the information stage. For example, not only can employees access reference information about the 401(k) plan and view their personal account balances—they can now change their contribution rate on line. Employee transactions like these are now Web-enabled in many areas of HR, such as benefits enrollment, 401(k)-account management, and name and address updates.

Beyond basic transactions, HR Internet solutions have begun to address broader, more complex processes that involve a series of transactions strung together across different users and user applications. In staffing and recruiting, for example, a number of software providers enable managers to create job requisitions, post jobs internally and externally, and view candidate applications and resumes as they arrive on-line. These software packages also allow setting the required workflow and approvals among managers, HR professionals, and recruiters, in accordance with the organization's preferred recruitment process.

In large, complex organizations today, the compensation-planning process often involves hundreds of managers working thousands of hours, cumulatively, on unwieldy, disconnected spreadsheets. Software for compensation planning allows hiring managers to access budgets for their specific groups, to model pay increases according to the plan rules that are built into the system, and to submit their proposed increases for the year. Their proposals are routed to senior managers and compensation planners, enabling them to roll up multiple group and division budgets and if necessary send back individual proposals for changes to the managers who issued them. There are many other such processes, including performance management, learning and development, succession planning, and career planning, that can be Web-enabled to save time and money and increase workforce productivity. Automation-stage solutions can also look at processes that involve participants outside the organization. In staffing and recruiting, for instance, software can integrate background checkers, drug screeners, and search firms into the Web-enabled workflow. In benefits, health planners, fund managers, investment advisers, and others can be wired into Web-based processes.

Transformation

Perhaps the best way to understand the truly transformational power of the Internet is to look at a recent development in the marketing profession, the widespread adoption of customer relationship management (CRM). CRM allows marketing staff to focus on deepening relationships with individual customers by learning as much about them as possible, institutionalizing the learning, and working to maximize the profitability of these relationships over the course of the customer lifecycle. Web-based CRM technologies have been developed that enable all employees who interface with customers to gain access to a complete database of customer information and to use Web-based tools that facilitate direct interactions with customers. For example, every time an Amazon.com customer makes an on-line purchase, the transaction is recorded in Amazon's database of customer information. The customer's purchasing history is then used to send e-mail messages to specific customers offering books and music the customer might want to purchase.

Beyond automating basic processes and distributing information, HR groups can concentrate their eTransformation efforts on "employee relationship management" (ERM) that enables their organizations to manage talent more effectively. We have extensively studied why employees choose to stay with an employer, to serve that employer with extra effort, and to say good things about the employer to others outside the organization—all of which are indicators of the high level of commitment required to drive organizational performance. These studies highlighted two factors that are nearly always among the few critical levers identified: (1) opportunities in the organization and (2) the employee's relationship with his or her manager. The insights offered by CRM show how HR might deploy Web-based technology to leverage opportunities and create more effective relationships between employees and managers.

Cisco's approach to eRecruiting on its corporate Internet site is an outstanding example of applying ERM principles. In addition to submitting their usual resumes on-line, job seekers who log on to Cisco's careers page

Automation-stage solutions can also look at processes that involve participants outside the organization.

can enter data about themselves—name, company, job interests, desired geographic locations, etc. Based on the information in the job seekers' profiles, the site asks pre-screening questions designed to round out information about their work experiences. Once the job seekers complete this exercise, they immediately receive an e-mail thanking them for the information. Within days, they begin to receive targeted job opportunities via e-mail. No more venturing out on the Web to search job databases repeatedly to see if anything new has been posted. Job seekers have a one-to-one relationship with Cisco. Without ever having interacted with a live person at Cisco, they are suddenly receiving more information, more relevant information than they may be receiving from their own employers, who know more about them than Cisco could imagine. Of course, it is difficult to build and maintain relationships entirely on-line. If job seekers wish, they may log onto Cisco's career site and access a "Make Friends at Cisco" tool that helps them connect with live Cisco employees (see http://www.CISCO.com/ for examples).

Cisco's Web-based recruiting approach is a great example, but it represents just the tip of the iceberg when it comes to ERM. HR in many organizations could deploy similar applications internally for employees who seek new opportunities. HR could deploy solutions to help employees navigate career opportunities, model development needs, and create "learning agents" that will alert them when appropriate development opportunities emerge.

Further, HR could create tools that help managers more effectively lead, develop, and manage people. In marketing's CRM evolution, the sales agent is the primary point of contact between the customer and the organization. CRM gives sales agents the tools to be more effective. In ERM, the manager is the primary point of contact between the employee and the organization.

These eTransformation-stage solutions will do more than simply help managers deploy cost-saving, self-service transactions. Transformational solutions will enable managers to access, at their fingertips, complete employee histories, goals and objectives, performance and pay records, disciplinary records, even project assignments and training needs. Ultimately, such information can be used to develop more productive, more engaged employees who are more closely aligned with the needs of the business.

One interesting finding from our work with clients is that in most global organizations the HR issues that tend to be associated with ERM, such as performance management, career development and planning, strategic staffing and succession planning, are also the issues most commonly addressed throughout the organization. As issues of data privacy and cultural differences emerge, it will be fascinating to see how the eTransformation stage of HR customer empowerment plays out in global companies. In the meantime, there are a few rare examples, like Cisco's recruiting model, of existing ERM solutions.

How are HR customers reacting?

Do employees and managers resent these technological solutions as attempts to push the work of HR onto them? Not at all. Our anecdotal experience shows that, where solutions are effectively developed and deployed, employees and managers clamor for more functionality, more information on-line, and more control over their own information. Of course, when solutions are poorly developed and deployed, the feedback is less encouraging. And as with any other initiative, there are detractors and people who resist any form of change.

But how will employees and managers react to the more transformational types of solutions suggested above? To find out, we recently conducted focus groups with managers and employees from organizations with low-turnover knowledge-workers and from organizations with high-turnover service employees. The *employees* in our focus groups were excited about the career development and training opportunities in the ERM model. They thought that if their companies deployed such solutions, they would have far better access to jobs, development projects, and training resources. On the other hand, they were concerned about confidentiality issues, and they expressed the fear that poor managers would use technology as a crutch. Meanwhile, the *managers* in our focus groups were excited about consolidating all employee information in one place and having the potential for faster resolution of people-related issues. On the other hand, they too were concerned about confidentiality issues and the lack of interpersonal interactions with employees, as managers begin to manage more of the employment relationship on-line.

In essence, many of our clients find that the demand for new, increasingly sophisticated customer-empowerment solutions outpaces HR's ability to develop and deploy their new capabilities. So far so good, at least from an HR customer standpoint. That leads us to the next dimension of HR eTransformation, enabling the new HR professional.

Enabling the (*new*) HR professional

A client recently shared an anecdote about an HR generalist's reaction to customer empowerment efforts. The HR generalist had contacted a member of the HR technology team to inquire about the best way to get a manager's reorganization of his department reflected in the system. The HR technology person informed the HR generalist that all managers could transfer employees from one group to another, on their own, at the click of a mouse. The generalist's response was, "*They* can't do that. What am *I* going to do?"

There are significant negatives for HR professionals in the eTransformation stage, particularly for those who were hired and trained to do purely administrative tasks. A shift in mindset is required if HR staff is to let go of the reins and enable employees and managers to solve problems on their own. But there are also significant positives for the HR professionals who want to take on the consultant and strategist roles.

The "take-aways"

As mentioned earlier, a study of one organization showed that 74 percent of HR activity continues to be devoted to administrative tasks. Whenever we have mentioned this finding to other HR executives, most thought the percentage in their organizations would be similar. When HR customer empowerment works, it truly eliminates the need for HR intervention in the majority of administrative tasks. For example, a recent Hunter Group (2000) report states that some organizations have seen up to a 50-percent reduction in process cycle times, a 59-percent reduction in inquiries to call centers, and a 75-percent reduction in headcount associated with Web solutions for employees and managers. The results are real. In organizations where HR customer-empowerment solutions have been effective, the impact on HR staff has been significant.

Compounding the issue of HR's changing role is a trend toward outsourcing HR's administrative work and technology management. Many organizations implemented pre-Web human resource information systems (HRIS). They have since built new solutions for advanced HR processes on top of their HRIS. Some organizations have had success with these add-on software products. Others have struggled. Many organizations have learned the hard way that when a start-up software company folds, HR and IT are left with the job of supporting the software themselves or rushing to implement a new system at break-neck speed. Because PeopleSoft, SAP, Oracle, Lawson, and others have released Web-native versions of their software, HR groups face a big decision: stick with the HRIS they have (and, potentially end up with software that is no longer supported) or migrate to Web-native versions (which potentially involve expensive and often painful implementations too closely on the heels of the last round of implementing new software). As a result, many HR groups are looking to combine their eTransformation and outsourcing efforts by joining with a partner who will deliver comprehensive, robust HR administrative services—thus shifting the burdens of HR administration management and constant upgrades to the outsourcing partner. Beyond basic application service providers, employers seek partners who will manage the technology and provide backroom processing and other supportive business services around HR administration systems. In our work, we have noted a trend from the types of outsourcing that are common today (benefits and payroll) to the types of outsourcing that stretch broadly across HR content areas and deeply into HR administrative activities.

The combined trends of outsourcing and customer empowerment will create a window of opportunity for HR to re-focus its talents and efforts and seize a more strategic role. As one HR executive said about the eTransformation efforts in his organization, "When the winds of change are blowing, some people will hide behind rocks, and some will build windmills." We have observed the truth of this executive's observation. Simply creating solutions and waiting for results will not be effective. If change-management issues are not addressed, reluctant HR staffers can slow the momentum and limit the results the change would otherwise yield. In our experience, staff reluctance to embrace change has been, more than any of the technology details and the process re-design issues, the "dark side" (as one of our clients ominously put it) of HR eTransformation.

Volumes have been written on effective change management, so we will not address the issue here—other than to acknowledge that effective HR eTransformation will require change management at its best. By implication, the change effort must focus on the HR function itself. Organizations that take HR eTransformation seriously will develop plans for re-skilling, re-staffing, and redeploying existing HR staff. We asked one executive what portion of the current HR staff would be effective at the far end of eTransformation. He predicted that 50 percent or less would make it. When we subsequently shared his prediction with other HR executives, the vast majority said that the same percentage or less would survive HR eTransformation in their organizations. The re-skilling and change-management issues associated with HR's eTransformation have just begun to be explored.

The "pluses"

As HR eTransformation efforts minimize their administrative activities, many HR professionals will acknowledge the change as positive. For HR generalists in the field, the change will mean having more time to focus on people-related needs. The HR professionals who are experts in such issues and who prefer to spend their time working to solve them will welcome the change.

Further, the HR professionals who take the consultant role will have tools and information at their fingertips. Whenever a process is automated on the Web, the technology produces a series of records that can be used to monitor trends and events as they occur. Turnover, performance levels, attendance—whatever factors are critical to the success of a given business—can be tracked and monitored in real-time. HR professionals and managers can have the information they need to make effective decisions, to change behaviors, and to target interventions in ways they never experienced before. Targets and warning signs can be set for critical measures and tied to HR systems. Automatic alerts can arrive at the HR professional's computer the moment a trend takes shape.

For example, an HR professional and a VP of sales for a medical systems company may together decide to set a warning-level for the number of involuntary separations in the North American region. As sales managers in the region initiate employee terminations and record these events in the system, they will code each event as voluntary or involuntary. If the number of involuntary separations hits the warning level, the HR professional will receive an instant alert on her computer. She can examine the data and find that the rate of involuntary separations has spiked in the Philadelphia area. She might then identify the fact that a Philadelphia area sales manager was promoted into his role three weeks ago, which is when the trend started. The HR professional now has a great set of data with which to begin analyzing the situation. If she uncovers a managerial effectiveness issue, she and the VP can intervene. If they decide to retrain the new sales manager, the HR professional can refer to expert content about managerial effectiveness on the Internet, identify several targeted tools, and put together a development plan. In a few months, she and the VP can review the involuntary separation data to determine if their intervention had been effective.

While this scenario may seem far-fetched, it is all possible today. A number of tools are available to analyze such workforce situations. However, few organizations have capitalized on opportunities to deploy these capabilities. Most have focused all their efforts on HR customer-empowerment issues and efforts. The successful approach to HR eTransformation will address the need to enable HR professionals in their new role of consultant/strategist through information and tools like those described above. For an eTransformation effort to have a real and lasting impact, HR must develop solutions to empower their customers and enable the new HR professional.

Making HR eTransformation happen

HR eTransformation is complex work. There is no simple recipe for success. But there are a few common building blocks that an organization must consider in planning eTransformation efforts:

- Strategy and Action Plan
- Wired Workforce
- Portal Solution
- HR Applications
- Business Services Operations

Strategy and action planning

When it comes to executing an HR eTransformation, one of the most common pitfalls is the lack of an integrated strategic plan and a vision for the transformation. Many organizations have made a number of disparate, disjointed efforts that either conflict with each other or fail to capture the potential synergies across process and content areas. We have used the framework depicted in Figure 2 to help clients define their priorities and organize their eTransformation efforts:

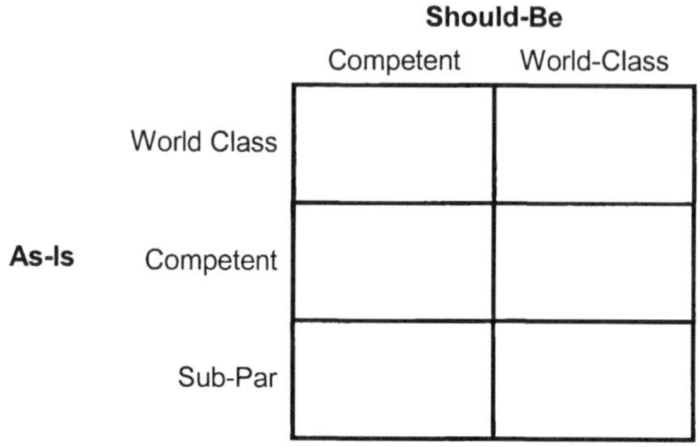

Should-Be
Competent   World-Class

World Class

As-Is   Competent

Sub-Par

Figure 2. HR eTranformation opportunity analysis framework

This framework enables HR executives to zero in on the areas where eTransformation will have the most impact. For example, if the organization should be world-class in its recruiting efforts but is sub-par today, HR ought to focus on developing innovative approaches to recruiting by leveraging technology and making process improvements. This approach to defining HR's focus is intended to prevent the knee-jerk reaction of simply Web-enabling that which exists today, without strategic consideration of what will matter most in the future.

While the framework helps in examining at the highest level what areas deserve HR focus, there is another step. Once the organization has identified its high-level focus, say recruiting or benefits, the change effort must be divided into discrete, executable projects. These projects must be prioritized and sequenced. We often use the matrix in Figure 3 for this work.

We suggest that clients give top priority to projects that fall in the "strike zone" (the upper right quadrant). These projects have significant impact and

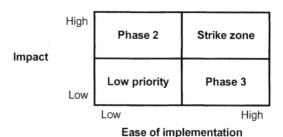

Figure 3. HR eTransformation project prioritization

are not insurmountable challenges. The intent is to execute important successes fast and build momentum. Next, we suggest focusing HR efforts on the projects that have high impact but are more difficult to execute (the upper left quadrant). Inertia might otherwise drive the HR staff to focus on the easier projects, even though they will have less impact (the lower right quadrant). After having worked through the process of defining priorities by direction and project level, the usual work of first-rate project planning and management begins. This planning work, which can be done in a few short days, will save months of wasted time and heaps of wasted money down the road.

Wired workforce

All efforts will be for naught if HR staff and organization managers do not have access to intranet-connected PCs. The eTransformation project team should know what portions of the workforce are wired. If this information is not readily available, the team must gather it. (Very few organizations will find that their workforce has 100 percent access to their intranets.) Once the wired-workforce gap is understood, the eTransformation team decides (or helps senior managers decide) what to do about it. A few common strategies can be used to address the wired-workforce gap:

- Aggressive connectivity plans. In late 1999 and throughout 2000, amid the e-business craze, a number of stories were widely circulated about organizations offering free, or virtually free, PCs and Internet access to all employees. This is certainly an approach to eliminating the wired-workforce gap, but one that most organizations' balance sheets will not support.
- PC purchase plans. Organizations can choose to offer PCs and Internet access to employees at a discount through a number of leading PC manufacturers. Dell's "Employee Purchase Program" is an example. PC purchase programs can be subsidized by the organization at whatever levels will encourage employees to participate. One concept that has been discussed but not yet implemented (to our knowledge) is building a PC purchase program into the enrollment periods for flexible benefits. Such an approach would certainly raise visibility and encourage participation in the plan.
- Shared workstations. Perhaps the most usual approach to addressing the wired workforce gap, particularly in manufacturing environments, is to set up intranet-connected PC workstations in common areas, such as break rooms. The shared-workstation approach is relatively low cost and easy to implement, but it has limitations. For example, employees may

be reluctant to conduct such transactions as benefits enrollment in the break room during lunch. Also, front-line managers may not be entirely supportive of employees taking time from other tasks to use the PC workstations. Nonetheless, shared workstations can certainly be one approach to a wired workforce.

- Targeting "wired" populations. Some organizations have opted to address the wired workforce gap by directing customer-empowerment efforts toward specific employee groups who are already connected to the Internet or the intranet. For example, one company decided to develop solutions for managers and HR staff because they had 100 percent access. A targeted approach may be a first step to building credibility and making the case for some combination of the broader approaches described above.

These approaches are not mutually exclusive. In particular, some combination of the latter three may expedite progress toward closing the wired-workforce gap. Analyzing the wired-workforce gap and developing a plan to address it, are critically important to HR eTransformation efforts.

Portal solution

Much has been written about portals and their role in a Web-enabled organization. A portal is a personalized gateway to information and applications. The portal itself is a fairly empty solution; it is simply a gateway to other things. Some organizations are developing enterprise-wide portals to serve as gateways to broad corporate information and applications. Others are developing functional portals within HR and other groups. The danger in the latter approach is that a series of disconnected, un-integrated portals will be developed within the organization—making it all the more difficult for employees to get what they need. The most effective HR eTransformation efforts are coordinated with the development of an enterprise-wide portal. In this approach HR can guarantee that its content and functions are delivered through the primary Web gateway to the organization. It is no wonder that HR often leads or catalyzes organization-wide portal efforts. HR groups' eTransformation success depends on their customers having easy access to information and applications.

HR applications

The preceding sections, "Empowering HR customers" and "Enabling the new HR Professional," presented a number of applications. When it comes to deploying these applications, organizations must set a directional strategy for HR information management and technology. There appear to be three fundamental approaches to building the foundation for HR eTransformation:

- The Web–enabled HRIS approach. Traditionally, HR groups (particularly in large organizations) have built their HR information and technology foundations around such information systems products as PeopleSoft, SAP, Oracle, and Lawson. In the past, these products were strong in data management and weak in HR processes. They also were not Web-enabled. However, new Web-enabled versions (for example, PeopleSoft's Version 8) offer far better functionality, and they have become truly viable options for Web-enabled HR.
- The "HRIS wrapper" approach. A number of software providers in the market offer products that sit between the company portal and the HRIS (or other source system) database. These middleware solutions offer functions that enable employees and managers to access and update a broad range of HR information. These products were developed around the gap that the formerly non-Web-enabled HRIS providers have now filled. For organizations that are seeking greater independence from their core HRIS solutions, these products may make sense.
- The "best in class" approach. In either of the two preceding approaches, most organizations will continue to use a few additional technology products beyond the core HRIS. The main advantage of using "best-in-class" applications is that their functionalities are robust for each specialized area of HR. For example, an organization may implement a Web–enabled HRIS for core data administration but implement separate software packages for specific areas like staffing, learning, compensation, etc. The main disadvantage is that they can be difficult and expensive to integrate and maintain. Ultimately, every organization must decide if it will take a best-in-class approach.
- HR will clearly need IT support in setting the stage for eTransformation. Appropriate IT resources may exist within HR, or HR may partner with an IT organization. A few organizations have formed e-business groups and made them available to support such important organization efforts as HR eTransformation. In any case, having access to a strong technology staff with knowledge of Web solutions and e-business principles is essential to the success of HR eTransformation.

Business services operations

As mentioned in the "Enabling the New HR Professional" section, there is an increasing trend toward outsourcing HR operations. There is also a continuing trend toward shared services models. In either case, an HR eTransformation effort will need to analyze alternative models and decide whether it makes more sense to insource or outsource, centralize or decentralize. Also, an eTransformation effort will impact existing HR operations. For example, a series of customer-empowerment solutions will eliminate the transactions that may currently be managed in a centralized service center. The organization should have a plan for handling this change and adjusting roles and staff accordingly.

Conclusion

Earlier, we looked at CRM, a trend in marketing that offers lessons for the HR profession. Another, different trend is underway across the corporate hallway in the IT group. This trend, too, offers lessons for the HR profession. Recall that IT used to be focused on keeping the mainframe running, fixing printers, and helping techno phobic workers solve software and hardware snags. Today, much of that work is outsourced, and the Chief Information Officer (CIO) has been charged with taking a strategic business-planning role and working closely with the CEO to shape business direction. The CIO's staff focuses on lines of business and other functional areas by providing supportive technologies for the business strategy as it is cascaded through the organization. Likewise, HR is shifting from being an administrative, tactical, procedural, compliance-driven function to being one that is more focused on developing strategic talent and supporting strategic employee management and recruitment.

Will a Chief People Officer be the next role to emerge on the organization chart? Such a role already exists in some organizations. The eTransformation efforts that many HR groups are engaged in will certainly help drive that change. To be successful, HR must focus on both dimensions of eTransformation, empowering HR customers and enabling the new HR professional. Simply launching Web-based solutions atop today's HRIS and creating thousands of pages of Web content will not be effective. Great work has already been done, but HR must get strategic and serious about what it will accomplish.

Lloyd Wilky, Director of Employee Services at Honeywell, recently reflected on his eTransformation work of the past few years: "The climb is steep, but the view is spectacular. This is the best work that HR can be doing right now." Let us begin the journey.

References

Dell. (2001, March). "HR Direct" Presentation.

Hunter Group. (2000). Human Resource Self-Service Study.

Wilky, L. (2000). *1:1 Relationship Management at Honeywell.* Presentation to Conference Board, October 4, 2000.

MANAGING INFORMATION TECHNOLOGY CHANGE IN THE WORKPLACE
A Systems Perspective

Linda K. Lawson
Williams Companies

Catherine M. Sleezer
Oklahoma State University

Abstract

In the networked world, many management models no longer presume face-to-face interactions within organizations. To further the prospects of managing today, we present research that describes information-technology changes in ten typical organizations. Our description relies on a systems perspective and incorporates the four levels of systems thinking described by Senge (1999, 2000): events, patterns/trends, structures, and mental models.

Whatever your role in your organization—employee, manager, customer, or investor—people-to-people and people-to-information connections have never seemed so fast or so transformative. Many people believe that advances in information technology (IT) are the driving force in moving society from the Industrial Age to the Information Age. In the Industrial Age, information was shared physically through meetings, printed documents, analog telephones, and so on. Today, information is transformed into bits and communicated across digital networks accessed by computers, faxes, e-mail, voicemail, pagers, cell phones, and personal digital assistants. Many organizations rely on digital information to produce the efficiencies that create competitive advantage. Some organizations combine digital information and employee knowledge to create competitive assets that are particularly difficult to emulate. (See Van Buren's and Ardichvili's chapters for more information on managing knowledge and intellectual capital.)

Authors in the business and popular press have enthusiastically described the New Economy and its opportunities for lowering costs and increasing productivity all along the e-commerce chain. Consider the many in-depth business stories about Internet companies and consider the major hype that surrounds a few well-known organizations like Cisco, Dell, and America Online. But becoming a success story is not easy,

> The American Dream has a new name: e-business. But the realities of internet business are harsh; look past the hype and the well-publicized stories and you'll find that many companies spend a great deal of money on their initiatives and have little to show for it. (*Net Ready*, 2000, Book Jacket).

In a special report published by *Fortune Magazine,* Vogelstein (2001) pointed out that when the economy was booming and few competitors understood the technology, failure could be redefined and repositioned as a "learning experience." But as the slowdown that began in late 2000 and early 2001 continues to affect the world economy, "there is little room to screw up" (p. 142). The report advised leaders that now is the time to "look around and learn."

We decided to take this advice and look around and learn from the IT experiences of typical business, education, and government organizations. Why do we focus our attention in this chapter on typical organizations? A sports analogy will provide the answer: In ice-skating, as in e-business, a few superstars deliver performances that are fascinating to watch. However, the world's rinks are full of typical skaters who could seriously injure themselves if they attempted the triple jumps, back flips, and spins that seem so effortless when the superstars do them. Most typical skaters could more effectively improve their performance by closely observing the strategies and techniques of skaters more like themselves. As they learn which techniques are effective and which are problematic, they develop the mental models and the skilled behaviors they need to improve their own performance. Similarly, decision makers and human resource development (HRD) professionals in most organizations can benefit by learning from the descriptions of IT applications and their results in typical organizations. To provide a background for our look around to learn from others' applications of IT, we will briefly examine the historical patterns of past technology adoptions.

Historical patterns for technology adoptions

In retrospect, it is easy to see that initially decision makers seriously underimagined the opportunities offered by technological advances. For example, television was first viewed as a medium for stage plays (Hagel & Armstrong, 1997), not as the ubiquitous source of entertainment and information it is today. Railroads too were first viewed as a means for transporting passengers, not as a means for transporting goods and commodities (Drucker, 1999). Watt's 1776 steam engine provides yet another example of a seriously underimagined, world-changing technology.

Initially, the steam engine was used in iron works to pump water and blow air for blast furnaces. The value of the steam engine's work was compared to the number of horses needed to do the same or similar work;

Initially decision makers seriously underimagined the opportunities offered by technological advances.

hence the derivation of the term *horsepower* for measuring the power of motors or engines (Wren, 1987). Only many years after their invention were steam engines used to power looms, an innovation that changed how work was done in the textile industry and that gave birth to the factory system. Work that had been performed by craft persons in their homes gradually moved to factories with steam-powered looms. As textile workers began laboring together in a common setting, the need to direct and coordinate their efforts became apparent. Then, in an increasingly competitive environment, many factories developed economies of scale by expanding in size or scope. When the maximum number of individual workers an entrepreneur could monitor appeared to be limiting business growth, the role of professional manager developed. Managers acquired, allocated, and employed human effort and other resources to accomplish business goals.

This example illustrates that new developments in technology can often be perceived and applied as the means for improving pre-existing processes (e.g., replacing horsepower with more efficient and less-expensive steam-generated power). They can also be perceived and applied in ways that fundamentally change the structure of work, which in turn produces new patterns of work and new outcomes. Indeed, the use of steam engines in the textile industry produced both such changes. Human perceptions have similarly influenced the creation of new applications for electricity, the automobile, the copy machine and so on.

Today's advances in IT present special challenges to human perception. Weick (1996) used the phrase "technology as equivoque" (p. 561) to characterize the existence of multiple interpretations of new technology. He noted that technological applications can be viewed simultaneously as continuous events, unexpected events, and abstract events. We use a familiar example to demonstrate these three qualities: the automated teller machine (ATM), an IT-enabled process, has changed the face of banking. Customer services that include the continuous processing of transactions are available 24 hours a day, 7 days a week. When an ATM is temporarily out of service, banking customers encounter what they perceive to be an unexpected event. Further, they gain little by standing around looking at an out-of-service ATM because the causes of the problem are neither concrete nor visible. So they interpret this impersonal event as if it were aimed at them and leave the scene muttering under their breath, "Why me? Does it break down because it knows I need money?"

Taking a systems perspective allows problem solvers to acknowledge the many possible interpretations and explanations that can be applied to complex systems. Senge (1999, 2000) presented a particularly useful graphic, the Iceberg, to help leaders look beneath the superficial events in any complex system into the underlying causes of problems. The Iceberg, with nine tenths of its bulk under the water line, illustrates four levels for viewing reality. Only the events level is above the water line. The large structure that supports the tip of the iceberg is below the water line and cannot be clearly seen.

At the *events level* of thinking about the world, attention is focused on observed events and on decisions about the best ways to react to them. Events explanations are common in contemporary organizations, hence the preponderance of reactive managers and the tendencies to misplace blame on the not guilty and the unsuspecting (Senge, 1990). Consider how IT applications are often described as isolated events (e.g., implement a database system, develop an expert system, create a Web link, provide on-line training).

In the Iceberg graphic, the *patterns level* is just beneath the water line; therefore, it is not readily visible (Senge, 2000). At the patterns level, attention is focused on observable trends or cycles of events and on considering ways to respond to or take advantage of these trends or cycles. For example, many business managers and stock market analysts closely monitor the latest e-business trends and anticipate exploiting them. Here is another example: We recently overheard an executive at an Academy of Human Resource Development (AHRD) conference say, "We installed a knowledge-sharing database—and spent millions doing it." She grimaced and added, "We are having problems getting our employees to use it, and we really need to think about the implications." This executive faced a problem that is evident in many organizations. According to a recent ASTD Trends Executive Summary (Van Buren, 1999),

The promises of learning technologies for many organizations have gone largely unfulfilled. They are discovering that a major issue that needs to be addressed before the full promise of learning technologies can be realized is the challenge of getting employees to accept and use technology-delivered learning" (p. 2).

Yes, understanding the patterns of events in a system allows us to adapt to the trends. However, to understand why the patterns occur, we must look deeper. Looking deeper beneath the Iceberg water line takes us to the level of system structures.

At the *structures level*, we focus on identifying the system structures that underlie and sustain the patterns of events, or the system's behaviors. Behind each pattern of behavior is a systemic structure—a set of factors that interact, even though they may be widely separated in time and place, and even though their relationships may be difficult to recognize. When studied, these structures reveal the best levers for change. (Senge, 2000, p. 82)

The executive who wished employees would utilize the knowledge database didn't say it, but she was looking at a pattern of system behavior that was supported by a system structure that was larger and more complex

Behind each pattern of behavior is a systemic structure.

than the knowledge database. System structures in organizations develop via socially constructed solutions to recurring problems in the organizational context (Symon, 2000). Over time, new problems arise. The socially constructed solutions to these new problems are layered onto the previous solutions and interact with them to create an increasingly complex system structure. Any new internal or external event then brings a multitude of interacting relationships and interdependencies into play. These complex interactions explain why seemingly reasonable actions sometimes create surprising or unintended results. Sometimes it is difficult to trace the interactions because initiating events and subsequent results are masked by distance and time.

Let's revisit the example of the lack of employee response to the knowledge-sharing database. In any organization, many factors interact. In this case, the knowledge-sharing database, the incentive structure, the management structure, and the training program, to name just a few, interact. These factors influence employee behavior. Decision makers and HRD professionals who "see" systemic structures are in a position to discern where to apply leverage that will change the system and produce the desired results. Systems thinkers are less vulnerable to the tendency to apply ineffective, quick-fix solutions. For example, if the knowledge-sharing database is supported by an out-of-date incentive structure or by a management structure that favors hard-copy resources, simply training employees to use the database is unlikely to produce the desired results.

The deepest level of the Iceberg represents the mental models. At the *mental models level*, attention is focused on the thinking and the vision that underlie the system structures. Mental models are internal images that an individual or group of individuals has of how the world works. Mental models include assumptions, values, attitudes, and beliefs. The more closely a mental model reflects reality, the more useful it is.

Gilovitch (1991) described how questionable and erroneous beliefs are formed and maintained in everyday life. He traced them to errors in processing information and drawing conclusions. His many examples included the erroneous belief in the "hot hand" in the game of basketball, which refers to the supposed tendencies of basket-making success (or failure) to be self-perpetuating. Such thinking is part of a widely held belief that "success breeds success," a premise that holds true in many areas (p. 11). In this case, as Gilovitch's research revealed, "a player's performance on a given shot is independent of his performance on previous shots" (p. 13). Superstitious beliefs are particularly costly because the mental models that we hold influence what we see, what we expect, and what we learn (Senge, 1990). As Kauffman (1980) succinctly stated, "It ain't what you don't know that hurts you; it's what you DO know that ain't so" (p. 38).

The mental models that people in organizations share, whether they are accurate or erroneous, are powerful. It is difficult to make substantive changes in system structures, patterns, or events without first changing the relevant mental models. Consider the mental models that might underlie the knowledge-sharing system in our example. Let's imagine that the creators of the underused system assumed that employees would value sharing their knowledge and would therefore be intrinsically motivated to use the

Are IT applications being used in typical organizations as a means for improving pre-existing processes?

database. Let's further imagine that employees believe hoarding information provides them with job security. The executive who lamented the issue could achieve substantive, long-term change in employee behaviors by bringing these inconsistent mental models to consciousness within the organization. She could facilitate dialogue to produce a shared mental model that better fit reality, and she could also negotiate changes in the structures so they better fit the shared mental model and produced the desired employee behaviors.

This overview of technology adoption suggests ways to view IT applications using a systems thinking perspective. It also highlights important questions to ask: Are IT applications being used in typical organizations as a means for improving pre-existing processes? Or are they being used to substantially change the structure of work systems, to produce new patterns of behavior, and to achieve new outcomes? To answer these questions we examined the IT applications in ten organizations and identified the events, the patterns, the system structures, and the mental models.

The ten organizations

We focused our looking around and learning on IT applications in four business organizations, four education organizations, and two government organizations. The individuals who provided the following stories about their organizations' particular applications of IT were purposefully selected for this research because a) they represented a variety of organizations and held a variety of staff and operational management positions and b) they had experience in using IT to improve learning processes and performance for their organizations and their customers. One individual worked in business and at the same time served as an adjunct faculty member. She provided information about both organizations, hence the nine participants in the study and the ten organization descriptions.

The nine participants and their names, titles, and organizational affiliations are listed in Table 1. Their organizations provided a variety of products and services to distinct customer and customer groups.

All nine participants actively contributed to the AHRD 2001 Technology Pre-Conference. Six of them also served as members of a pre-conference panel that discussed IT applications. Following the pre-conference, all participants completed an open-ended survey in which they described the uses of IT in their organizations during the last five years, including what had changed for their organizations as a result of using IT, what had remained the same, and how using IT had altered the organization's structure and management practices. The survey also asked participants to describe expected future uses of IT and the implications for their organizations and HRD professionals. This survey data is the basis for our describing IT applications in the ten organizations at Senge's (1999, 2000) four levels: events, patterns, structures, and mental models. To assure the accuracy of the descriptions, all participants reviewed the chapter and provided feedback.

Table 1. Participant names, job titles, and affiliations

Participant	Job title, organization information
John W. Bing	President, ITAP International. Provides research and consulting services for measuring and improving human processes in global businesses
Rose Bonjour	Telecommunications Training Coordinator, Oklahoma Department of Career and Technology Education. Provides leadership, resources, and assures standards of excellence for a comprehensive statewide system of career and technology education
Loretta L. Donovan	Director Corporate Learning and Development, ClientSoft. Provides e-business solutions for remodeling existing applications to seamlessly integrate traditional legacy transactions with new sources of data. existing
	Adjunct Faculty Member and Distance Learning Consultant, Columbia University, Teachers College. Provides graduate degrees with foci in adult learning and leadership
Larry Dooley	Professor at the Center for Distance Learning Research (collaboration between Texas A&M University and Verizon) and Chair, Human Resource Development Program, Texas A&M University department of Educational Administration and Human Resource Development, Texas A&M University. Provides graduate and a proposed undergraduate degree in human resource development
Art Johnson	Chief Auxiliary Administration Division, Office of Auxiliary, U. S. Coast Guard. Provides training and information services to the 35,000 men and women who volunteer their time and expertise to support the Coast Guard and improve boating safety.
Sandra Massey	Dean, Student Support and Development, OSU Okmulgee. Provides 2-year degrees
Jennifer Peacock	Information System Educator and E-Learning Super-System Administrator for Web-Based Training, Cox Health Systems. Provides patient health care through its hospitals, home-health care organization, insurance company, clinics, and educational systems.
Billy B. Ray	Team Leader of Human Resource and Administrative Systems, Williams Gas Pipeline. Provides natural gas transportation
Kimberly A. Shaw	Claims Specialist, City of Tulsa, Human Resources Department. Provides municipal government services

Viewing IT applications from the events level

In this section, we look at IT applications in each organization at the events level. Participants identified using a total of 24 IT applications during the last 5 years. The number of IT applications identified by participants ranged from 1 to 7. (See Table 2.)

Table 2. IT applications in ten typical organizations

Organization	IT uses
1	Communicate processes/protocols/preparations/standards, etc.
2	Communicate with colleagues and customers.
3	Move system and infrastructure applications from the mainframe to client server and the Web.
	Provide wireless, handheld e-mail solutions so managers can stay in touch with the organization wherever they go.
4	Support global customers by measuring processes on global teams
	Maintain customer work, partnerships, and conduct other business transactions through the Internet.
	Monitor internal processes
5	Offer an on-line course
6	Use technology in the delivery of on-campus and distance instruction
	Offer courses at a distance
	Manage the organization more virtually using electronic communication, e-mail, and document sharing
7	Streamline paperwork for customers
8	Provide employees with forms, policies, and information
	Schedule meetings within divisions
	Meet with employees and customers
	Communicate with customers and organizations
	Provide customers with forms and information
	Establish a virtual learning system
	Provide customers with IT training
9	Provide training
	Supervise instructors
10	Provide a telephonic reporting system for our employees to report injuries
	Provide electronic mail
	Provide benefits and employment information

The IT applications were aimed at achieving the organization mission. We discovered, for example, that a portion of the mission of the Texas A&M Center for Distance Learning Research is "to provide timely and appropriate information on the development, application, and maintenance of technology systems that directly enhance education and training. The Center's services are available to all public agencies and private businesses that are interested in the welfare and education of people through appropriate information technology and distance education." IT applications there are used to offer courses. The following reported change after implementing IT was consistent with the Center's mission,

> Classes offered at a distance are now offered in a multiple of modalities ranging from Internet delivery to videoconferencing. Moreover, classrooms on campus now have computers, LCD projectors, and document cameras.

The mission of ITAP International is to provide consulting, tools, and research to customers and to leaders in the international consulting industry for the purpose of measuring and improving human processes in global business. IT applications that ITAP developed to support its global customers also support its own operations.

All the IT applications described by our participants directly or indirectly supported the achievement of their organizations' missions.

In summary, the events perspective provides information about the number and the types of actual IT applications and their perceived link to the organizations' missions.

Viewing IT applications from the patterns-of-events level

We scanned all the descriptions of events for underlying patterns by asking the following six questions: What purposes were IT applications meeting? What levels of empowerment did IT uses enable? As a result of using IT, what changed and what remained the same? How had the structure and the management changed? What future developments were expected? Were there differences among the IT-driven changes in education, business, and government? To answer each of the questions, we reviewed participants' descriptions, grouped them according to themes, and identified categories. The following are the patterns that we found.

IT purposes

The IT applications in participants' organizations were meeting a variety of declared purposes. They were directed to facilitating communication (N=9), providing training (N=6), enabling monitoring and support of customers and employees (N=4), making information available (N=4), and other (N=1).

IT levels of empowerment

We determined the levels of empowerment enabled by IT applications by using the stages of empowerment that Christie described in his chapter, "HR to the Power of $_e$: Internet-Powered Transformation of Human Resources." IT applications can empower customers by giving them direct access to and ownership of information and outcomes. Christie describes three progressive stages of HR customer empowerment: information, automation, and transformation. We extend Christie's model to describe the stages of customer empowerment in other organizational units. In the information stage, IT provides the tools to disseminate, gather, and share information. In the automation stage, IT facilitates simple and complex transactions and processes among people. In the transformation stage, IT enables relationship management. Of the 24 reported IT applications, we determined that 11 were at the information stage; 2 were at the automation stage, and only 1 was at the transformation stage. Many IT applications were simultaneously at the information and the automation phases (e.g., an IT application that provided information also automated some interactions).

IT-driven changes in work

We learned that in all ten organizations some aspects of work changed and some remained constant. The changes were as follows: 1) more efficient employee-employee and employee-customer interactions; 2) fewer duplicative efforts for customers; 3) new approaches to working with customers; and 4) different customer services. Note: we use the term *customer* to mean both internal and external clients. For example, IT applications that made information available on the Internet and through wireless communications contributed to more efficient and faster interactions between employees and between employees and their customers. IT applications also contributed to eliminating duplicate efforts for customers. As one participant commented,

> The paperwork is more streamlined, eliminating redundancy, so the customer no longer has to go to five different offices and provide name, social, address, and major at each.

IT applications also enabled employees to use new approaches when working with customers, which in turn changed these relationships. For example, a participant reported,

> My company now considers its partners in Europe, the Americas, and Asia as colleagues and professionals, and we often work together on the same project. Once again, communications technology makes this possible; without it, we would be separate organizations working together only when we were in the same place at the same time.

In some organizations, IT applications led to working with different customers. For example, an education institution that offered courses on line found that distance learning helped them begin to serve those who were not traditional full-time, on-campus students. A participant reported,

> Our students are also different in that most are not residential at this point and are shuffling jobs, classes, family and other career initiatives.

Aspects of the organizations that remained the same in these organizations included the dynamics of human interactions, the focus on customer service, the use of analysis and planning, and the use of paper documents. Some participants' comments about human interactions reflected a certain resignation or frustration. For example, a participant expressed frustration in this comment,

> Human dynamics remained the same...the 'luddites' are all-powerful and consistent in undermining technology transfer.

Most participants also focused on the continued need to support and develop people. Furthermore, they often identified training in their organizations as the mechanism for providing this support.

Some aspects of work changed
and some remained constant.

The focus and the emphasis on customer service also remained, even though the methods of providing services had changed. The same held true for analysis, planning, and research and development. For example, one participant stated,

> Sound research and development of the tools and methods we use are required whether or not the tools and methods are delivered face to face or over the Internet.

Finally, paper systems remain firmly in place. The constraints to going paperless include government policy, union contracts, and fear. As one participant commented,

The organization is still very 'paper dependant' in procedures. Technophobe if you will—they don't trust the electronic system to always work.

In summary, some aspects of the workplace changed and some stayed the same for all ten organizations. However, no consistent change patterns emerged across all organizations.

IT-driven changes in structure and management

We discovered that IT applications affected physical or social structure changes in eight of the ten organizations. The reported changes were as follows: flatter organization structures; new assignments for support staff; and modified assignments for and hiring of IT staff.

Several participants indicated that IT applications resulted in the need for fewer layers of management in their organizations. For example, a participant commented that cross-communication between departments was easy and the "big gun manager" typically did not need to be involved. IT applications also resulted in less need for support staff to provide professional workers with clerical services. For example, in several organizations professionals assumed responsibility for their own correspondence, and their support staff were assigned other duties. In general, the described changes involved middle managers, support personnel, and employees at lower organization levels. Also, most of the described changes involved small groups of employees and their work processes, not large organization units. Many comments focused on changes in the IT function. In some organizations, the changes involved creating and filling high-level IT positions. In other organizations, the changes involved shifting IT support personal from completed projects to new projects.

Next we look at management changes. Seven of the ten participants described management changes in their organizations. They described managing across distances, sharing information, and communicating with greater speed. Managers had to adapt to managing employees, colleagues, and customers at a distance. A typical comment was,

> Because of technological changes and the new company benefits all staff may not be on site everyday of the week. How are these employees included in staff and project meetings? How is employee effectiveness measured?

Another participant related how managing at a distance could be paradoxically described as hands-off and controlling,

> Employees can work more independently as the information is literally at their fingertips; however, with technology, managers have the ability to run reports and use tracking devices to "see" what employees are doing during

their daily routines. Individuals can be monitored on everything from how many files they open to how many changes they actually make in only one file. While management may not be as visible physically, they definitely have more ways to "see" what employees are doing. Through technology, they also have the capability to tap into phone lines and e-mail with not much more than a flick of the switch. While most managers elect not to use this big brother approach, technology has definitely given them the capability to become more of a micro-manager.

Several participants indicated that managers in their organizations now share information. They described a democratization of information, increased collaboration, and sharing of timely information. Often, this information sharing involved real-time data that could be quickly analyzed in many ways. Some participants expressed a positive view of this change. One, however, commented,

> I think mostly things are moving faster and less efficiently. Kind of helter-skelter.

Many commented on the absence of management change. A participant from education captured this concern,

> It seems that although the organizations themselves have radically changed, how they are administered has rarely changed....

A participant from business echoed this view,

> I don't see a vast change in management style. In fact, those who were bureaucratic may be more so.

In many organizations, employees had access to information, but they lacked the authority to act on that information.

Future developments

All nine participants anticipated IT developments in their organizations in the next three to five years. Seven noted that developments of on-line services would continue. In contrast to the previously described finding that most current IT applications in the ten organization are at the information and automation stages, participants expected to see changes that will

> *Participants expect to see changes*
> *that will transform relationships.*

transform relationships. They described telecommuting, access to real-time data, and availability of information from any location. Most commented about the ongoing requirements to keep up with the current technology and decide what technology is needed and by whom.

Five participants predicted changes in HRD activities in their organizations, including the reality of on-line learning that will be available 24 hours a day and 7 days a week, the Internet as a supplement or alternative to classroom instruction, and accreditation for all the organization's training. One participant anticipated mandatory education taken via distance education "on the employees' time/dollar."

Participants anticipated that individuals will face control issues. One participant predicted that individuals will have increased control because they will work alone and in private. But other participants predicted less individual control. For example,

> The new system allows the information to be tracked fairly easily, so it is much more difficult for something to "slip through the cracks" or to be on someone else's desk.

Another participant based her prediction on a recent IT project,

> As we converted to a new streamlined system, many managers and supervisors found it hard to let go of their traditional methods and policies. By using technology, we empowered the employees. The dependency is taken away and supervisors and managers are more easily held accountable for not completing information.

Leaders' resistance to change, which is expected to be a continuing issue for organizations, was captured in the following comment:

> It [IT] is forcing higher management to learn or get out before they get run over in the technology frenzy. There is going to have to be a shift in trust and responsibility. Leadership positions are going to have to give up some of their control to help expedite change. Many are resisting all around change.

All participants commented on the ongoing need for individuals to have technology skills. Seven noted that although their organizations are providing training for current employees, they expect new job applicants to have the skills.

Some comments focused on organizational forms and resources. For example,

> Technology also makes possible collections of organizations in molecule-like fashion, which are created for specific functions and then may either reform with other organizations or may form a more permanent structure. Smaller organizations/companies may therefore be able to serve as virtual segments of larger ones for shorter or longer periods of time. Larger organizations will become more porous as they make use of such devices to improve their productivity and competitiveness.

This prediction is consistent with collaborations among organizations for the specific purpose of developing knowledge networks. See the chapter,

"Building a Competitive Workforce for the New Economy," by Meeder and Cude.

Several participants commented on saving or using time. For example,

Resources that have been developed by others are available for sharing, which eliminates duplication of services and saves faculty and staff time for new projects.

One respondent expressed a bit of cynicism about saved time,

I think we will see instructors moving away from curriculum development and more into coaching/mentoring roles with their newfound extra time. (ha/ha).

In summary, an overview of the effects of IT applications in a number of organizations provided a richer view than could be gained by reviewing the same in a single organization. Our looking around for patterns of change that resulted from IT applications allowed a glimpse of changes in work behaviors and organization structures that could not otherwise have been observed. Furthermore, we were interested to note that participants from business, education, and government expressed similar views. However, we were unable to identify any consistent patterns of change that affected multiple organizations.

Viewing IT applications from the structures level

In this section, we focus on the systemic structures that underlie or contribute to patterns of behavior. The participants' comments revealed an ongoing tension between the organization's growth in capacity and outputs and the limits to its growth.

Participants described cycles of increasing organizational capabilities and outputs. As shown in Figure 1, the growth cycle, which can be called a virtuous circle using systems language, begins with new IT applications that increase employee capacity. For example, IT applications enable employees to more efficiently obtain and share information. When using these IT capabilities, employees inevitably span old boundaries of space and time. They also span boundaries within the organization because working with new technology requires them to ignore some cultural norms, formal policies and traditional work practices. Employees develop new patterns of acting and interacting that may require changes in work roles, reporting relationships, and work processes. As they use IT capabilities to improve organizational processes or customer relationships, they increase the organization's capacity and output for providing new customer services. The organization may supply the same customers with more services or recruit

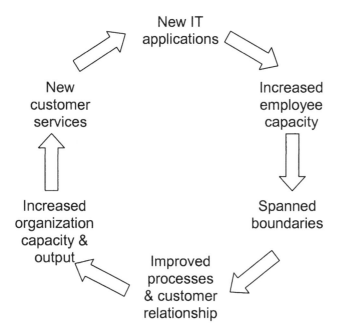

Figure 1. Virtuous circle of increasing organizational capacity and output

new customers and customer groups. Eventually, working effectively with customers requires purchasing new IT applications. And so the cycle continues.

Unchecked growth, however, can destroy an organization. Some of the effects of IT applications may actually serve to slow growth. The capabilities supplied by IT are often balanced by the lack of readiness of decision makers to take advantage of available IT capabilities. In this case, the term *decision makers* includes managers and employees at all levels of the organization.

When managers authorize individuals and groups to use IT applications, one result can be a redistribution of authority. Fewer managers may be needed, and those who remain may lose control of crucial work processes to individual employees and groups who use IT applications to contribute in new ways to organization performance. The multilevel theory of organizational performance (Fisher, 2000) identifies many pathways by which individuals use their capacities to contribute to organization performance. For example individuals may combine their own resources with organizational resources to produce accomplishments that are deployed by the organization, or they may share a skill or idea that is used by another group to modify a production process. Individuals who use their IT-enhanced capacities to work more independently, to expand their job roles, to change their reporting relationships, or to increase their contributions to an organization's performance could gain increased authority. Decision makers may slow this process and dissipate the gains for the organization by resisting changes, implementing bureaucratic processes, and focusing resources internally. Decision makers may focus IT-driven changes exclusively on lower levels of the organization. They may also keep change at a manageable level by providing employees with information without giving them the authority to act on the information. In this way, they limit the benefits of using IT applications on behalf of customers. Finally, those who use IT applications only to improve the efficiency of current processes could squander much of the potential for using IT to create new processes.

Looking at IT applications from the structures level provides insight into the events and the patterns of events that occurred in the 24 IT applications. According to Senge (1990), structural changes are more effective than superficial changes. In this case, the structures level of analysis revealed a potential leverage point for change: prevent decision makers from squandering IT capacity. Using this leverage point may be less costly and more effective than using the training strategy described by many participants in the survey.

Viewing IT applications from the mental-models level

In this section, we asked four questions that were designed to bring to consciousness the thinking that underlies IT structures. Specifically, we sought to identify inconsistencies, questionable beliefs, and unexpressed assumptions. Mental models are usually tacit, but when they are made visible they can be discussed, shaped, and changed.

First, what assumptions result in IT applications being used more often to improve pre-existing processes than to fundamentally change the structure of work? Hammer & Champy's (1996) insight could enhance this discussion,

> The fundamental error that most companies commit when they look at technology is to view it through the lens of their existing processes. They ask, "How can we use these new technological capabilities to enhance or streamline or improve what we are already doing?" Instead, they should be asking, "How can we use technology to allow us to do things that we are *not* already doing" (p. 607).

Second, what assumptions lead to framing IT applications in terms of organization mission rather than in terms of larger economic systems? Many participants reported that their organizations were trying to better serve customers and be more competitive by using a readily available tool, IT

Mental models are usually tacit but when they become visible they can be discussed, shaped and changed.

applications. However it is difficult for leaders to differentiate their organizations in the marketplace when they use similar tools in similar ways (e.g., enhance information sharing and create efficiencies at lower levels of the organization). Hamel (2001) provides pertinent insights. He reminds his readers that turning productivity into profits is not easy, especially when their competitors are using the same strategy. He also points out that customer ignorance has been a competitive advantage for many companies: "For banks, insurance companies, and auto dealers, customer ignorance has long been a reliable profit center" (p. 176). Hamel also notes that this source of profits may disappear when people use IT to become informed consumers. Also many organizations (e.g., educational institutions) compete based on providing information that customers may now be able to access at lower costs on the Internet. Consumers can now use the Internet to quickly compare products, services, organization missions, and so forth. The absence of comments from participants regarding the shift in power from organizations to consumers should be discussed.

Third, what are the mental models that support continued reliance on traditional forms of organizational structure and management? In general, our participants identified superficial rather than deep structural changes. By contrast, many business experts state that IT applications require organizations to move beyond the traditional bureaucracy to other organizational structures (e.g., Williamson & Boyle, 2000; Symon, 2000; Tapscott &Caston, 1998). For example, Man Jit Singh, President and CEO of Futurestep unequivocally stated, "The hierarchy command-and-control bureaucracy is gone. Now it is self-managed teams, it is enlightened teams, it is people with information, knowledge workers who use information productively to get things moving forward" (Sikes, 2000, p.168).

Participants at the (AHRD) Technology Pre-Conference offered insights about the interaction of IT and national and organizational cultures. For example, John W. Bing, President of ITAP International, pointed out that the term *mental model,* as it is used in cross-cultural studies, refers to patterns of values and beliefs that determine how views of reality are influenced by national cultures. Governmental systems in China monitor on-line behavior to a much greater degree than do governmental systems in the U.S., where such monitoring activities are perceived to interfere with strong values of individualism and individual choice. Using Hofstede's (1991) model, the differences stem from how IT is applied in China, a low individualistic/high power-distance/high need for certainty culture, as distinct from how IT is applied in the U.S. a high individualistic/low power-distance/low need for certainty culture. The culture and subcultures of the organization also

Decision makers' mental models served to limit the application of IT capabilities.

interact with IT applications. For example, Tanuja Agarwala from the University of Delhi, India noted that in some organizations IT applications are being questioned and resisted rather than being institutionalized in ways that integrate people and work processes. Additional examples of how organizational culture and IT interact to influence work processes and results can be found in the chapter titled "Making Knowledge Count: Knowledge Management Systems and the Human Element."

Given these insights, we believe that discussions of mental models related to IT applications and organizational structure should be informed by critically revisiting the relationships between culture, knowledge, and power. Shafritz and Ott (1996) identified the tensions that we saw in these typical organizations: "The informating process sets knowledge and authority on a collision course. In the absence of a strategy to synthesize their force, neither can emerge as a clear victor, but neither can emerge unscathed" (pg. 542). The informating process also emphasizes results-oriented rather than social-oriented organizational structures. Any review of systems, power, authority, accountability, and the role of people in organizations should acknowledge the systems heuristic "Beware of the Tragedy of the Commons" (Kaufman, 1980, p. 41). This heuristic demonstrates how, in a competitive environment, individuals make decisions that are in their own best interests and by so doing harm the larger system (e.g., upper-level decision makers may make IT decisions that best meet their individual needs rather than the needs of the organization). Another heuristic that could inform this discussion is "Don't try to control the players, just change the rules" (Kaufman, 1980, p. 39). Small changes in a few organization rules could encourage adopting a new concept of management authority or a redistribution of authority. Rule changes could support dual roles of decision makers—sometimes encouraging the use of IT to increase organization capacities; other times limiting it. Furthermore, rule changes could illuminate the mental models that underlie the criteria for decisions.

Fourth, how do participants conceptually integrate IT's advantages with the corresponding responsibilities? Many participants described using IT to obtain increased freedom, increased connection, or increased control. They seldom considered the likelihood of unintended consequences to themselves or others. They provided few descriptions of the costs and personal responsibilities that accompany the benefits of IT.

The mental models that underlie IT decisions in the ten organizations seemed to limit the possibilities for action. Mental models that better represent current reality could provide opportunities to more effectively utilize IT capabilities.

Conclusion

Viewing IT applications from Senge's four levels of systems thinking provided a number of insights. At the events level, we saw the many IT applications to organizational missions. At the patterns level, we observed how organizations are actually using and managing IT applications. At the structures level, we saw the tensions between the available technology and the readiness of decision makers at all levels to use the technology to change work processes. We identified structural levers for change. By looking at events, patterns of events, and structures across organizations, we surmised the mental models that underlie IT decisions.

This study was based on ten typical organizations. The differences between the perspectives from which participants made their comments and the perspectives from which we interpreted those comments could have influenced our findings. Therefore, this study should be replicated by other researchers who take a systems view of IT.

In the meantime, decision makers should use IT strategically. They could compare the uses of IT in their organizations to those in the organizations described in this chapter and answer some important questions: What other IT applications could we be using? What are the potential benefits and risks of these applications? How could we design our organization structures to take full advantage of IT capabilities to provide goods and services to our customers that better meet their preferences? What are our mental models and how do they serve us? Which of our mental models should we revise to better reflect reality?

HRD professionals who are charged with supporting and improving human and organization performance can compare the patterns of events in their organizations with the patterns of events in the ten cases. They can also reflect on how underlying structures support the uses of IT applications in their organizations. Upon reflection, they can consider how to apply IT to the breadth of their human performance technology responsibilities, including "training and education, job design, feedback systems, incentives and rewards, selection and staffing, and environmental engineering" (Rosenberg, Coscarelli, and Hutchison, 1999). As Loretta Donovan (personal communication, February 27, 2001) pointed out, "IT interacts with the traditional HPT problems. There is still too much work to do, and never

HRD professionals can help decision makers reframe their use of IT applications.

enough time." To address this issue, HRD professionals must figure out how their organizations work as performance systems and promote a general awareness of the activities that dissipate human and IT capacities. Through strategic planning and organization development, they can help decision makers reframe their uses of IT applications.

Finally, all readers of this chapter know that views of reality at each of Senge's four levels of systems thinking will be different and enlightening. Caution: skipping immediately to the deepest level is impossible. Rather, systems thinking requires beginning at the most superficial level, observing events, and working through the patterns level to the structures level to the mental models level. Understanding IT use and management from the four levels depicted in the Iceberg analogy allows us to improve the prospects of managing in today's networked world. We invite readers to examine the chapters in this book and other works and identify the levels at which the authors perceive reality.

References

Drucker, P. (1999). Beyond the information revolution. *The Atlantic Monthly, 284*(4), 47-57.

Fisher, S. (2000). *A multilevel theory of organization performance.* Unpublished Doctoral Dissertation, Oklahoma State University, Stillwater.

Gilovich, T. (1991). *How we know what isn't so: The fallibility of human reason in everyday life.* New York: The Free Press.

Hagel, J. III, & Armstrong, A. G. (1997). *Net gain: Expanding markets through virtual communities.* Boston: Harvard Business School Press.

Hamel, G. (2001). The think tank. *Fortune, 143*(5), 175-176.

Hammer, M., & Champy, J. (1996). Reengineering the corporation: The enabling role of information technology. In J. M. Shafritz & J. S. Ott (Eds.), *Classics of organization theory* (4th ed., pp. 607-616). New York: Harcourt Brace.

Hartman, A., & Sifonis, J. (2000). *Net ready.* New York: McGraw-Hill.

Hofstede, G. (1991). *Cultures and organizations: Software of the mind.* McGraw-Hill: Berskshire, England.

Kauffman, D. L. (1980). *Systems one: An introduction to systems thinking.* Mpls: Future Systems Inc.

Rosenberg, M. J., Coscarelli, W. C., & Hutchison, C. S. (1999). The origins and evolution of the field. In H. D. Stolovitch &. E. J. Keeps (Eds.), *Handbook of human performance technology: A comprehensive guide for analyzing and solving performance problems in organizations* (2nd ed.) (pp. 24-46). San Francisco: Jossey-Bass.

Senge, P. (1990). *The fifth discipline: The art and practice of the learning organization.* New York: Doubleday.

Senge, P. (1999). *The dance of change: The challenges to sustaining momentum in learning organizations.* New York: Doubleday.

Senge, P. (2000). *Schools that Learn.* New York: Doubleday.

Shafritz, J. M., & Ott, J. S. (Eds.). (1996). *Classics of organization theory (*4th ed.). New York: Harcourt.

Sikes, A. C. (2000). *Fast forward.* New York: William Morrow.

Symon, G. (2000). Information and communication technologies and network organization: A critical analysis. *Journal of Occupational and Organizational Psychology, 73*(4), 389-414.

Tapscott, D., & Caston, A. (1998). Paradigm shift: Introduction. In G. R. Hickman (Ed.), *Leading organizations: Perspectives for a new era.* . Thousand Oaks: Sage.

Van Buren, M. (Ed.). (1999). *Learning a new game, technically speaking.* Alexandria, VA: ASTD.

Vogelstein, F. (2001). E-Corp special report: Flying on the Web in a turbulent economy. *Fortune, 143*(9), 142-146.

Weick, K. E. (1996). *Technology as equivoque: Sensemaking in new technologies.In J. M. Shafritz and J. S. Ott (Eds). Classics of organization theory.* (4th ed.). New York: Harcourt Brace.

Williamson, E., & Boyle, A. (2000). A new structure for the new millennium. *Management Services, 44*(10), 14-16.

Wren, D. (1987). *The evolution of management thought* (3rd ed.). New York: Wiley and Sons.

Authors' Note: The authors acknowledge the contributions of Peter Kuchinké, Assistant Professor at the University of Illinois in co-facilitating the panel discussion.

THE ROLE OF HUMAN RESOURCE DEVELOPMENT IN TRANSITIONING FROM TECHNOLOGY-FOCUSED TO PEOPLE-CENTERED KNOWLEDGE MANAGEMENT

Alexander Ardichvili
University of Illinois

Abstract

Communities of practice supported by on-line interactive technologies rapidly become one of the most efficient knowledge management tools in organizations. This chapter demonstrates that the Human Resource Development (HRD) function is uniquely positioned to implement the enabling systems for realizing the community-of-practice metaphor, which is grounded in the human capital theory and the resource-based theory of the firm. Examples of knowledge-sharing communities of practice demonstrate their central role in mobilizing the potential of the intellectual resources of the organization. The chapter includes a discussion of seven areas where HRD can play a central role in creating knowledge-sharing communities of practice. The chapter ends with a discussion of the HRD competencies and skills needed to fulfill this role.

Knowledge management (KM) has received unprecedented attention in the business press and academic publications since the mid-1990s. It is viewed as the key to long-term business growth, increased competitiveness, and organizational effectiveness (Davenport & Prusak, 1998). Today, the field of KM is dominated by the information systems perspective, which emphasizes data collection and storage in computer databases, with organized processes and rules for disseminating these data (Myers, 1996).[1] Thousands of consulting firms and technology vendors have flooded the market with KM-

---

[1] For an overview of definitions, theoretical underpinnings, current practices, and criticism of knowledge management, see Davenport & Prusak (1998), Gourley (2001), and Von Krogh, Ichijo, & Nonaka (2000).

related products based on new software, databases, and other technological solutions. However, since late 1999, the initial euphoria has given way to disillusionment with the results of KM efforts so far and to a realistic assessment of the impact of KM technologies. For example, annual surveys by the consulting firm Bain & Co., which measured executive satisfaction with 25 management techniques, showed that in 1998 and 1999, knowledge management ranked at or near the bottom in every category (Garner, 1999). Among the chief reasons for this failure were an overemphasis on technology-based solutions—from search-and-retrieval tools to decision-support systems, data mining, data visualization, and intelligent search agents—and a lack of attention to the human side of the equation, especially the relationship between learning and knowledge creation, dissemination, and use at the individual, group, and organizational levels (De Long & Seeman, 2000; Dixon, 2000; Gourley, 2001; Pfeffer & Sutton, 2000).

One strategy for overcoming the deficiencies referenced is to move away from the "data capturing and dissemination" metaphor in KM to that of a socio-technical system that helps people generate, share, and use knowledge in specific organizational contexts (Von Krogh, Ichijo, & Nonaka, 2000). In socio-technical systems, individual, group, and organizational learning and knowledge management become interwoven and inseparable. How do organizations implement a people-centered approach to KM? And do they have the mechanisms, qualified personnel, and resources for implementing such an approach? The central argument of this chapter is

A people-centered approach to knowledge management requires using different metaphors, tools, and expertise.

that moving from a technology-centered to a people-centered approach to KM requires using different metaphors, tools, and expertise. One useful metaphor appears to be communities of practice supported by on-line interactive technologies.

This chapter demonstrates that the human resource development (HRD) function of a business organization is uniquely positioned to implement enabling systems to realize the communities-of-practice metaphor. HRD has expertise in the three domains that need to be integrated to create efficient communities of practice: adult learning (especially the constructivist model of learning); the use of learning and communication technologies; and change management and organization development methods (especially teamwork facilitation and building organizational culture). HRD professionals can and should play a leading role in conceptualizing, designing, and implementing a knowledge-management strategy and the knowledge-enabling systems of the organization.

The chapter begins with a brief overview of the theoretical base for understanding three main types of intellectual resources of the company. Second is an explanation of the role of communities of practice in mobilizing the potential of these intellectual resources. Third are descriptions of specific examples of knowledge-sharing communities of practice in business organizations. The chapter concludes with a discussion of the role of HRD in creating knowledge-sharing communities and the HRD competencies and skills needed to fulfill this role.

Three types of intellectual capital of the company[2]

The realization that KM plays a central role in ensuring competitiveness of the company rests on the perception that in today's business world the only truly unique resource of a company is its intellectual and human capital (Von Krogh, Ichijo, & Nonaka, 2000). This perception is grounded in the resource-based view (RBV) (Penrose, 1959; Wernfelt, 1984). The RBV depicts a company as a collection of productive resources that attains a competitive advantage by virtue of its unique combination of heterogeneous resources (Penrose, 1959). Wernfelt (1984) pointed out that these resources could be both tangible and intangible. By extension of the RBV, the knowledge-based view (KBV), conceptualizes organizations as heterogeneous, knowledge-bearing entities. It suggests that companies achieve sustainable competitive advantage when they develop and leverage knowledge-based competencies (e.g., Barney, 1991; Dierickx & Cool, 1989; Prahalad & Hamel, 1990). Human capital theory underlies much of this view. Its major postulate is that the utility of investments in employee skills and knowledge depends on their potential payoff to the company (e.g., Backer, 1976; Flamholtz & Lacey, 1981). Several theorists have expanded the concept of human capital to show that the human resources of a company include not only the knowledge and skills of individual employees, but also their relationships, knowledge flows, and networks (Snell, Lepak, & Youndt, 1999). These theorists use the term *intellectual capital* (IC) to describe the entire scope of an organization's knowledge, skills, and information (Edvinsson & Malone, 1997; Stewart, 1997). Underlying the broad concept of IC are three constructs: human capital, social capital, and organizational capital.

---

[2] A more detailed discussion of the theory of intellectual capital and its practical applications is provided in Van Buren's chapter, "Making Knowledge Count: Management Systems and the Human Element."

Human capital represents the knowledge, skills, and abilities of individual employees (Becker, 1964; Schultz, 1961).

Social capital represents the knowledge flows among individuals within networks (e.g., Burt, 1997; Bontis, 1996; Coleman, 1988, Stewart, 1997). It is defined as "the actual and potential resources individuals obtain from knowing others, being part of a social network with them, or merely being known to them and having a good reputation" (Baron & Markman, 2000, p. 107). Social capital encompasses both actual and potential resources flowing through a relationship network established either individually or collectively, either consciously or unconsciously (Bourdieu, 1983; Coleman, 1988). Social capital is an instrumental resource that helps individuals acquire other types of resources, even additional social capital.

Organizational capital represents knowledge that is codified and stored in databases, patents, manuals, and procedures, and is imbedded in organizational cultures (Hall, 1992; Itami, 1987). Kogut and Zander (1992) indicate that a company is a repository of capabilities in which individual and shared expertise is transformed into economically valuable products. Much of this knowledge and expertise is tacit (Polanyi, 1967) and not traceable to individuals (Kogut & Zander, 1992).

It follows that organizations are the bearers of tacit, social, and path-dependent organizational knowledge that makes them unique and competitive. Promoting the growth of social capital and organizational intellectual capital is especially important for building competitive advantage because it helps to create knowledge assets that are shared among multiple parties, assets that are larger than those possessed by any individual member of the organization (Teece, 1996; Teece & Chesbrough, 1996). In addition, the truly valuable strategic assets of an organization are embedded in the social architecture that results from ongoing skill-building activities, forms of spontaneous and informal cooperation and learning, and the tacit knowledge that accumulates in this cooperation (Mueller, 1996).

Communities of practice: A metaphor for integrating human, social, and organizational capital

Most existing KM approaches are based on the premise that the knowledge of individual employees must be, and can be, captured and stored in databases and made accessible to other members of the organization through a variety of technological tools. However, as Sternberg and Horvath (1999) pointed out, human competence is largely tacit and is inseparable from individuals and groups. Therefore, attempts to capture knowledge, separate it from people operating in specific contexts, and put it in storage are futile. Another reason why attempts to capture and store knowledge and human competence are problematic is associated with the rapid changes in today's business environment, technologies, and products. Most knowledge becomes obsolete faster than one can capture and catalogue it (McGrath & Macmillan, 2000). Furthermore, it is extremely difficult to predict which parts of the existing individual or organizational knowledge will be needed and useful in the future and which parts will become useless or even harmful if institutionalized and legitimated by their addition to organizational databases.

The above discussion suggests that technology-driven KM systems deal with only one of the three domains of an organization's intellectual capital— the human capital domain—and even in this domain, KM systems fail to

One potentially useful metaphor for describing a supportive context is community of practice.

provide efficient "management" of an organization's knowledge. To realize the full potential of all three components of an organization's intellectual capital, new approaches and a new metaphor are needed.

Several leading KM theorists have proposed strategies for closing the gap between available KM solutions and the real needs of an organization. Von Krogh, Ichijo and Nonaka (2000) introduced the term *knowledge enabling*, which they defined as a set of organizational activities that promote knowledge creation. They described five key knowledge enablers: creating a company-wide knowledge vision, facilitating conversations between all organizational players, mobilizing knowledge activists, creating contexts for knowledge creation, and globalizing local knowledge. Dixon (2000) described various types of transfer of "common knowledge" (tacit knowledge that employees learn from doing the organizational tasks, and that is inseparable from specific organizational contexts) between teams and organizational units. Davenport et al. (1998), in their overview of practices of KM in various organizations, concluded that culture, teamwork, and other human resource management and development issues are critical to the success of knowledge-management projects.

Underlying all these contributions is the insight that it is impossible to develop and grow intellectual capital and institute efficient knowledge transfer and sharing without creating an organization-wide supportive context for such activities. One potentially useful metaphor for describing and conceptualizing a supportive context is *community of practice* (Liedtka, 1999). The term was coined by Lave and Wenger (1991) to describe an activity system that includes those individuals who are united in action and in the meaning that action has, both for them and for the larger collective. Lave and Wenger argue that communities of practice are concerned with producing practical outcomes and with learning from the process. Furthermore, learning and the generation of knowledge in communities of practice occurs when people participate in problem solving and share not only the knowledge necessary to solve the problems, but also insights into the doing itself (Wenger, 1998). The community's activity results in the mutual development of individual and collective capabilities in the process. Thus, it is in the social interaction of the community, not in the individual heads of its members, that the community's knowledge exists and evolves. With its emphasis on systems outcomes, such a community appears especially well suited for ongoing value creation in a time of change.

Furthermore, communities are efficient because they are built on trust, which promotes the exchange of resources (Fukuyama, 1995). To see a group of organization's employees as a community of practice is to see them as held together by a shared concern for achieving the outcomes for stakeholders, the personal development and growth of its members, and the collective growth and development of the community. An important feature of a community of practice is that meaning, purpose, and learning are tied to the doing. Therefore, everything that is important is local and contextual and cannot be packaged and shipped to a remote location beyond the community's borders for consumption by outsiders. The communities-of-practice model allows organizations to overcome a barrier to sharing information that conventional, technology-based KM systems often encounter. That is people who are reluctant to contribute when they are asked to write something to send to a database are willing to share information when asked by a colleague (Dixon, 2000).

Communities of practice are not formal structures, such as departments or even project teams. They exist in the minds of their members in the connections they have with each other, the larger institution in which they

In a community of practice, meaning, purpose, and learning are tied to the doing.

reside, and the specific problems or area of interest they share. Researchers have observed that creating or supporting communities of practice is a powerful alternative to building teams (Nirenberg, 1995), especially in the context of new-product development and other knowledge work (Stewart, 1997).

Communities of practice have been called "stealth knowledge management architecture" (Dove, 1999). This term suggests that communities offer a natural, rather than a directed, way to create and nurture a culture of collaborative learning and knowledge generation that meets the organization's strategic knowledge management needs and its grass roots operational priorities. In addition to providing a natural venue for knowledge sharing, communities help to initiate a collaborative culture and to strengthen a culture of sharing. As Dixon (2000) observed,

> Which comes first, the learning culture or the exchange of knowledge? Given many organizations' rather abysmal success rate at changing their culture, I would put my money on having the exchange impact the culture rather than waiting for the culture to change (p. 6).

Another reason why communities of practice are efficient tools for knowledge generation and sharing is that tacit knowledge is embedded in the stories people tell (Horvath, 1999, p. 47). Competencies do not exist apart from the people who develop them (Dougherty, 1995). Not only new knowledge, but also new skills are discursively produced in conversations in a number of ways (Weick & Westley, 1996). What is more, conversations disseminate skills (Brown & Duguid, 1991). Therefore, one of the ways to help people share and internalize tacit knowledge is to allow them to talk about their experiences. Opportunities for face-to-face interactions are rather limited in today's globally dispersed multinational organizations (Taulbert 2001). Therefore, communities of practice that are supported by on-line technologies become the only viable alternative to live, informal conversations.

Examples of successful implementation of on-line communities of practice

Examples of successful implementations of on-line communities of practice in business organizations abound. The first, rudimentary forms of such communities emerged in the early to mid-1990s, when Hewlett Packard created, by using Lotus Notes, its Trainer's Trading System, a discussion database on training topics (Davenport, 1996). This database was used by HP educators to post questions and to contribute answers on topics related to training. Incentives (e.g., free airline miles) were offered for questions, responses, and contributions. British Petroleum developed a network, which it named Virtual Teamwork, to connect employees who had complementary expertise and to encourage knowledge sharing (Cohen & Prusak, 1996). Network tools included desktop videoconferencing, multimedia e-mail, application sharing, shared chalkboards, video-clip recording, groupware, and a web browser. The network was connected through ISDN lines and satellite links. To encourage knowledge sharing, the company developed on-line yellow pages, which listed employees according to their interests and expertise. The yellow pages allowed seekers to find the most useful sources of help. The company developed a program to train employees in using the high-tech network and called it coaching, instead of training, to emphasize teamwork and interaction between players.

Ernst & Young formed what it called Knowledge Networks of small groups of consultants who had expertise or strong interest in specific knowledge-management domains (Davenport, 1997). At one timer there were about 22 networks in the U.S. practice, one for each key domain of knowledge in the consulting practice.

Each network

- Met face-to-face occasionally
- Had on-line discussions
- Maintained a document database in Lotus Notes
- Was assigned a facilitator to capture the knowledge acquired from engagements, to prompt consultants to add their learning, and to edit and prune the discussion and document databases.

The facilitators, who were experts in the field of the network, were rotated into knowledge facilitator positions and back into consulting positions.

More recently, Shell International Exploration and Production (a division of Shell Oil) formed multiple communities of practice that use collaborative software to share information, insight, and advice about a common interest or practice. With the new system, Shell is solving problems and reaping value as people share and apply talents, learning, and resources globally. Haimila (2001) quoted a Shell executive, Arjan van Unnik:

> We hook up people who are working in related disciplines in Shell companies around the world so they can problem solve and share learnings and ideas. The big trick is to go further than connecting people in the same disciplines. We get excellent cross-fertilization of disciplines--for example, pipeline engineers and corrosion engineers sharing information and ideas, thereby coming up with better and more complete solutions—that's how we get great value (p. 1).

Shell's 13 communities of practice encompass more than 10,000 users in 3 major communities for the sub-surface, wells, and surface disciplines and 10 smaller communities for supporting such cross-disciplines as finance; procurement; human resources; and health, safety and environment. Based on a value review completed in 2000, Shell's Exploration and Production business realized benefits of at least $200 million per year through its knowledge-sharing initiative. It all began with a seed group of members who recognized the benefits and formed a natural community of interest. Today, each community has a community manager, whose task it is to support and energize the group to keep up interest and build content.

Caterpillar's first communities of practice (or communities of knowledge sharing, as the company employees prefer to call them) emerged in 1997 (Ziemba & Coffey, 2001). Today, there are more than 300 on-line communities with more than 14,000 members worldwide. Dedicated software, community managers, a group of KM technology experts, and learning "gurus" support Caterpillar's communities. Most of the communities formed as a result of employee initiative, not as the result of interventions planned by the KM group or the executive team. As with Shell's communities, Caterpillar's communities tend to form around specific subject matter expertise or professional activity areas. They are open to all interested employees.

Many units and individuals within business organizations play a role in establishing and maintaining knowledge sharing systems. IT units, HR units, corporate communications units, and HRD units have all been involved.

The role of HRD in creating and supporting on-line communities of practice and knowledge sharing

The challenges in enabling communities of practice are not so much that of creating them (since most communities emerge spontaneously) but that of preserving, supporting, and enriching the development of each individual's uniqueness within the context of the community and extracting tangible value from the community by linking that uniqueness with the community purpose. Therefore, under the communities-of-practice model of KM, the role of HRD professionals is not so much to capture or distribute knowledge, but to create conditions for its generation and dissemination. This work is achieved by enabling community interactions, by promoting conditions for an open exchange of ideas and information, by creating time and space for storytelling, and by supporting innovative thinking.

What are the elements of the enabling system that need to be put in place? And what is the role of HRD professionals in developing and maintaining this system? Figure 1 demonstrates that a KM-enabling system should include seven major elements. Circular placement of the elements in the model suggests there is no one right sequence for introducing the elements. Rather, developing an enabling system for KM is an interactive process requiring multiple feedback loops, frequent evaluations of system status, and rapid adjustments to the system as needed. Therefore, the circle numbers in Figure 1 are used to facilitate referring to the diagram, not to prescribe a rigid sequence of steps.

Figure 1. The role of HRD in supporting communities of practice

Circle 1 addresses the need to develop and maintain a technology platform for synchronous and asynchronous interaction between the members of the community. It is advisable to make this system easily accessible through the company's intranet and to link to the elements of knowledge storage (circle 3), learning modules (circle 6), and "ask the expert" subsystems (circle 7). In this enabling role, HRD professionals cooperate closely with the IT function of the company to select and implement the most appropriate technological solution and to ensure compatibility with the company's existing databases. For example, the background information about community members should be easy to download into the community system from existing HR databases.

Circle 2 addresses the need to provide encouragement and support and to energize the community discussions. This need, which is likely to be greater at the initial stages of community formation, will diminish as communities develop and become self-sufficient. The role of community facilitator is generally assumed by one of the members. The role of the HRD professional is to provide this individual with training in teamwork facilitation skills, conflict resolution, on-line communication etiquette, and so on.

Circle 3 addresses the need to facilitate the transformation of the new knowledge generated by the community interactions into organizational capital. The most important information is captured and made available in the form of knowledge objects residing in on-line databases. The key to this activity is to make sure that only accurate information (verified by multiple community members) is stored for access by community members. A crucial role for HRD practitioners is to ensure the user friendliness of knowledge objects. To achieve such a goal, HRD professionals need to utilize their understanding of the knowledge-acquisition strategies of adult learners, theories of cognition, and constructivist models of education.

Circle 4 addresses the need to develop teamwork skills. One of the most important roles for HRD professionals is to participate in community-building efforts to help develop teamwork skills among the community members, and to help build a culture of sharing. In this role, HRD professionals use techniques and approaches common to organization development interventions.

Circle 5 addresses the need to equip community members with skills to use the technologies that support community interactions. In this role, HRD professionals develop and make available on-line, self-paced learning modules and provide just-in-time synchronous or asynchronous tutoring in technology skills.

Circle 6 addresses the need to monitor the evolving learning needs of community members. For example, discussions about the technical problems encountered by community members as they work may suggest a role for HRD professionals to provide training in new technological processes. Observations of inter-cultural problems in community interactions across national boundaries may suggest a role for HRD professionals in improving cultural awareness among community members by providing cross-cultural sensitivity training.

Circle 7 addresses the need to integrate an "ask the expert" subsystem within the technological platform that supports the communities of practice. The "ask the expert" subsystem connects community members with a pool of volunteer experts on specific subjects whenever they need assistance or tutoring and cannot get help from other community members or through the knowledge and learning object database. HRD professionals who have a long history of finding and using experts as needed will have much of the required expertise for this role.

Competencies of HRD professionals involved in community-building efforts

It follows from the above descriptions that to provide an effective support system for communities of practice, HRD practitioners need a whole set of competencies, most of which are already in the arsenal of the HRD profession. Some competencies, however, may need to be acquired or further developed. The areas where most HRD professionals have the requisite competencies for building on-line communities of practice are as follows:

- Understanding how adults learn individually and in groups and their motivations to share information and expertise (Sternberg & Horvath, 1999).
- Understanding how people develop new knowledge structures in informal and incidental learning situations (Marsick & Watkins, 1990).
- Understanding how people use their competence, knowledge, and skills in various work situations.
- Facilitating the telling of stories and building a culture of sharing in communities of practice. (HRD professionals with a background in OD are especially well positioned to fulfill this enabling role.)
- Facilitating the generation of knowledge by using constructivist learning theory. Most existing corporate KM and e-learning systems are based on delivering pre-packaged modules, with an underlying assumption that knowledge is static. The community of practice metaphor, on the other hand, is based on an assumption that knowledge continually emerges out of community interactions.

Additional competencies that HRD professionals may not already possess and may need to develop include the use of technologies for synchronous or asynchronous on-line collaboration, the use of software for developing and delivering on-line learning and knowledge objects, and understanding the principles of on-line databases, learning management systems, and expert systems.

There is evidence that in companies that have adopted the communities-of-practice model for KM, the HRD function takes a leading role in implementing relevant activities. Thus, Motorola regards on-line communities of practice as key to the company's global learning strategy, along with CD-ROM and e-learning systems and video and satellite conferencing. These strategic learning activities are coordinated by Motorola's corporate university (Rucker, 1999). The same model emerged at Caterpillar, where knowledge-sharing communities of practice are supported jointly by the corporate university and a KM technology group. Their communities-of-practice efforts are an integral part of the company's strategy for becoming a global learning organization (Ziemba & Coffey, 2001, personal communication).

As the above examples suggest, the KM-enabling activities of a company could be housed in its corporate university or its HRD department. However, either arrangement is not required to ensure HRD's central role in KM efforts. More important is HRD's role in ensuring the full support and leadership of the company's executive team. HRD's goal is to help executives actively embrace a knowledge-management approach and realize the importance of communities of practice. Without executive support, KM could become isolated in the HRD department as easily as it has sometimes been isolated in the IT department. Therefore, an important challenge for HRD professionals is to play an active role in providing a link between the corporate strategy and the knowledge-management strategy through a combination of approaches: strategic planning, scenario planning, and advocacy.

References

Barney, J. (1991). Firm resources and sustained competitive advantage. *Journal of Management,* 17(1): 99-120.

Baron, R. A & Markman, G. D (2000). Beyond Social Capital: How social skills can enhance entrepreneurs' success. *Academy of Management Executive, 14*(1): 106-116.

Becker, G. S. (1966). Human capital. New York: Columbia University Press. In Becker, S. W., & Gordon, G. (1966). An entrepreneurial theory of formal organizations. Part I: Patterns of formal organizations. *Administrative Science Quarterly*, Dec., 315- 344.

Becker, G. (1976). *The economic approach to human behavior*. Chicago: The University of Chicago Press.

Bontis, N. (1996). There's a price on your head: Managing intellectual capital strategically. *Business Quarterly, 60*(4): 40-47.

Brown, J. S., & Duguid, P. (1991). Organizational learning and communities of practice. *Organization Science, 2*(1): 40-57.

Bourdieu, P. (1983). Forms of capital: In J. Richardson (Ed.), *Handbook of theory and research for the sociology of education*, pp. 241-258. New York: Greenwood Press.

Burt, R. (1997). The contingent value of social capital. *Administrative Science Quarterly, 42*(2): 339-365.

Cohen, D., & Prusak, L. (1996). *British Petroleum's Virtual Teamwork Program*, Center for Business Innovation, Ernst and Young LLP. Available: http://www.businessinnovation.ey.com/research/researchf.html

Coleman, J. (1988). Social capital in the creation of human capital. *American Journal of Sociology, 94* (Supplement), S95-S120.

Davenport, T. (1996). *Knowledge Management at Hewlett-Packard*, Center for Business Innovation, Ernst and Young LLP. Available: http://www.businessinnovation.ey.com/research/researchf.html

Davenport, T. (1997). Knowledge Management at Ernst & Young, Center for Business Innovation, Ernst and Young LLP. Available: http://www.bus.utexas.edu/kman/e_y.htm

Davenport, T., & Prusak, L. (1998). *Working knowledge: How organizations manage what they know*. Boston, MA: Harvard Business School Press.

Davenport, T., De Long, D. W., & Beers, M. C. (1998). Successful knowledge management projects. *Sloan Management Review, 39*(2): 43-57.

De Long, D., & Seeman, P. (2000). Confronting conceptual confusion and conflict in knowledge management. *Organizational Dynamics, 29*(1): 33-44.

Dierickx, I., & Cool, K. (1989). Asset stock accumulation and sustainability of competitive advantage. *Management Science, 35*, 1504-1511.

Dixon, N. (2000). *Common Knowledge: How companies thrive by sharing what they know*. Boston: Harvard Business School Press.

Dougherty, D. (1995). Managing your core incompetencies for corporate venturing. *Entrepreneurship Theory and Practice*, 19(3): 113-135.

Dove, R. (1999). Implementing stealth knowledge management, *Automotive Manufacturing and Production, 111*(6): 16-17.

Edvinsson, L., & Malone, M. S. (1997). *Intellectual capital: Realizing your company's true value by finding its hidden brainpower*. New York: Harper Business.

Flamholtz, E., & Lacey, J. (1981). *Personnel management: Human capital theory and human resource accounting*. Los Angeles, CA: UCLA.

Fukuyama, F. (1995). Social capital and the global economy. *Foreign Affairs, 74*(5): 89-103.

Garner, R. (1999, August). Please don't call it knowledge management! *Computerworld*, 50.

Gourley, S. (2001). Knowledge management and HRD. *Human Resource Development International, 4*(1): 27-46.

Haimila, S. (2001, February 19). Shell creates communities of practice. *KM World*, 1-2.

Hall, R. (1992). The strategic analysis of intangible resources. *Strategic Management Journal, 13*, 135-144.

Hansen, M. T., Nohria, N., & Tierney, T. (1999, March-April). What's your strategy for managing knowledge? *Harvard Business Review*, 106-116.

Horvath, J. A. (1999). Tacit knowledge in the profession. In: Sternberg, R., & Horvath, J. (1999). *Tacit knowledge in professional practice*. London: Laurence Erlbaum.

Itami, H. (1987). *Mobilizing invisible assets*. Cambridge, MA: Harvard University Press.

Kogut, B., & Zander, U. (1992). Knowledge of the firm, combinative capabilities, and the replication of technology. *Organization Science, 3*(3), 383-397.

Lave, J., & Wenger, E. (1991). *Situated learning: Legitimate peripheral participation*. New York: Cambridge University Press.

Liedtka, J. (1999). Linking competitive advantage with communities of practice. *Journal of Management Inquiry, 8*(1), 5-16.

Marsick, V. J., & Watkins, K. (1990). *Informal and incidental learning in the workplace.* London: Routledge.

McGrath, R., & Macmillan, I. (2000). *The entrepreneurial mindset.* Boston: Harvard University Press.

Mueller, F. (1996). Human resources as strategic assets: An evolutionary resource-based theory. *Journal of Management Studies, 33*(6), 757-785.

Myers, P. S. (1996). *Knowledge management and organizational design.* Boston, MA: Butterworth-Heinemann.

Nirenberg, J. (1994/1995, Winter). From team building to community building. *National Productivity Review*, 51-62.

Penrose, E. (1959). *The theory of the growth of the firm.* London: Basil Blackwell.

Pfeffer, J., & Sutton, R. (2000). *The knowing-doing gap: how smart companies turn knowledge into action.* Boston, MA: Harvard Business School Press.

Polanyi, M. (1967). *The tacit dimension.* Garden City, NY: Anchor Books.

Prahalad, C. K., & Hamel, G. (1990). The core competence of the organization. *Harvard Business Review, 68*, 79-91.

Rucker, R. (1999). Maintaining market leadership through learning: How Motorola uses technology to provide the right knowledge at the right time to its globally dispersed personnel. *Supervision, 60*(9), 3-6.

Schultz, T. (1961). Investment in human capital. *American Economic Review*, 51, 1-57.

Snell, S. A., Lepak, D. P., & Youndt, M. (1999). Managing the architecture of intellectual capital. *Research in Personnel and Human Resource Management*, Supplement *4*, 175-193.

Sternberg, R., & Horvath, J. (1999). *Tacit knowledge in professional practice.* London: Laurence Erlbaum.

Stewart, T. (1997, August 5). The invisible key to success. *Fortune,* 173-176.

Teece, D. J. (1996). Firm organization, industrial structure, and technological innovation. *Journal of Economic Behavior and Organization, 31*(2): 193-224.

Teece, D. J., & Chesbrough, H. W. (1996). When is virtual virtuous? Organizing for Innovation. *Harvard Business Review, 74*(1), 65-71.

Von Krogh, G., Ichijo, K., & Nonaka, I. (2000). Enabling knowledge creation: How to unlock the mystery of tacit knowledge and release the power of innovation. NY: Oxford University Press.

Weick, K., & Westley, F. (1996). Organizational learning: Reaffirming an oxymoron. In S. Clegg, C. Hardy, & W. Nord (eds.), *Handbook of Organization Studies.* London: Sage.

Wenger, E. (1998). *Communities of practice: Learning, meaning and identity.* Cambridge: Cambridge University Press.

Wernerfelt, B. (1984). A resource-based view of the firm. *Strategic Management Journal*, 5: 171-180.

Ziemba, R., & Coffey, J. (2001). *Communities of practice and KM at Caterpillar*. A presentation at the BrainTrust 2001 conference.

MAKING KNOWLEDGE COUNT

Knowledge Management Systems and the Human Element

Mark E. Van Buren
American Society for Training and Development (ASTD)

Abstract

The management of intellectual capital has been hampered by the lack of sound methods for measuring stocks of intellectual capital, their value, and the impacts of investing in intellectual capital. In 1997 seven large U.S. corporations that had made significant investments in intellectual capital management initiatives began a collaborative cross-industry study with ASTD. Working together, these organizations created a widely applicable and accessible framework for measuring intellectual capital. The framework identifies key measures of the economic value that stocks of intellectual capital bring to organizations. ASTD included the core intellectual capital indicators in their 1999 Benchmarking Study. This study presents the results, which are the bases for measures of each of the core indicators. This study also presents case studies of three companies at varying stages in their introducing and using knowledge management systems—Polaroid, PricewaterhouseCoopers, and Unisys.

The importance of measuring and managing intellectual capital

In the grand scheme of economic history, the knowledge era has unfolded with remarkable speed. Its evolution has been so rapid that development of some of the most basic tools for creating and managing wealth has lagged far behind the need. Fundamental among these tools is a framework for measuring the effectiveness with which knowledge—the cornerstone of wealth creation in the knowledge era—is managed.

Without good measurement, truly effective management is all but impossible. Initiatives to manage intellectual capital are hampered by the lack of sound methods for measuring stocks of intellectual capital, their value, and the impacts of investing in intellectual capital. Most organizations have, at best, only a dim notion of the value of their intellectual capital assets, even if they have clearly identified such assets. Furthermore, standard accounting systems do not allow for easy estimation of the value of investments in intellectual capital. Sound measurement requires information sharing, common definitions and metrics, and shared measurement methodologies—none of which can be addressed by market forces or by the work of isolated organizations.

The importance of measurement is difficult to overstate. In a report from The Conference Board and the American Society for Training & Development entitled *Leveraging Human Capital,* Bassi & Hackett (1997) observe, "Measurement is a critical issue for executives. They realize that even if they are not expected to present measurable deliverables today, they probably will be tomorrow" (p. 9). The significance of and the lack of progress on this issue are clear from the results of a survey, *Twenty Questions on Knowledge in the Organization,* by Ernst and Young's Center for Business Innovation (Ernst & Young, 1997). Measuring the value and

Without good measurement,
truly effective management is all but impossible

performance of knowledge assets ranked as the second most important challenge companies face today, exceeded only by changing people's behavior (54 and 43 percent respectively). On the other hand, only 4 percent of organizations claimed to be good or excellent at "measuring the value of knowledge assets and/or impact of knowledge management" (p. 8).

With this perspective in mind, the American Society for Training and Development (ASTD) has been working to develop a system for benchmarking a set of intellectual capital indicators—the Intellectual Capital Management Model. Seven large U.S. corporations that had made significant investments in intellectual capital management initiatives began a collaborative cross-industry study with ASTD 1997. The member organizations of the Effective Knowledge Management Working Group included Charles Schwab, Chevron, Dow Chemical, EDS, Motorola, Polaroid, and PricewaterhouseCoopers. Working together, these organizations created a widely applicable and accessible framework for the measurement of intellectual capital.

Intellectual capital management defined

In general, taxonomies of intellectual capital acknowledge three primary types of capital: human capital, structural capital, and customer capital. The chapter by Ardichvili in this book provides an excellent example of one such taxonomy. Despite their differences, definitions of intellectual capital have in common a focus on the intangible assets, which are distinct from the tangible assets that make up the physical and financial forms of capital, by which organizations have traditionally competed.

Another way to distinguish various perspectives on intellectual capital involves the degree to which they explicitly equate intellectual capital with knowledge. Some authors use the terms interchangeably. Karl-Erik Sveiby, author of *The New Organizational Wealth* (1997), for instance, views knowledge management as the art of creating value from an organization's intangible assets. Other authors explicitly define knowledge management as the management of only codified, formalized, explicit forms of knowledge, such as repositories of lessons learned, documents, databases, and company yellow pages. Thus, David Skyrme and Debra Amidon (1997) define knowledge management as "the explicit and systematic management of vital knowledge and its associated processes of creating, gathering, organizing, diffusion, use, and exploitation" (p. 32). Adapting Skyrme and Amidon's definition, we define *intellectual capital management* as the explicit and systematic management of intellectual capital and the associated processes of creating, gathering, organizing, disseminating, leveraging, and using intellectual capital.

Measuring intellectual capital

Efforts to address the measurement challenges surrounding intellectual capital fall into two basic, but overlapping types. The first type is focused on measuring the *stocks*, or the quantities, of intellectual capital. The simplest form of this type of measurement is a straightforward enumeration of the intellectual capital of an organization—the number of patents, Ph.D. professionals, or Fortune 500 contracts. Enumeration results in an inventory of intangible assets, which tells an organization relatively little other than the types and amounts of assets it "possesses."

Usually, organizations are more interested in measuring the *value* of their intellectual capital stocks. Such efforts attempt to assign monetary values to intangible assets. However, the intangible qualities of these assets make such valuations exceedingly difficult. Thus, most attempts at valuation provide an approximation of the aggregate value of an organization's entire intellectual capital stock without enumerating each and every intangible asset. One formula for measuring the value of intellectual capital is Paul Strassman's method for valuing "Knowledge Capital." With this formula, the value of knowledge capital can be estimated as the ratio of "management value-added" to the price of capital, where management value-added is essentially profits after tax minus shareholder equity. (Strassmann, 1996)

One especially popular approximate measure of intellectual capital, which explicitly compares the value of an organization's intellectual capital to its financial and physical capital, is the market-to-book value (based upon, and often referred, to Tobin's q). Market value is a company's stock price multiplied by the number of outstanding shares, while book value is the replacement value of its physical assets. The portion of an organization's market value that is in excess of its book value is assumed to be the value the market places on its intangible assets. According to Charles Handy (1989), the intellectual capital values of most organizations assessed in this manner are worth three to four times their book values. This measure, which constantly changes as an organization's stock price fluctuates, may reflect other factors, such as takeover rumors or global volatility, and can only be constructed for publicly traded firms. The major drawback to such aggregate measures of intellectual capital is the inability to see how certain actions and changes affect specific types of intangible assets.

A second basic type of measurement goes beyond approximating the value of the stocks of intellectual capital themselves to estimating the value of the goods and services they produce or create. The emphasis shifts away from intellectual capital stocks to the processes by which they are managed (i.e., intellectual capital management). From stocks to *flows*. Likening management processes to production functions, this form of measurement looks at the output side of the equation as well as the input side. The purpose of measurement becomes one of ascertaining the effectiveness of knowledge-management activities. Recently, there have been a number of calls for greater progress on the measurement of effectiveness. For instance, the Conference Board's report *Managing Knowledge for Business Success* argues that "Measuring the economic value of knowledge and knowledge management initiatives is a critical challenge for organizations" (Cohen, Smith, Prusak & Azzarello, 1997, p. 14).

Effectiveness measures fall into two different classes. On the one hand, effectiveness can be measured as *changes* in an organization's stocks (quantity or quality) of intangible assets. This class of effectiveness measures leads one, by necessity, to undertake the first type of measurement discussed above as well. It is relatively easy to see how some intellectual capital management activities, such as selection and recruitment or marketing, that are aimed at creating additional intellectual capital lend themselves to this class of measures.

The second class of effectiveness measures assesses how knowledge management affects performance, that is, how well intellectual capital assets are leveraged. Performance can be assessed by various levels (e.g., individual, team, and organization); units/functions (e.g., human resources and finance), product lines, markets, and so on. Those who use performance measures are particularly interested in the economic value produced by a firm's intellectual capital. Inevitably, discussions about economic value turn to the "Holy Grail" of measures—Return on Investment (ROI). However, financial assessments of effectiveness, such as ROI, are particularly difficult to make. A recent study by the American Productivity and Quality Center (1996) found that 80 percent of organizations do not calculate ROI on their knowledge management activities.

One example of this form of measurement comes from Ante Pulic of the Institute for International Management in Austria (1996). Pulic proposes using the "value added intellectual capital coefficient" (VAIC) which he defined simply as value added divided by intellectual capital. Like

Those who use performance measures
are particularly interested in the economic value
produced by a firm's intellectual capital.

Strassman's formula, Pulic's formula relies upon proxies for both parts of the ratio. Value added is loosely defined as the difference between sales and all inputs except labor expenses. Intellectual capital is approximated by total labor expenses. The higher the ratio, the more efficient the use of intellectual capital.

As with the first type of measurement, the intangible nature of intellectual capital makes the measurement of its effectiveness very challenging. The *Managing Knowledge for Business Success* report (Cohen, Smith, Prusak & Azzarello, 1997) observes that because knowledge is continually evolving and so deeply woven into the fabric of organizations, "the effects of using it better can never really be measured as a simple one-to-one correspondence (so much knowledge in, so much product out). That kind of measure belongs to an older, industrial business model. Clinging to it in today's world may prove to be a liability" (p. 14). Moreover, an excessive emphasis on quantitative financial measures of success can undermine activities that promise much larger returns in the long term. The report concludes that "measuring the impact of knowledge on business performance is both essential and difficult, and that gauging the success even of individual knowledge projects can be a baffling problem" (p. 32).

Some have chosen approaches to measuring the effectiveness of intellectual capital management that do not focus exclusively on financial measures—Skandia's Navigator (Edvinsson & Malone, 1997) and Sveiby's Intangible Asset Monitor (Sveiby, 1997), for example. Charles Lucier, Booz-Allen & Hamilton's first chief knowledge officer, and Janet Torsilieri (Lucier & Torsilieri, 1997) suggest two tiers of non-financial outcome measures: operating performance outcomes and direct measures of learning. Operating performance outcomes include such items as lead times, customer satisfaction, employee productivity. Direct measures of learning include such items as the number of participants in communities of practice, people trained, and customers impacted by the use of knowledge.

A general model of intellectual capital management

The Effective Knowledge Management Working Group tackled the issue of measuring intellectual capital in both ways—as an intangible asset that is available for creating economic value and as the management of such an asset. After a year of work, the group produced a framework containing a core set of indicators of intellectual capital stocks common to most organizations. The framework identifies several key measures of the economic value these stocks bring to organizations. The framework goes a step further to help organizations understand the flow from such stocks into something of value.

The framework, which is situated within a model of intellectual capital management, was developed by the group from the collective experience of

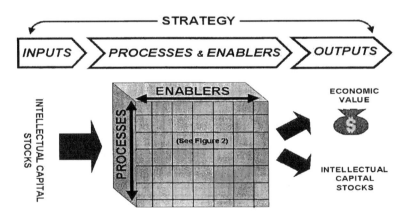

Figure 1. Intellectual Capital Management Model

the members and the best thinking on intellectual capital measurement today. Working from left to right, Figure 1 illustrates that an organization begins with its existing stocks of intellectual capital. These stocks become inputs to the organization's intellectual capital management processes. The knowledge management processes and their enablers produce two types of outputs: 1) changes in the stocks of intellectual capital themselves and 2) economic value.

With the Intellectual Capital Management Model in hand, it becomes possible to address measurement of intellectual capital stocks, knowledge-management processes, and outputs. On the front end, the model requires measuring existing stocks of intellectual capital and over time the changes in those stocks. On the back end, the model requires measuring the economic value produced by intellectual capital management processes and enablers.

By building upon the measures of intellectual capital stocks that others have proposed or used, we identified two sets of intellectual capital indicators: a core set and an elective set. Our final sets of core and elective indicators were created through a conceptual exercise of ranking a universe of possible intellectual capital indicators. The indicators were ranked first on the basis of their relevance to the intellectual capital management objectives of most organizations. Indicators that ranked roughly in the top quartile were considered core indicators. Indicators that ranked in the second quartile were considered elective indicators because they are not relevant to all organizations, only to organizations in certain industries or lines of business.

To trim the first list of core indicators and develop a parsimonious set of key intellectual capital measures, we subjected the list to a second ranking process. Each core indicator was ranked according to the following criteria:

- Strategic importance to top executives and external stakeholders
- Availability of information/data
- Applicability to a wide variety of organizations

The second ranking process resulted in the final set of core indicators that appears in Table 1. Indicators that failed to meet the three criteria were placed into the set of elective indicators that appears in Table 2. A similar two-staged process was undertaken to identify sets of core and elective financial performance outcomes (i.e., measures of economic value). The resulting sets of financial performance measures appear in Table 3.

The heart of the Intellectual Capital Management Model is the middle section, which consists of processes and enablers. Heretofore, much of the effort to describe the management of intellectual capital has treated this area as a black box. Yet, both processes and enablers are critical leverage points for enhancing an organization's intellectual capital management capability.

Table 1: Core Intellectual Capital Indicators

Indicator	Measure
	Human Capital
Retention of key personnel	Percentage of employees most essential to the organization retained during the previous year.
Ability to attract talented people	Percentage of openings requiring advanced degrees or substantial experience filled in the previous year.
IT literacy	Percentage of employees with a basic level of proficiency in standard office computer applications.
Training expenditures as a percent of payroll	Total expenditures on training in the previous year as a percent of the organization's annual payroll.
Replacement costs of key personnel	Average cost to recruit, hire, and train a someone to fill an essential job in the organization.
Employee satisfaction	Percentage of employees' highly satisfied with the organization and their jobs.
Employee commitment	Percentage of employees' highly dedicated and committed to the organization.
	Innovation Capital
R&D expenditures	Total expenditures on conceiving and designing new products and/or services in the previous year.
Percent of workforce involved in innovation	Percentage of employees with responsibility for conception and design of new products and/or services.
Product freshness	Percentage of all current products and/or services introduced in the last three years.
	Process Capital
Processes documented and mapped	Percentage of business-critical processes documented and analyzed.
Use of documented processes	Percentage of document processes being fully utilized.
	Customer Capital
Customer satisfaction	Percentage of customers completely satisfied with products and/or services.
Customer retention	Percentage of top customers ending sales contract in the previous year.
Average duration of customer relationship	Average number of years existing customers have been purchasing products and/or services.
Repeat orders	Percentage current customers that previously purchased products and/or services.

Table 2: Elective Intellectual Capital Indicators

Human Capital	Process Capital
Organizational learning measure	Strategy execution
Effectiveness of learning transfer in key areas	Quality of decisions
Management credibility	Percent of revenues invested in knowledge management
Employee wages and salaries	Percent of company effectively engaged with customer
Educational levels - % college graduates	IT access (/ employee)
Employee empowerment	Strategy innovativeness
Management experience	Cycle time
Time in training	IT investment / employee
Percentage of employees with X+ years of service	Process quality (e.g., defects, error rates)
Empowered teams	Time to market
	Collaboration levels
	IT capacity (CPU/DASD/MB)
	IT capacity / employee
	Operating expense ratio
	Administrative expense / total revenues

Innovation Capital	Customer Capital
Number of copyrights/trademarks	Market growth
Number of patents used effectively	Customer needs met
Planned obsolescence	Marketing effectiveness
New opportunities exploited	Annual sales / customer
New markets development investment	Market share
R&D productivity	Average customer size ($)
Sales from products in released last 5 years	Five largest customers as % of revenues
Research leadership	Days spent visiting customers
Net present value (NPV) of patents	Support expense / customer
Effectiveness of feedback mechanisms	Image enhancing customers as % of revenues
Average age of patents	
R&D invested in product design (%)	
Number of patents pending	
Number of new ideas in KM database	
Direct communications to customer / year	

Table 3: Core and Elective Financial Performance Measures

Core Measures	Elective Measures
Return on equity	Market capitalization
Earnings per share	Return on assets
Growth rank in industry	Revenue growth
Total shareholder return	Market share
	Revenue per employee
	New product sales
	Value added per employee
	Market value

The Intellectual Capital Management Matrix in Figure 2 begins to unpack the black box. Down the left-hand side of the matrix we identify five general categories of processes.

- Define: Identifying IC types, needs, and requirements
- Create: Creating new IC and uncovering existing IC
- Capture: Compiling, gathering, representing, codifying, and reorganizing IC
- Share: Disseminating, distributing, and transferring IC
- Use: Applying, incorporating, reusing, exploiting, and leveraging IC

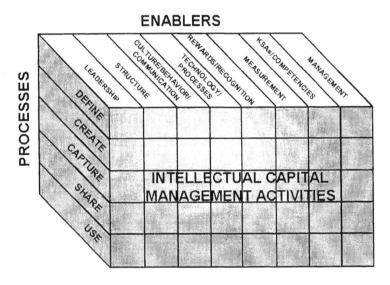

Figure 2. Intellectual Capital Management Matrix

Although the process categories are listed sequentially, in reality, the activities within these processes overlap and reinforce one another (i.e., they are non-linear).

Across the top of the matrix we identify eight categories of intellectual capital management enablers.

- Leadership: The actions and statements of a company's leaders that demonstrate a strong belief in, understanding of, and commitment to the values and business objectives of the company
- Structure: The organization of individuals, work groups, teams, and business units within and across the company
- Culture (Behavior/Communications): Widely shared beliefs, norms, and values about appropriate ways of behaving and conducting work within the company
- Technology/Processes: The formal tools and methods employed by the company in carrying out its core business activities
- Rewards & Recognition Systems: The methods of positive reinforcement used by the company to encourage desired behaviors
- Measurement: The tools and methods used to record, monitor, and track the performance of individuals, units, and the company as a whole
- Knowledge, Skills & Abilities/Competencies: The existing capabilities of employees to carry out the work of the company
- Management: The tasks associated with ensuring that the activities of the company are performed as planned

While the process categories and the enablers are not in any way new, the matrix represents a novel way of thinking about their interaction and the intellectual capital management process as a whole. Each cell of the Intellectual Capital Management Matrix can be used to identify particular activities that firms undertake as part of a given process with a given enabler. For example, in the Share-Leadership cell, one activity that an organization may undertake is to have the CEO or President model knowledge-sharing behaviors through widely visible participation in popular communities of practice within the firm.

Assessing the value of intellectual capital

ASTD embedded the core set of intellectual capital indicators as questions in a module of the 1999 ASTD *Measurement Kit*™, which was publicly released in March of that year. The *Measurement Kit* serves as the data collection instrument for ASTD's Benchmarking Service, which is offered to all organizations that choose to submit the data they derived by using a common set of metrics defined within the *Measurement Kit*. To the organizations that participate in ASTD's Benchmarking Service, the Intellectual Capital Module is a tool for continuous improvement.

The module consists of two parts. Part one contains 16 items that collect data on all of the core measures of intellectual capital, with the exception of training expenditures and employee satisfaction and commitment.[1] Training expenditure data is measured by items elsewhere in the *Measurement Kit*. Part two contains 4 items for measuring employee satisfaction and five items for measuring employee commitment. Part one is completed by someone responsible for training within the organization, while part two is administered by the training department to all employees in the organization. Employee responses are summarized (e.g., the percent who "strongly agree" with an item), and the summaries are entered into the *Measurement Kit*.

Descriptive statistics

In 1999, 276 organizations in the United States responded to at least a portion of the Intellectual Capital Module of the ASTD *Measurement Kit*. Figures 3 and 4 show the distribution of these enterprises by size of organization and by industry sector. Respondents were roughly distributed by thirds across small, medium, and large organizations, with the largest percentage of organizations employing fewer than 500 employees. The high level of interest in benchmarking intellectual capital among small employers was surprising, given that the most widely publicized examples of intellectual capital management tend to be from large companies. Small

Firms by Number of Employees

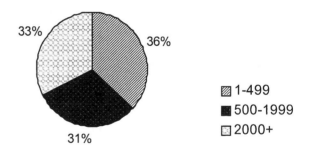

Figure 3. Size distribution, Intellectual Capital Module respondents

---

[1]   Due to the length of the Intellectual Capital Module, the items are not reproduced here. For copies of the items, please contact the author.

organizations appear to value knowledge as much as or more than large ones. The largest percentage of respondents were in the Technology sector (16 percent), followed the Service sector and the Finance/Insurance/Real Estate sector.

The most elementary results to emerge from this first-ever attempt to benchmark intellectual capital are the basic measures on each of the core indicators. The means of the responses of the 16 items in part one of the module and the item on training expenditures are summarized in Table 4.[2]

An examination of the means by industry sector reveals that they did not vary substantially on any item except training expenditures and IT literacy. Not surprisingly, organizations in the Technology sector reported the highest level of IT literacy (72 percent), which is more than 32 percentage points above the lowest scoring sector (Health Care). Nonetheless, it is interesting to note the variation across industry sectors on each of the items. As more data are collected in the years 2000 and beyond from a larger sample of organizations, we anticipate that additional statistically significant differences will emerge.

Firms by Industry

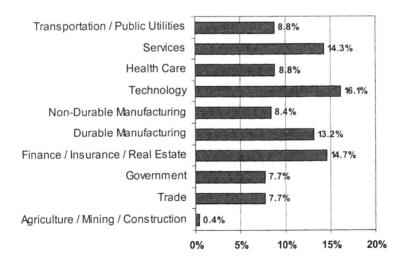

Figure 4. Industry distribution, Intellectual Capital Module respondents

---

[2] Less than a third of respondents completed the items for the indicators on employee satisfaction and commitment. These items were not included in the analyses reported here.

Table 4: Maximum Industry Deviations from Overall Average

	Number of Respondents	Overall Mean	Lowest Industry Mean	Highest Industry Mean
Training expenditures as a percent of payroll	234	2.2%	Health Care (1.0%)	TPU (3.1%)
Retention of key personnel	234	88.5%	Non-Durable Manufacturing (81.4%)	TPU (93.4%)
Ability to attract talented people	221	44.0%	Trade (30.4%)	Technology (54.3%)
IT literacy	245	55.9%	Health Care (38.0%)	Technology (71.9%)
Replacement cost of key personnel	185	$72,419	Services ($12,539)	FIRE ($249,580)
R&D expenditure	127	$25,532,456	TPU ($107,273)	Non-Durable Manufacturing ($74,290,000)
Percent of workforce involved in innovation	202	9.1%	Health Care (2.26%)	Services (13.6%)
Product freshness	180	32.6%	Health Care (11.3%)	Technology (49.3%)
Processes documented and mapped	208	51.0%	Services (38.7%)	Non-Durable Manufacturing (59.2%)
Use of documented processes	192	56.4%	Services (48.4%)	Durable Manufacturing (66.5%)
Customer satisfaction	196	78.4%	FIRE (68.0%)	Non-Durable Manufacturing (87.95)
Customer retention	124	94.7%	Technology (85.0%)	Government (100%)
Quality of products and services	181	92.1%	Non-Durable Manufacturing (89.7%)	TPU (96.7%)
Average duration of customer relationship (in years)	158	14.3	Trade (9.2)	Government (23.2)
Repeat orders	161	78.7%	FIRE (65.8%)	Non-Durable Manufacturing (90.6%)

Note: FIRE is an abbreviation for Finance/Insurance/Real Estate. TPU is an abbreviation for Transportation/Public Utilities

Identifying the core indicators

We observed a number of significant correlations among the core indicators (see Table 5). For instance, among the human capital indicators, we found that training expenditures as a percent of payroll were significantly related to IT literacy, the percentage of employees involved in innovation, product freshness, process documentation, process utilization, and customer retention. The level of IT literacy in an organization was positively related to its ability to attract talented people. Retention of key personnel was positively related to the quality of products and services and to the level of process utilization, but negatively related to the share of employees involved in innovation.

Table 5: Relationships Between Core Indicators

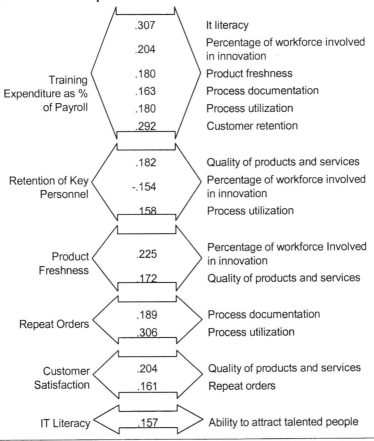

	.307	It literacy
	.204	Percentage of workforce involved in innovation
Training Expenditure as % of Payroll	.180	Product freshness
	.163	Process documentation
	.180	Process utilization
	.292	Customer retention
	.182	Quality of products and services
Retention of Key Personnel	-.154	Percentage of workforce involved in innovation
	158	Process utilization
Product Freshness	.225	Percentage of workforce Involved in innovation
	.172	Quality of products and services
Repeat Orders	.189	Process documentation
	.306	Process utilization
Customer Satisfaction	.204	Quality of products and services
	.161	Repeat orders
IT Literacy	.157	Ability to attract talented people

Note: Numbers shown are Pearson correlation coefficients

Product freshness was strongly related to higher percentages of employees involved in innovation and to higher quality of products and services. Both the level of process documentation and the level of process utilization were positively correlated with the percentage of repeat orders. The correlations with the customer capital measures revealed strong positive relationships between customer satisfaction and both the quality of products and services and the percentage of repeat orders.

The link to organization performance

Since its inception in 1997, the Measurement Kit has been used to collect data on subjective assessments of organization performance. Although these measures of performance do not coincide with those of the Intellectual Capital Management Model, they are nonetheless helpful for understanding the kinds of outcomes experienced by organizations that invest in various forms of intellectual capital.

Respondents were asked to measure and report on five indicators of their organization's performance:

- Profitability (if applicable)
- Quality of products and services
- Customer satisfaction
- Employee satisfaction
- Ability to retain essential employees

They assessed whether their organization's performance on each indicator in 1998 was (1) better, worse, or no different from 1997 and (2) better, worse, or no different from similar organizations in 1998. Two indices of overall performance were created from these measures: change in performance from 1997 to 1998, and 1998 performance versus their peers.

Correlations between the core intellectual capital indicators and the measures of subjective performance displayed a number of interesting relationships (see Table 6). For example, it is encouraging to note that the measure of employee satisfaction and commitment was positively correlated with both scales of overall performance. The only other measure of human capital to display such strong relationships with both scales of overall performance was the ability of an organization to retain key personnel. Training expenditures as a percent of payroll was associated with overall improvements in organization performance between 1997 and 1998, but it was negatively related to an organization's profitability in comparison with others.

Table 6: Correlations Between Core Indicators and Subjective Measures of Performance

	Scale of Performance Vs Other Organizations	Scale of Performance, 1997 Vs 1998
Retention of key personnel	**.246**	**.143**
Ability to attract talented people	.050	.008
IT literacy	.034	.025
Replacement costs of key personnel	-.032	.029
Training expenditures as a percent of payroll	-.065	**.162**
Employee satisfaction and commitment	**.762**	**.391**
Innovation capital scale	.101	.059
Process capital scale	**.238**	.088
Customer retention	-.058	-.106
Quality of products and services	.141	.100
Average duration of customer relationship	-.088	-.038
Repeat orders	.012	-.092

Note: Numbers shown are Pearson correlation coefficients. Coefficients in bold are statistically significant at p<.05.

The innovation capital measure did not display significant relationships with any of the subjective measures of performance. By contrast, the process capital measure was positively correlated with nearly every measure of an organization's performance versus their peers, except their self-reported ability to attract and retain workers (of all types). With several exceptions, the customer capital indicators also exhibited few correlations with the subjective measures of performance. Respondents that reported higher quality products and services versus their peers scored highly on three measures of customer capital: high customer satisfaction, low product/service complaints, and longer customer relationships. Higher customer satisfaction levels were also associated with overall performance versus their peers. Low product/service complaints were correlated with higher assessments of employee satisfaction.

Finally, for the subset of 102 organizations in the sample that were publicly-traded, it was possible to examine the relationship between the core intellectual capital indicators and a variety of objective measures of financial performance. The financial performance variables examined for these organizations included

- Total Shareholder Return
- Return on Equity
- Sales per Employee
- Price to Earnings Ratio (for Earnings per Share)
- Gross Profit Margin
- Market Capitalization Per Employee (Minus Book Value)

Data for these variables were collected for the 1998 calendar year and into mid-1999. The 1999 data allow us to begin to assess the timing of the relationship between investments in intellectual capital and organization performance. Given the wide variability of financial performance across industry sectors, we elected to compute each individual organization's performance in terms of its departure from the average for the industry sector on that particular measure. For each measure, organizations that scored above the average for their industry sector obtained a positive value. Organizations that scored below the average for their industry sector received a negative value.

This analysis revealed relatively few significant associations (see Table 7). For the human capital indicators, we found a positive relationship between the retention of key personnel and both sales (1998 and 1999) and market capitalization (1998 and 1998). We also found a significant relationship between the ability to attract essential employees and gross profit margin (1998 only). Somewhat surprisingly, however, training expenditures were negatively associated with market capitalization in 1999.

Unlike the subjective assessments of performance, for which we detected numerous positive relationships between process capital and performance, process capital was not correlated with any objective measures of performance in 1998. Instead, the measure of innovation capital, which was not related to the subjective measures, was positively associated with gross profit margins in 1998 and 1999. Our analyses also failed to detect any significant relationships between the core indicators of customer capital and the objective measures of performance.

Table 7: Relationships to Financial Performance

	1998	1999
Retention of key personnel	Sales per employee vs. sector (+)	Sales per employee vs. sector (+)
	Market capitalization per employee after book vs. sector (+)	Market capitalization per employee after book vs. sector (+)
Innovation capital scale	Gross profit margin vs. sector (+)	Gross profit margin versus.sector (+)
Ability to attract talented people	Gross profit margin vs. sector (+)	
Process capital scale		Gross profit margin vs. sector (+)
Training expenditures as a percent of payroll		Market capitalization per employee after book vs. sector (-)

Managing intellectual capital through technology

In the 1990s organizations increasingly turned to technology to manage their intellectual capital. They created intranets, introduced groupware (e.g., Lotus Notes™), or developed some other propriety system. Unfortunately, in some organizations these systems wound up barren and useless, rather like an electronic ghost town into which the occasional drifter comes once, never to return. In these organizations, the water cooler remained the center of knowledge sharing. In other organizations, these systems became so popular that every person, every team, every division had its own site, resulting in an overgrown garden sorely in need of weeding.

In either case, organizations with knowledge management systems face a fundamental question: How does one address the human side of managing intellectual capital through technology? In 1997 ASTD explored this question by conducting case studies of three companies at varying stages in their introducing and using knowledge management systems—Polaroid, PricewaterhouseCoopers, and Unisys. We looked specifically at the activities and systems these companies used to transform individual knowledge into organizational knowledge, such as discussion groups, lessons learned, and best practice repositories. Our findings are summarized as six critical success factors. While none of the companies had all six success factors in place, the more factors they had, the better they leveraged their knowledge management systems.

Case study companies

Polaroid

In 1997, Polaroid was a leading manufacturer of instant photographic imaging products with sales of $2.1 billion. The company employed just over 10,000 people. Its knowledge management system, until relatively recently, was limited to its ProTech (Professional Technical Markets)

ASTD conducted case studies of three companies—
Polaroid, PricewaterhouseCoopers, and Unisys.

business unit. Introduced in mid-1997, the system consisted of fewer than a dozen Lotus Notes databases that could be accessed through the company's newly formed intranet. The ProTech Discussion Forum, the interactive portion of the web site, contained discussion areas for sharing success stories, best practices, and lessons learned, organized by market segment or product line. Once a best practice became certified as an accepted procedure, it moved to the site's ProTech KnowledgeBase database.

PricewaterhouseCoopers

Prior to its merger with Price Waterhouse in July 1998, the Coopers & Lybrand part of the international professional services firm had more than 82,000 employees in 138 countries. As a test site for Lotus Notes, Coopers & Lybrand, in the late 1980s, began using Notes for such knowledge management activities as email and discussions. In 1994 the firm committed to the largest Notes installation anywhere. By late 1997 the firm boasted a total of 150 servers in the United States that supported over 3,000 Notes databases. In 1995 the company introduced its award-winning intranet, KnowledgeCurve. Another excellent example of PricewaterhouseCoopers' knowledge management applications was Globe, a database of best practices within its business assurance group.

Unisys

Unisys, an information management company with nearly 32,000 employees and over $6.6 billion in sales in 1997, had the full repertoire of knowledge management systems and technology available. The company had more than 3,000 Lotus Notes databases and a state-of-the-art intranet with over 7,000 web pages. The corporate Information Technology department owned the physical hardware and was responsible for the technological infrastructure and operating systems. Unisys' three business groups largely determined the content of the company's knowledge management systems. The most concrete illustration of a knowledge management application was The Idea Factory, which was conceived as an incubator of new products. The Idea Factory web site contained a place for employees to suggest new product ideas and a threaded discussion area for others to comment on or build on the ideas.

Findings

In 1997 Larry Prusak of the IBM Consulting Group warned, "When it comes to successfully managing knowledge, culture trumps all other factors" (Cohen, Smith, Prusak & Azzarello, 1997, p. 7). While a knowledge-sharing culture is essential to realizing the potential of a knowledge management system, only a few organizations are fortunate to have pre-existing cultures that value knowledge sharing.

Larry Prusak warned, "When it comes to successfully managing knowledge, culture trumps all other factors."

PricewaterhouseCoopers was a case in point. In the early 1980s, even before it introduced its first knowledge management system (the Knowledge Network), the company already had a history of sharing. Rather than concentrating knowledge in a priestly elite, the company relied on an apprentice-mentor model for developing talent, through which knowledge naturally flowed. PricewaterhouseCoopers' knowledge-sharing culture can be best illustrated by its informal "gift economy," in which people understood that if they shared their knowledge, they could expect to get help when they needed to know something in return. Over time, the culture of reciprocity supported many communities of practice founded on a high level of trust.

Some organizations, however, do not have this head start and must transform their existing culture into one that values knowledge sharing. One way to start is to find those isolated pockets or groups that already value and promote knowledge sharing. For example, at Unisys, these pockets consisted primarily of engineers and consultants who traditionally relied extensively on their communities of practice for help in carrying out their work. They eagerly created their own databases or web sites for exchanging knowledge. After identifying pockets of sharing, the key challenge is to spread this willingness to share knowledge throughout the organization.

Success factor #1: Management practices

Perhaps the most critical condition for creating a knowledge-sharing culture is senior management support. Knowledge management must be owned by the top, lead by the top, and practiced by the top.

Senior management's support for and participation in knowledge management was a crucial underpinning of PricewaterhouseCoopers' knowledge-sharing culture. In the beginning, only PricewaterhouseCoopers' partners used its Knowledge Network. When the organization moved to using Notes and put this capability on its intranet, KnowledgeCurve, the partners continued to be regular users of the company's knowledge management systems. The moderators of discussion groups tended to be senior managers and partners who had developed a high level of expertise on given topics. Their active participation in knowledge sharing gave the firm's knowledge management systems a level of credibility that encouraged their use throughout the organization.

The corporate vice president of Polaroid's North American commercial imaging division became the primary sponsor of the knowledge management system and facilitated its expansion beyond the pilot stage. However, support requires more than just sponsorship; it requires leadership and participation. The success of knowledge management systems in all three organizations depended on the ability of senior managers to articulate a compelling vision or a business case in support of knowledge sharing. Where senior managers did not actively and routinely encourage employees to share their knowledge or did not model the behaviors that would promote knowledge sharing throughout the company, the use of the knowledge management system remained less than optimal.

Success factor #2: A knowledge management strategy

Instead of simply introducing intranet or Lotus Notes to meet a specific learning need, Polaroid's knowledge management team started from the top and worked its way down. The team began by clearly identifying the business priorities of the company. And they crafted a knowledge management strategy that supported those priorities. By doing so, they were able to provide strong justification for the technological infrastructure that would support knowledge sharing. The strategy also provided a compelling business need for knowledge management that not only was instrumental in winning the support of other senior managers, but also helped employees see how knowledge sharing could benefit them and the organization.

Perhaps the most observable knowledge management obstacle in companies is the lack of a well-defined corporate strategy for knowledge management. Without an integrated, corporate-wide knowledge management strategy to coordinate sharing activities across units, companies have witnessed the emergence of thousands of databases and web sites. Navigation across the repositories and sites can become extremely unwieldy, and the knowledge management systems can become populated with hundreds of redundant, orphaned, and dormant locations.

Success factor #3: Knowledge management roles

Whether or not knowledge management is given a seat of its own in the boardroom, large organizations in particular have quickly discovered a need for a host of new knowledge management roles. Although the most visible roles may be given the title of Chief Knowledge Officer or Chief Learning Officer, other roles are often established.

At the time of this study, over 400 people in PricewaterhouseCoopers' knowledge management organization, under the leadership of Ellen Knapp, the firm's CKO, managed and maintained its intranet and its Lotus Notes databases. These 400 people were critical to capturing the best knowledge in the organization, ensuring the quality of knowledge in the depositories, and supporting the smooth operation of the entire system. Aiding them were the hundreds of individuals who served as owners, moderators, and administrators of the discussion groups.

At other organizations, much of the progress on knowledge management was accomplished by a small team of energetic people. Sometimes, the demands for expanding the system exceeded the team's ability to keep up. They had little time to address such issues as flagging participation and constraints on employees' time for knowledge sharing. As a result, deployment of the knowledge management systems in these organizations failed to progress as quickly as it could have, enhancements to the system waited for implementation, and people did not make full use of the system.

Success factor #4: Rewards and incentives

Individuals want assurance that their contributions to the knowledge base will be valued and recognized. Some organizations cultivate a knowledge-sharing culture by providing an environment that encourages and rewards the sharing and use of knowledge.

PricewaterhouseCoopers' International Tax Practice area, to ensure that new ideas were widely shared, began to tie knowledge sharing to annual performance evaluations. Although the measures of performance were fairly simplistic (e.g., number of contributions), they became a formal part of the performance evaluations of its consultants. At Unisys, weekly contests were initiated to sustain and grow the use of its Idea Factory. These contests became extremely popular, and prizes, such as pocket protectors and screwdrivers and especially a winner's certificate, were highly coveted.

Building knowledge sharing into the performance management practices of its sales and marketing employees contributed to the early success of Polaroid's knowledge management system. Contributions to the knowledge management databases were used as a criterion for ranking the performance

Individuals want assurance that their contributions to the knowledge base will be valued and recognized.

of sales personnel. Rankings were shared with senior managers, who used them to assess the overall advancement potential of personnel. By making knowledge sharing an essential aspect of the performance of individual employees and of the organization, Polaroid made effective use of both push and pull strategies for fostering knowledge sharing.

Success factor #5: Communication

The expression "build it and they will come" does not always hold true for knowledge management systems. As for any other new initiative in an organization, promotion efforts are critical to attracting and keeping users. To encourage use of its Idea Factory, Unisys kicked off the site with a large promotional event and with such marketing materials as T-shirts and mousepads.

When PricewaterhouseCoopers rolled out a new content architecture for its KnowledgeCurve, it employed a vast array of communication vehicles to promote its use, including broadcast email announcements, electronic marketing on the intranet's "What's New" section, posts to discussion groups about relevant new features, posters, mailings, and even mousepads. The company also held demonstrations at places where people regularly gather, such as training sessions and orientation meetings at branch offices. Information on how to use the knowledge management system was embedded in other employee training. For instance, participants in training sessions on new auditing regulations were shown how KnowledgeCurve could help them stay abreast of the latest regulations.

Success factor #6: Measurement

Measuring knowledge management systems can serve three purposes. The first is to test and evaluate new designs or enhancements before they are rolled out. At PricewaterhouseCoopers, usability testing was especially helpful. In the summer of 1997, the company found that end users were particularly concerned about clutter and information overload. After enhancements and modifications Knowledge Curve's usefulness to end users dramatically increased, and hits on the intranet soared to over 10 million per month.

Another purpose of measurement is simply to track the level of use and identify problem areas. PricewaterhouseCoopers monitored the use of its discussion groups. If a certain discussion group was inactive for 60 days, the moderator of the group was contacted to determine its status. Orphan and inactive discussion groups were removed.

Certainly the most difficult objective of measurement, but also the most important, is to determine the impact of the knowledge management system. None of the companies we studied had made much progress on addressing this objective. Their knowledge management functions had not been asked to provide hard evidence to show the bottom-line impact of their knowledge management systems. Therefore, the bulk of the evidence of impact in all three cases was anecdotal. While the lack of hard evidence of impact is not a problem at present, at some point in the future it is indeed likely that the utility and value of knowledge management systems may come into question. Individuals who see little value for or benefit from the use of knowledge-sharing systems may stop contributing to or using them. Without evidence of value, support for and use of knowledge management systems may erode over time and their ability to foster true organization-wide learning will be diminished.

Conclusion

While the results of ASTD's combined research on intellectual capital and its management have not yet demonstrated anything conclusive, they are tantalizing. In sum, they provide compelling evidence that investing in intellectual capital does matter and that managing the knowledge of organizations and their employees is a valuable, yet difficult endeavor. We believe that only those organizations that succeed at this critical undertaking will survive in an era where knowledge counts. Since much of this knowledge resides in the skills, competencies, knowledge, and abilities of individual employees, clearly this is a critical juncture in time for those who are tasked with human resource development in organizations all around the world.

References

American Productivity and Quality Center. (1996). *Knowledge Management*, Houston, TX.

Bassi, L., & Hackett, B. (1997). "Leveraging Intellectual Capital," *HR Executive Review*, *5*(3).

Cohen, D.,Smith, D., E., Prusak, L., & Azzarello, A. (1997). *Managing Knowledge for Business Success* (Report No. 1194-97-CH). New York: The Conference Board, Inc.

Edvinsson, L., & Malone, M. (1997). *Intellectual Capital: Realizing Your Company's True Value by Finding Its Hidden Brainpower*. New York: Harper Business.

Ernst & Young, LLP. (1997). *Executive Perspectives on Knowledge in the Organization*. Cambridge, MA: Ernst & Young.

Handy, Ch. (1989). *The Age of Unreason*, London: Arrow Books Ltd.

Lucier, C., & Torsilieri, J. (1997) "Why Knowledge Programs Fail: A CEOs Guide to Managing Learning," *Strategy & Business*, *9*(4).

Pulic, A. (1996). *The Physical and Intellectual Capital of Austrian Banks*, Unpublished manuscript, University Graz, Austria: Institute for International Management.

Skyrme, D., & Amidon ,D. (1997). *Creating the Knowledge-Based Business*. London: Business Intelligence.

Strassmann, P. (1996). *The Value of Computers, Information, and Knowledge*, Unpublished manuscript.

Sveiby, K.,E. (1997). *The New Organizational Wealth: Managing and Measuring Knowledge-Based Assets*. San Francisco: Berrett-Koehler.

WEB-BASED LEADERSHIP TRAINING: DETERMINING SUCCESS FACTORS AND EFFECTIVENESS

Darlene Russ-Eft
Achieve Global

Kathleen Hurson
Independent Contractor

Ruth Pangilinan
Independent Contractor

Tori Egherman
36 Partners

Abstract

This chapter describes an evaluation that examines the process, the success factors, and the initial outcomes of an implementation of leadership training. It compares two different delivery methods: a local, classroom-based training and a blended strategy of asynchronous and synchronous remote, Web-based training. The study uses a longitudinal case-study method that incorporates both quantitative and qualitative analyses. The authors report their qualitative analyses of initial telephone interviews and mid-term in-person interviews. Variables of technical reliability, perceived usefulness of training, learner expectations, individual learning styles, time and workload issues, and management support—all emerged as potentially critical to achieving learning outcomes and on-the-job use of learned skills.

In the past several decades, various distance learning and distance education methods have been developed, for example, computer-based training, two-way video, groupware, and now Internet- or Web-based, training (Chute, Thompson, & Hancock, 1999; Russ-Eft, 1994). Indeed, Web-based instruction is being used increasingly in management education (Alavi, Yoo, & Vogel, 1997; Rahm & Reed, 1997). Organizations, too, are demanding that more and more training be made available to local and remote learners through computer-based means (Flannery, Wagner, & Ellinger, 2000). As some evidence of this increasing demand, Herther (1997) reported that altogether, U.S. organizations invest billions of dollars in Web-based training.

Reasons for increasing use of Web-based training

Various reasons have been offered for the increasing interest in Web-based training. One is that on-line learning can take place "just-in-time and at *your* convenience" (Herther, 1997, p. 63), which means that employees can obtain the training whenever they feel it's needed. Also, they can take the training at times that fit their schedules rather than having to fit their schedules to those of the trainer.

Another reason for the shift from classroom-based to Web-based training is the opportunity to reduce the amount of time spent delivering basic information (Partee, 1996). The time spent in the group setting can be reduced to the time needed for discussion, debate, and skill practice.

From the organization's viewpoint, however, the primary reason for embracing Web-based training is reduced costs for travel for trainees and

> *Organizations invest billions of dollars in Web-based training.*

instructors and for time off the job related to such travel. The question then turns to one of effectiveness. According to Chute, Thompson, and Hancock (1999, p. 15), researchers have tried to answer this question for almost 70 years.

After looking first at correspondence instruction and then at instruction using technologies such as radio, television, and interactive audio-conferencing, videoconferencing, and computer conferencing, these researchers have overwhelmingly reported that *there is no significant difference in the achievement of students in well-designed distance learning programs and the achievement of those in traditional face-to-face programs, based on standard performance measures* (p. 15).

Ravishankar (1999) also reported this finding of "no-significant difference" in achievement in a comparison of classroom training, CD-ROM training combined with a classroom meeting, and CD-ROM training only.

That finding appeared for those who completed the training. Nevertheless, the completion rates among the three groups were vastly different. Almost 99 percent of the classroom trainees completed the training. About 85 percent of the combined CD-ROM and classroom trainees completed the training. Only 67 percent of the CD-ROM-only group completed the training.

Success factors

Although Chute, Thompson, and Hancock (1999) indicated that no differences should appear between Web-based training and classroom-based training, there may be certain factors beyond those of instructional design that lead to the success or failure of the training. Flannery, Wagner, and Ellinger (2001) reviewed the research literature on human-computer interaction, information management, business management, and adult education. Based on this review, they identified a variety of factors affecting user acceptance of the technology. They then tested these factors with both civilian and military sample groups from a government agency and found the following variables to be significant: software anxiety, information support, self-determination, attitudes toward use, management support, educational level, perceived usefulness, browser experience, and behavioral intentions.

User acceptance of the training is important, and equally important is whether or not the trainee uses the learned skills on the job. From an organization's standpoint, the training becomes less cost-effective if the trainees refuse to participate or if they neglect to use the skills.

Research questions

The major research questions for this study were

- What factors affect the success of asynchronous and synchronous Web-based training?
- What are the results of asynchronous and synchronous Web-based training, particularly as compared with traditional classroom training?

Methods

Organizational context

The organization is a large Internet company providing services throughout the world. Because of rapid company growth, employees within the customer service operation had been hired and promoted but had not received training. This situation led to somewhat reduced employee satisfaction and somewhat higher than expected employee turnover. The purpose of the leadership training program was to provide human resource

User acceptance of the training is important, but equally important is whether or not the trainee uses the learned skills on the job.

development opportunities to employees regardless of their location. In addition to improved leadership skills, upper management hoped that the use of learned skills would lead to greater stability within the organization and that results could be realized through less costly, more efficient and effective ways of delivering training.

Because of a dispersed workforce, the training took place using two different methods:

- Typical classroom sessions (for the trainees who are locally based)
- Web-based training, supplemented by coaching, synchronous Web meetings, and quarterly group meetings (for the trainees who are based in remote locations)

Training program

The training program for both groups was similar. It consisted of the following topics: an introduction to leadership, coaching, giving and receiving feedback, recognizing others, influencing others, correcting performance problems, conducting performance reviews, managing priorities, understanding organization goals and identifying priorities and setting goals. At the time of the researchers' mid-term interviews, the trainees had completed the introduction to leadership, coaching, and giving and receiving feedback. The same instructor led both groups.

Classroom training group

The local trainees, who were situated in the same geographic location, were 60 customer service managers, supervisors, and leads. Their training was scheduled one session a month, for ten months, with the first session taking place in July 2000 (one month prior to the start of the Web-based training sessions). The classroom-based group experienced the following training:

- Gathering and analysis of 360-degree feedback data
- Classroom session, with a role-play practice included

- They also received the following kinds of coaching and reinforcement:
  - Live and virtual coaching with the instructor
  - Manager-led follow-up sessions
  - Availability of workbook materials from classroom session
  - E-mail follow-up messages
  - Use of a just-in-time planner

The 360-degree feedback occurred only at the beginning of training; and the classroom session took place each month, with one topic covered each time (such as coaching).

Web-based training group

The remote trainees, who were located in different parts of the country, were 12 customer service managers, supervisors, and leads. They held similar positions and had similar backgrounds to those trainees in the classroom-based group. Their first Web-based training session took place in August 2000. As with the classroom-based group, the synchronous sessions covered one topic per month for ten months. The remote group experienced the following training:

- Gathering, analysis, and feedback of 360-degree feedback data
- A session called "Learning How to Learn On-line" to acquaint trainees with how to participate in and access the tools for the synchronous Web-classroom session.
- Asynchronous Web-training, during which each person completed a "Just-in-Time Planner. Upon completion, each trainee was asked to e-mail the instructor with a summary of that planning material.
- Synchronous Web classroom and role-play practice session. The role-play practice took place in separate break-out rooms. It should be noted that each trainee received a short workbook that included a listing of key steps, role-play worksheets, and future planning worksheets. They did not receive the complete workbook provided to the classroom-based trainees.
- Coaching and reinforcement of the following types:
  - Live and virtual coaching with the instructor
  - Manager-led follow-up sessions
  - Availability of asynchronous Web training modules
  - E-mail follow-up messages
  - Use of a just-in-time planner

The 360-degree feedback and the "Learning How to Learn On-line" occurred only at the beginning of training. A different asynchronous and synchronous training session took place each month, with one topic covered each time (such as coaching).

Design

As discussed by Russ-Eft and Preskill (2001), evaluation designs must be derived from the research questions and from the practical limitations of the situation. Because of the very different sample sizes, n=60 and n=12, we decided to undertake a longitudinal case study. Mixed-methods were used to gather both quantitative and qualitative data. (Caracelli & Greene, 1997; Greene & Caracelli, 1997; Simonson, 1997). The evaluation compared both the process and the effectiveness of the two training methods. This information will lead to some understanding of the advantages and limitations of classroom-based training and Web-based training.

The design of the longitudinal study calls for gathering data and analyzing the process, the success factors, and the initial outcomes of the two methods. It then calls for gathering and comparing data for the two methods on attitude change, behavioral change, and organizational outcomes over an entire year. This chapter reports the process, the success factors, and the initial outcomes of the two methods based on the initial and mid-term interviews.

Types of data gathered

Attitudes towards training

Trainees' attitudes can affect their willingness to engage in training and to learn from training. This study compared trainees' expectations concerning the training and their reactions, as obtained by the trainer during the synchronous Web sessions (for the remote trainees) and during the classroom sessions (for the local trainees). In addition, once each quarter during the training, individual in-person or telephone interviews were held with each trainee.

Behavior change

Improvement in the trainees' behaviors on the job is a critical outcome of the training. To measure behavior levels and gains, we used on-line Web-based assessment tools with both groups. Because of the small numbers of remote trainees, we can examine the direction, but not the statistical significance, of the changes by using these instruments. In addition, we gathered trainees' descriptions of the ways in which they have used or not used the skills learned during training.

Organizational outcomes

Another desired outcome of the training is a change in the organization itself. Establishing such a change could involve such measures as reduced turnover and improved employee morale. This archival data is potentially available from the organization. If these data are not available in archival form, they will be gathered using survey methods.

Results to date

Initial telephone interviews

Seventy-two trainees participated in the telephone interviews, 60 from the classroom-based group and 12 from the Web-based group. Participants in the training had the following job titles: Project lead, Supervisor, and Manager. Some Directors and a Vice President were also interviewed, but these data are not included in the description of the results.

Table 1. Respondents' Expectations for the Anticipated Training

Expectations for Future Training	Percentage of Classroom Trainees (N=56)	Percentage of Remote Trainess (N=8)
Improved effectiveness and communication	61	75
To become a more effective, supportive leader	60	
Maximizing employees' potentials and performances	30	13
Dealing more effectively with challenges	21	
How to approach problems successfully	21	
Strategies to reward, recognize, and motivate	7	

(Because each respondent can provide multiple responses, the percentages can add to more than 100%)

All of the trainees expressed enthusiasm for the training. Several trainees indicated that this was the first training they had received from the organization and that they understood its importance.

Expectations of the training

As a total group, the respondents anticipated that the training would enhance their leadership skills. (See Table 1.)

One respondent noted,

I'm hoping to learn more of what my strengths and weaknesses are and what my opportunities are to improve.... More importantly, to overcome the opportunities that I have and work on those to become a better leader and be more effective for the team and for the company.

Another commented,

It's the whole ability to stop for that very brief moment to reevaluate where you are and... can help you grow to that next level, can help you be that better manager.... I'm hoping that through this we'll have that little brief second for us where you're able to focus not in the day-to-day but the ability to kind of reinvest in yourself.

In Table 1, however, note that the local trainees expressed a greater variety of expectations than did the remote trainees. The reduced variety of expectations expressed by the remote trainees may have resulted from some software anxiety. As a further probe to determine any anxieties about the training, the remote trainees were asked about their expectations of Web-based training. (See Table 2.) Most trainees had no expectations or focused

Table 2. Respondents' Expectations of Web-based Training

Expectations of Web-based Training	Percentage of Remote Trainees (N=8)
No expectations	38
Not as effective as classroom	25
Dynamic instructor not present	13
Not able to ask questions	13
Optimistic	13
Not have a captive audience	13
Lack of visual tools	13

(Because each respondent can provide multiple responses, the percentages can add to more than 100%)

on what the Web training lacked as compared with the local training. Thus, unlike the local trainees, the remote trainees had somewhat negative expectations of the training.

Some remote respondents expressed general uneasiness about the anticipated Web-based training. Specifically, one said,

> It's just when you're remote, you just sometimes think you're out of the loop a little bit. I think you get more out of it when you're sitting next to somebody in a group and you're taking this great class.

However, they felt that any training would be beneficial. As one respondent stated,

> Like I said earlier …[I'm] 'cautiously optimistic,' and [that] really nails it. Because I just get a lot more when I'm in person, but we'll see how it all ends up.

These comments indicated no software anxiety, but some anxiety as to the effectiveness of the training.

Links between training and the goals of the work group

As shown in Table 3, participants agreed that links exist between the prospective training and the goals of their work groups.

Respondents felt that the training would help them succeed in accomplishing present and future workgroup goals. One respondent said,

Table 3. Links Between Training and the Goals of the Work Group

Links Between Training and Work Group Goals	Percentage of Classroom Trainees (N=55)	Percentage of Remote Trainees (N=10)
Guiding change and furthering work group goals	25	
Building trust	25	
Becoming more effective communicators and motivators	19	20
Improving work environments	12	60
Increasing team productivity	9	10
Increasing customer focus	5	

(Because each respondent can provide multiple responses, the percentages can add to more than 100%)

I think the training [will help] to keep me a little more focused on the broader issues, not just what my team is doing today but what my team needs to be able to be doing next year.

Overall, trainees saw a link between the training and the goals of their workgroup. Again, the local trainees described more possible links than the remote trainees did.

Links between the training and the organization's goals

Respondents to our telephone interviews identified links between the training and the overall goals of the organization. (See Table 4.)

Table 4. Respondents' Responses in Identifying Links Between the Training and Organizational Goals

Links Between Training and Organizational Goals	Percentage of Classroom Participants (N=55)	Percentage of Remote Participants (N=10)
Increases job satisfaction	49	
Strengthens management team	37	50
Maximizes abilities and productivity	33	
Aids in adapting to rapid change	18	
Improves employee retention	14	
Improves morale and motivation	14	10
Facilitates motivated and competent teams	14	
Improves customer relations and performance	9	10
Improves communication	7	20
Includes the remote users		10

(Because each respondent can provide multiple responses, the percentages can add to more than 100%)

Respondents generally felt that the training would benefit the organization in a variety of ways: by increasing job satisfaction; by strengthening management; and by maximizing abilities and productivity. Additionally, they felt that the training would advance the company in the desired direction. One respondent stated,

> This is one of our aces in the hole, provide training for those who come on board, so that we can retain the best leaders that there are to lead our company into the new horizon. It's kind of an exciting opportunity.

Overall, the respondents were able to articulate a link between the training and the goals of the organization, and they indicated that the training would ultimately benefit the organization. As with the previously described results, these findings showed that local trainees described more varied links between the training and the organizational goals.

Mid-term in-person interviews

Sixty-eight trainees participated in in-person interviews. Of those, 62 had had the classroom-based training and six had had the Web-based training. The classroom-based group increased in size because people were added to the classes. Fewer people in the Web-based group were available to participate in the in-person interviews, given their travel and meeting schedules. Thus, only half of the remote trainees were able to participate in the mid-term in-person interviews because of scheduling conflicts.

Overall reactions

Nearly all of the local trainees raved about the instructor. Very few of them had anything critical to say about the training. By contrast, the remote trainees were much more critical. This difference could be attributed to a combination of problems with technical reliability and the general awkwardness of conducting a live Internet class.

Problems with technical reliability

The biggest problems with the Web-based training stemmed from technical difficulties with the live, synchronous sessions. Five of the six respondents identified technical difficulties as a problem with the training. Those on both sides of the Internet divide experienced problems. Some of the problems were due to trainees' connections to the Internet. Some were due to the instructor's difficulties with the technology. One respondent stated,

> To be really honest with you, the [training on] coaching was a terrible session. A lot of us had technical problems; we didn't get to the role-playing. I'm not sure I used much of it. The second one was better, but [instructor] had technical problems. So they haven't been the best sessions.

Another respondent stated,

They've been frustrating. The on-line modules on the phone have been riddled with technical problems and breakdowns in communication.

Despite the technical problems, respondents seem certain that these problems are being resolved.

Issues concerning learning style

All of the local respondents (62) and most of the remote respondents (4 of 6) had positive things to say about the training. One remote respondent said,

The most beneficial part to me was the asynchronous part: the Web modules, self-paced. I liked it all as a whole.

Another stated that the work the remote trainees do before the on-line class helps them prepare better:

I think the people in the [classroom location] miss a lot by not being able to do that interactive Web-based module. But I think we miss out a little bit because it is better in person. ... it's a good training program, but I think it's still more effective if you're there in person, on the actual role-playing and things like that. I actually think because of that pre-Web module, you're bringing something in there that's even more important, and that is that you've already thought about it, you've already looked at it, you've already done your homework. From my understanding of the [classroom location] ones, they walk in blind. So that's a benefit for the way our training is going.

Although classroom trainees did have materials in advance, they were not required, as were the remote trainees, to review and complete exercises in advance of the session. This preparation may be a major benefit of the Web-based training.

Nevertheless, reminiscent of remote trainee's initial concerns about the effectiveness of Web-based training, one or two respondents indicated that the learning style required by the synchronous sessions caused some problems for them. One respondent stated,

Web-based training is awkward. You have a conversation, then you have like a little quiz, and then it goes back to the conversation. And we're so worried about answering it wrong.

This latter issue may be an issue of individual learning style, or it may reflect upon the instructional design of the synchronous Web-based sessions.

Instructional design issues

The local trainees were much more likely to list specific aspects of the training that made it easier to use the learned skills. Among the remote trainees, two stated that the just-in-time planners helped them prepare for the synchronous classroom session. One said the role-playing helped. Another said that learning the skills on their own in advance of the synchronous training created a better learning environment.

Workload issues

One of the factors that emerged from the interviews involved the conflict between time to participate in the training and time to complete the workload expected on the job. Furthermore, this conflict appeared for both the remote and the local trainees. As one of the remote trainees said,

> If I remember right, the last one I looked at took about an hour to go through the whole reading, the questions, the whole Web module. And that's a lot of time when you're a manager, when you're already given 80 hours of work to do in a 40-hour week, and then you're given this.

In fact, half of the remote respondents commented that the heavy workload and the lack of time posed a challenge regarding implementing the training. The local trainees echoed this sentiment. A trainee summed it up this way,

> We had to move so fast with [our company]; we put it together like you wouldn't believe. It was a zoo, and it still is sort of a zoo. Not because no one is trying or not because talented people are not here, it's just because of the sheer speed. You just simply can't keep up with it.

Concerns regarding management support

One of the remote trainees responded with a concern that the training was creating somewhat confused expectations about their roles.

> To be quite frank, the thing I saw that kind of concerned me was my supervisors and leads who almost had the perception that the things that I ask them to do as a manager are wrong to ask them to do...

Expectations concerning the role of managers could be established by additional management support. Furthermore, both the remote and the local trainees expressed concerns about the level of involvement of top management in the training. They felt that top management was not implementing the skills, not reinforcing the skills, and not giving full attention to the training.

Skills used

Training participants at this Internet company frequently encounter situations where they must give and receive feedback. They work with customer service representatives (CSRs) who assist customers in the company. The trainees conduct regular "one-on-ones" with the CSRs, where they examine the CSRs' performance and the content of their interactions with customers. Because the remote trainees have to do much of their work over the telephone and via e-mail, their communications must be clear and precise. Therefore, it was no surprise that they found the skills of giving and receiving feedback to be the most useful.

As one trainee stated,

> I think the training that we had on giving and receiving feedback, the most recent training, . . . is probably the most beneficial of all the training we've had so far.

The trainees responded to such questions as "Think of a recent time when you used your new skills. What were the circumstances?" "And think of a time when you failed to use the skills that you learned. What were the circumstances?" Their responses showed that the trainees clearly understood how and why to use the skills they had learned on giving and receiving feedback. They could describe both the impact of using the skills and the impact of not using the skills. A typical response follows:

> I used constructive feedback when one of the members on my team had some problems *[with the organization's customer satisfaction effort]* and I kind of went through the seven steps, the key action items, and had sort of a game plan set up before I even made the phone call and had them written down, so it made it a lot smoother than normal.

Impact

Trainees were asked about the impact of the training on their workgroups and on the organization as a whole.

Among the remote trainees, these percentages dropped somewhat. Half of the remote trainees could see an impact on their work groups, and about half could see an impact on the organization. One remote respondent explained that this could be due to the fact that their work teams communicate remotely:

> Because we're remote, we communicate by e-mail and conference calls. I've only met maybe two folks on the team. We only might interact with them on telephone conversation perhaps once a week, where people here it's day-to-day, so it's easier to use the skills a lot quicker. So for us, it's a little slower process.

Although differences appeared between the two groups in the percentage of trainees citing impacts on their workgroups, there was a great deal of agreement concerning the types of impact on the workgroup. The most frequently cited impact on the work group was that the training improved communication.

As with the impacts on the workgroup, both groups reported somewhat similar impacts on the company. They reported that the culture is improving and there is more staff development. They also saw better teamwork.

Summary of the mid-term interviews

The local trainees expressed more excitement about the training than the remote trainees. This may be related to the problems with technical reliability experienced by some of the remote trainees. Furthermore, such

The local trainees expressed more excitement about the
training than the remote trainees.

problems may indicate that the remote trainees have somewhat different training needs from the local trainees. They may, for example, need more instruction and assistance with how to use both the asynchronous and the synchronous Web-based tools. In addition, because they have less live class time, they want to see materials that are more tailored to their experiences.

In general, the local trainees used more of the skills and were more specific about the results of training. However, the remote trainees were definitely learning and using the skills they learned. They do not use the skills as often as the local trainees do, because they do not have day-to-day contact with others.

The remote trainees are also less likely to see an impact on the company from the training; although most believe they will. Once again, this is due, in part, to the fact that most of the remote trainees work from home and are slower to use their skills.

Discussion

This study presented preliminary findings from an implementation of leadership training using both classroom-based and Web-based training at an Internet company. Preliminary observations from initial and mid-term interviews of trainees showed initial enthusiasm from both classroom-based and Web-based groups. The enthusiasm of trainees in the Web-based training group was, however, tempered by a few expressions of concern. Since all of these trainees were highly computer literate, their concerns do not seem to be related to the factors of software anxiety, computer anxiety, or browser experience, as identified in the work of Flannery, Wagner, and Ellinger (2001). Rather, their concerns revolved around a perception that such training would prove less effective than in-person, classroom-based training.

Both the local trainees and the remote trainees were able to articulate the goals of the training and the links between the training and the goals of their work group and the organization. Thus, both groups understood the importance of the training and the reasons for the use of the different training methodologies. However, the local trainees were able to identify more links between training and the work group and the organization goals.

Success factors

Although the remote trainees did not initially express concerns over problems with technical reliability, the mid-term interviews revealed that actual incidents of problems with the technology seemed to have an effect on trainee attitudes and possibly on learning outcomes. Such results are consistent with the findings of Webster and Hackley (1997) in their study of two-way audio/video/graphic links in university courses in accounting, chemistry, computer science, engineering, mathematics, physics, political science, and sociology. Specifically, they found that reliability of the technology was positively related to learning outcomes. In the present study, the reliability of the asynchronous training led trainees to comment on the usefulness of the materials. By contrast, the technical difficulties in the initial sessions of the synchronous classroom training led some of the

Time conflict appeared as an important factor.

trainees to question the usefulness of the program. Thus, in the present study, the variable of technical reliability (identified by Webster & Hackley, 1997) appeared to be related to the variable of perceived usefulness (identified by Flannery, Wagner, and Ellison, 2001). Whether perceived usefulness affects learning outcomes and on-the-job use of learned skills will require future data collection.

A second factor that emerged involved trainee expectations. The local trainees were able to articulate more varied expectations for the training and were able to describe the links between the training and the goals of the workgroup and the organization. Such expectations may have an effect on the learning and performance outcomes. This factor did not emerge from the Flannery, Wagner, and Ellison (2001) study, but Bandura (1977) and others (Gist, 1987; Gist, Schwoerer, & Rosen, 1989) described how expectations could have consequences. Calling it the Pygmalion effect, Eden (1990) showed that a person's expectations could affect how that person behaves in ways that lead to achieving those expectations. The results from the mid-term interviews, in which a larger percentage of the local trainees, as compared with the remote trainees, were able to describe impacts on the workgroup and on the organization, may be related to their earlier expectations.

Another factor that emerged was individual learning styles. It appeared that the asynchronous Web-based training proved to be an effective method for some, but not for all, remote trainees. Related to the individual learning styles factor was the factor of the instructional design. Neither the learning styles factor nor the instructional design factor appeared in the Flannery, Wagner, and Ellison (2001) study. Lima and Hoff (2000) and Aragon, Johnson, and Shaik (2000), however, examined the impact of learning style preferences in on-line university courses. Whether such factors affect learning outcomes from the leadership training course and on-the-job use of learned leadership skills will be investigated in future data collection.

The issue of conflict between the time involved in preparing for and taking the class and the time needed to fulfill job responsibilities appeared as an important factor for both the remote and the local trainees. Again, the workload factor did not appear in the work of Flannery, Wagner, and Ellison (2001), but workload has been shown to affect the success of training (Decker & Nathan, 1985; Porras & Hargis, 1982). Also, Cahoon (1998) identified the constraints of time in adult-learning situations, whether these are conventional classroom based or Internet based.

A final factor that emerged in the mid-term interviews was management support. This factor was consistent with findings of the Flannery, Wagner, and Ellinger (2001) study. Unless trainees receive management support, the reliability of the technology and the quality of the instructional design employed in the training program may be irrelevant to learning outcomes and on-the-job use of learned skills.

A few factors identified by Flannery, Wagner, and Ellinger (2001) did not appear to be important: self-determination, attitude toward use, educational level, perceived usefulness, and behavioral intentions. These factors may, however, emerge in future data collection, along with additional data on the behavioral and organizational impacts of this training.

Results

Preliminary results on the learning outcomes or the organizational impact of training suggested that problems with technical reliability, particularly with the synchronous training, as well as the fewer positive expectations among the Web-based group, might have had a negative effect on learning and performance for this group. As the technical problems are resolved in upcoming sessions, future data collection may confirm the "no significant difference" finding that was characteristic of previous research; that is, there is no significant difference between technology-based training and classroom-based training (Chute, Thompson, & Hancock, 1999; Ravishankar, 1999). On the other hand, the results may show specific differences between the groups in their knowledge, skills, and use of the skills on the job. Such differences may result from the earlier technological problems experienced by the remote trainees or from the differences in the expectations of the two groups. These differences in the training results may imply the need for modifications to the instructional design and for additional management support.

Conclusion

This study compares Web-based and classroom-based leadership training within one Internet company. The measure of training results or outcomes for the organization not only focused on whether trainees engaged in the Web-based experiences but also on whether trainees applied the learned skills on the job. It suggests that certain training factors, such as improving technical reliability, matching the instructional design with individual learning styles, and clarifying expectations regarding the training can influence the success of Web-based training. These findings contribute to the theory-building work of Flannery, Wagner, and Ellinger (2001) and to that of Sharda, Romano, and Lucca (in this book). They also indicate factors that may have influenced the results in the studies reported by Wang, Rossett, and Wangemann (in this book) and Scheets and Weiser (in this book). The results suggest that certain organizational factors, such as reducing the

Web-based training is not a "magic pill."

workloads of trainees and increasing management support for the trainees and the training, can have a positive impact for both local and remote trainees. Such findings confirm the previous findings from studies of traditional classroom training (Porras & Hargis, 1982; Taylor, 1992) and expand these findings to Web-based training. Furthermore, the emergence of workload as a success factor tends to contradict the notions that Web-based training can more easily fit into an employee's schedule. At the very least, it reveals that employees still need to have some amount of time available for training. In other words, Web-based training is not a "magic pill."

Identification of other success factors and the ultimate results of the training (in terms of on-the-job behavior changes among the trainees and potential improvements in employee morale among their subordinates) will require additional data collection and research. Furthermore, whether the success factors generated in this study generalize to other organizations and situations will require undertaking similar studies in other contexts.

In terms of implications for practice, this study suggests that HRD professionals should do more than simply implement a Web-based training program and assume that they have accomplished their responsibilities. Rather, HRD professionals should systematically evaluate their proposed Web-based training programs to determine whether issues exist that relate to technical reliability, individual learning styles and the expectations regarding training results. If so, HRD professionals should be prepared to intervene to address these issues. For example, with issues regarding technical reliability, there may be a need for additional resources to provide technical support. With issues concerning learning styles, HRD professionals should consider modifying Web-based training modules or providing paper-based options. As for expectations prior to training, HRD professionals should create plans for providing telephone- and e-mail-based coaching and support. HRD professionals should also determine the extent to which management support exists for trainees and be prepared to intervene to obtain needed support. Finally, HRD professionals should examine whether trainees are provided the needed time to complete the training, whether classroom, asynchronous, or synchronous. If trainees lack adequate time and needed management support, any training program, no matter how well it is designed and implemented, will be doomed to failure for the individuals, their groups, and the organization.

Thus, this study contributes to HRD knowledge and experience with Web-based training.

References

Alavi, M., Yoo, Y., & Vogel, D. R. (1997). Using information technology to add value to management education. *Academy of Management Journal, 40*(6), 1310-1333.

Aragon, S. R., Johnson, S. D., & Shaik, N. (2000). The influence of learning style preferences on student success in on-line vs. face-to-face environments. In K. P. Kuchinke (Ed.) *Proceedings of the Academy of Human Resource Development*, Baton Rouge, LA: AHRD, 958-966.

Bandura, A. (1977). *Social learning theory*. Englewood Cliffs, NJ: Prentice-Hall.

Cahoon, B. (1998). Adult learning and the Internet: Themes and things to come. *New Directions for Adult and Continuing Education*, No. 78 (Summer), 71-76.

Caracelli, V. J., & Jennifer, J. C. (1997). Crafting mixed-method evaluation designs. In J. C. Greene & V. J. Caracelli (Eds.) *Advances in mixed-method evaluation: The challenges and benefits of integrating diverse paradigms,* New Directions in Evaluation, no. 74, San Francisco: Jossey-Bass, 19-32.

Chute, Al. G., Thompson, M. M., & Hancock, B. W. (1999). *The McGraw-Hill handbook of distance learning*. New York: McGraw.

Decker, P. J., & Nathan, B. R. (1985). *Behavior modeling training: Principles and applications*. New York: Praeger.

Eden, D. *Pygmalion in management: Productivity is a self-fulfilling prophecy.* Lexington, MA: Lexington, 1990.

Flannery, D. D., Wagner, D. G., & Ellinger, A. D. (2001). Accessing learning in the workplace: A quantitative study of factors affecting learner acceptance of a computer-based training (CBT) support tool. In J. N. Streumer (Ed.) *Perspectives on learning at the workplace: Theoretical positions, organizational factors, learning processes and effects.* In J. Streumer (Ed.) *Proceedings of the Second Conference HRD Research and Practice across Europe.* Enschede, The Netherlands: University of Twente.

Gist, M. E. (1987). Self-efficacy: Implications for organizational behavior and human resource management. *Academy of Management Review, 12*, 472-485.

Gist, M. E., Schwoerer, C., & Rosen, B. (1989). Effects of alternative training methods on self-efficacy and performance in computer software training. *Journal of Applied Psychology, 74*, 884-891.

Greene, J. C., & Caracelli, V. J. (1997). Defining and describing the paradigm issue in mixed-method evaluation. In J. C. Greene & V. J. Caracelli (Eds.) *Advances in mixed-method evaluation: The challenges and benefits of integrating diverse paradigms*, New Directions in Evaluation, no. 74, San Francisco: Jossey-Bass, 19-32.

Herther, N. K. (1997, Sept/Oct). Education over the web: Distance learning and the information professional. *On-line*, 63-72.

Lima, L. A. C., & Hoff, K. S. (2000). Teaching strategies in a synchronous learning environment for adult students. In K. P. Kuchinke (Ed.) *Proceedings of the Academy of Human Resource Development*, Baton Rouge, LA: AHRD, 950-957.

Partee, M. H. (1996, June). Using email, web sites & newsgroups to enhance traditional classroom instruction. *T. H. E. Journal*, 79-82.

Porras, J. L., & Hargis, K. (1982). Precursors of individual change: Responses to a social learning theory based on organization intervention. *Human Relations, 35*, 973-990.

Rahm, D., & Reed, (1997). Going remote: The use of distance learning, the World Wide Web, and the Internet in graduate programs of public affairs and administration. *Public Productivity and Management Review, 20*(4), 459-471.

Ravishankar, L. (1999). *High tech training: Investigating non-response.* (AchieveGlobal Working Paper). San Jose: AchieveGlobal.

Russ-Eft, D. (1996). CBT, CAI, EPSS, and DejaVu. *Human Resource Development Quarterly, 5*(3), 207-212.

Russ-Eft, D., & Preskill, H. (2001). *Evaluation in organizations: A systematic approach to enhancing learning, performance, and change.* Cambridge, MA: Perseus.

Scheets, G., & Weiser, M. *Implementing a remote and collaborative "hands-on" learning environment.*

Sharda, R., Romano, N. C., Jr., & Lucca, J. *A conceptual framework for computer supported collaborative learning requiring immediate presence* (CSCLIP).

Simonson, M. R. (1997). Evaluating teaching and learning at a distance. *New Directions for Teaching and Learning*, No. 71 (Fall), 87-94.

Wang, M., Rossett, A., & Wangemann, P. *Do people engage when solving problems on-line?*

Webster, J., & Hackley, P. (1997). Teaching effectiveness in technology-mediated distance learning. *Academy of Management Journal, 40,* 1282-1309.

AN EXPLORATION OF ENGAGEMENT AND MENTORING IN ON-LINE PROBLEM SOLVING[1]

Minjuan Wang
San Diego State University

Allison Rossett
San Diego State University

Paul Wangemann
Motorola University

Abstract

This chapter examines some of the emotional and engagement aspects of on-line communicating and problem solving. We report our findings from an exploratory study of participant interactions in an on-line problem-solving program—the Motorola Internet-based Expeditions. The program provides youth with a non-school experience in solving problems situated on line with real-life aspects and under the guidance of on-line mentors.

Here we explore the degree of the youths' engagement in the 5-week problem-solving program by examining their patterns of communication, ways of talking, emotional markers, and social talk. We posit that more communication, exploratory talk, and emotional markers suggest greater engagement with on-line problem solving. In addition, we identify the strategies used by on-line mentors to keep youth engaged in on-line discussions and joint activities. We examine the mentoring strategies used in mediating exploratory talk, which involves negotiation and rational debate. Finally, we suggest ways to better rivet the attention of youth and others on on-line problem-solving activities, and we identify the strategies that on-line mentors use to facilitate communication, team building, and problem solving.

---

[1] The authors wish to acknowledge the iExpeditions 1999 project team at the Center for Technology Innovations in Education (CTIE), University of Missouri–Columbia. Under the strong leadership of Dr. James Laffey, the team cooperated in successfully designing, developing, and implementing the iExpeditions system.

Introduction

There is ample enthusiasm for the wonders of on-line communities of practice and on-line activities and problem solving. Many international corporations, from Motorola to IBM to Eli Lilly to PricewaterhouseCoopers, now engage their international employees in problem-solving tasks via intranet communications. Many organizations place high hopes on the Internet as a means to involve employees, no matter their locations, tasks, teams, learning, or corporate initiatives. What happens when people are challenged to solve a real-world business problem posed to them on line? Are they engaged by the experience? Or do they simply fulfill their obligations?

Human resource professionals, not surprisingly, are concerned about the tradeoffs associated with on-line problem solving. Can on-line environments sustain the same quality of human contact as traditional settings (Lowell & Persichitte, 2000)? Lowell and Persichitte answered this question by providing anecdotal evidence to show that well-designed and well-delivered on-line experiences can create engaging communities. Souder's (1993) study of traditional versus satellite delivery in three management of technology programs discovered that students bond with each other in asynchronous environments even more than they do in traditional, synchronous settings. Miller and Miller (1999) noted that many researchers believe that computer-mediated communication (CMC) helps participants transcend the interaction barriers that occur in traditional classroom settings and that it fosters greater participation.

Are on-line tasks emotionally engaging for participants? A handful of studies, such as Chapman, Selvarajah, and Webster (1999) and Laurel (1991), have examined user engagement in multimedia training systems. User engagement in this case refers to the user's emotional state, such as

What happens when people are challenged to solve a real-world business problem posed to them on-line?

curiosity, interest, confidence, and surprise when interacting with an engaging system (Chapman et al., 1999). The notion of defining user engagement as learner interest and participation in tasks (Reeves, 1999; Wang, 2001) is recently formed and has not been extensively studied in on-line problem solving. In Wang's (2001) dissertation study of Motorola's Expeditions program, for example, participants' engagement was considered a background factor in interpreting knowledge construction.

This chapter is a follow-up of that dissertation study. We further define learner engagement as the state of being emotionally involved in conversations and tasks. Involvement is indicated by interaction patterns and emotional cues in on-line communications. In other words, engagement is a variation of emotional involvement, concentration, or motivation. We posit that human touch, mentoring, on-line mentor preparation, team-forming processes, and strong social bonds are enablers of engagement. We provide some evidence that on-line activities do indeed engage participants, based on the quantity and the nature of on-line interaction as defined by Mercer (1995). In congruence with prior researchers in information systems (Chapman et al., 1999; Laurel, 1991), we found in this exploratory study that greater participant engagement in on-line problem solving appeared to lead to better task performance, perhaps because of increased concentration and motivation.

From our perspective, on-line engagement should not only be promoted by the software employed, it should also be cultivated by human touch, such as mentoring and peer interaction. Effective strategies for boosting engagement in on-line activities may include better preparing on-line mentors for their roles and better motivating participants by strengthening the social bonds in their on-line communities.

Internet-based Expeditions

The program—the Internet-based Expeditions program—was developed by Motorola University for youth (primarily the children of Motorola employees) who engage in a 4-to 5-week problem-solving experience using computer-supported collaborative tools. In Expeditions, participants access an on-line learning community through the Internet from their home computers or from designated computer labs. The goal for the youth is to present solutions to an actual business-related challenge faced by one of Motorola's businesses. The youth receive the challenging assignment and share their ideas and solutions with the actual stakeholders, the Motorola sponsors of the program. They participate as volunteers in this non-school experience and are expected to learn how to develop relationships, share information, make decisions, and present their ideas as a team while connected on-line. Their on-line mentors (pre-service educators from a collaborating university) are expected to guide the learning process and provide important feedback and support. Throughout the program, the mentors guide youth in developing their abilities to work as members of a team, solve problems, and communicate ideas.

The youth involved in these collaborative teams deal with relevant business issues, such as customer identification, product design and function, management, manufacturing, marketing, and defining requirements for satisfying customers. They are asked to contribute their thinking and their creativity by developing solutions for current, unresolved issues facing a business unit. The challenges are real, and the contributions and perspectives of the youth are valued and thoroughly reviewed. In this particular Expedition, the president of Motorola University acknowledged to the youth the importance of their insights, ideas, and applications and stated that they were expected to join a global community of consultants and advisors that help Motorola be successful. Expeditions is designed to be fun and challenging and to encourage youth to think about their futures.

The initial purpose of the Expeditions program was to find ways to help prepare the children of employees for future employment opportunities and in particular, to contribute to the development of potential leaders. Over the years, the on-line Expeditions and a related classroom-based version called Explorations have been used by Motorola as means for influencing customers, community, and employees and for deriving marketing information from future customers. Although the program has from time to time been positioned differently, the guiding philosophy has remained essentially the same. Motorola believes that young people, in order to become lifelong learners, require direct experience with such critical skills as problem solving and teamwork. They believe that youth learn best when they are engaged in challenges of interest and relevance while they simultaneously receive appropriate feedback. They also posit that youth need to feel ownership in the learning process and accountability for results. These are a few of the ideas that formed the underpinnings of the program. We believe that our findings will be valuable for other organizations seeking ways to engage their employees or youth in problem-solving tasks through on-line communications.

Literature review

With the increasing popularity of social constructivism in the 1990s, learner interaction has been placed under a spotlight for study. Social constructivists (Ernest, 1995; Rogoff, 1990; Vygotsky, 1978, 1986) believe that knowledge develops through discourse and joint activity. Appropriating this social constructivist view of knowledge and knowledge construction, cognitive and educational researchers (Barnes, 1976; Edwards & Furlong, 1978; Edwards & Mercer, 1987; Edwards & Westgate, 1987; Mehan, 1979) have come to perceive education as a communicative process and have accorded classroom discourse a central place in the process of learning and in research about learning. Edwards and Mercer (1987) discovered that classroom dialogues could help a community of learners construct shared understanding and adopt a common knowledge base.

This belief in conversation and communication extends to corporate settings where managers are eager to teach employees how things are done and to capture and share lessons across time and space. Prahalad and Hammel (1990) concluded that the core competencies—or the collective learnings—of an organization are the essence of competitive advantage. Unlike physical assets, competencies do not deteriorate as they are applied and shared. In fact they grow.

Enter the Web. Theoreticians and practitioners in educational technology have been intrigued by the ability of CMC tools to create and define complex social environments (Feenberg & Bellman, 1990) and interaction on line (Harasim, 1990). Mason and Kaye (1990) found that CMC facilitated the development of community by providing opportunities for people to inform, question, socialize, and engage in serendipitous exchange. Community adds emotional color to rational content (Mason & Kaye, 1990).

An on-line environment offers unique opportunities for elective and active participation.

In addition, group interaction allows people to exchange ideas, negotiate, and debate and to make leaps in understanding (Mason, 1994). Harasim, Hiltz, Teles, and Turoff (1995) also found that the asynchronicity of an on-line environment offers unique opportunities for elective and active participation, leading to thoughtful responses and reflection.

Koschmann (1996) and Roschelle and Pea (1999) called researchers' attentions to learner interactions; collaborative, graphical, and verbal representations; and other social factors in a computer-supported collaborative learning (CSCL) environment. They identified the need to better understand the processes of collaborative work and learning and to build better tools to support these emerging interactive processes. This tool-building approach is congruent with research in information systems. (See the chapter titled, "Conceptual Framework for Computer Supported Collaborative Learning Requiring Immediate Presence.")

As Chapman et al. (1999) noted,

> There have been calls to create systems for which users' interactions are pleasurably engaging, fun, and intrinsically motivating, to design multimedia systems to be more lively, intriguing, or fascinating, and to recognize the achievement of engagement as an important goal in the design of systems (p. 1).

While many studies about learner interactions on line have emerged, few have addressed learner emotion and engagement with tasks. The topic is intriguing because emotion and engagement have the potential to enhance learner persistence and thus to reduce the dropout rate from on-line activities, which is a critical problem facing many organizations with high hopes for technology-based learning and work (Rossett, 2000).

Researchers in the field of educational technology have continuously explored persistence and the dropout problem. For instance, Reeves (1999) noted that every emergent educational technology has promised to be intrinsically motivating, but the effective design of learning experiences is the real motivating factor. Harasim and her colleagues (1995) suggested that the learner control afforded by an on-line learning environment, because of its learner-centeredness, has the potential to enhance motivation.

From our perspective, it is critical that an on-line program involving voluntary participation be interesting, engaging, and stimulating. It is also critical that mentors be prepared to guide participants in an on-line program. The freedom the Web provides to surf to a site, a task, or a learning experience is also the freedom to exit. The Expeditions program is representative of many Internet-based collaborative learning and work programs that are predicated on voluntary participation. Expeditions participants, like participants in many other on-line programs, get to choose if they will stay, engage, contribute, and learn.

The invention of Expeditions

The Expeditions program was developed to provide youth with a voluntary, on-line, non-school experience that would encourage them to work with others to solve real-world problems. The term *Expeditions* is a metaphor for working with ill-defined problems that must be solved over time as conditions and circumstances evolve. The Expeditions under study here involved 39 youth who responded to a request by a chief executive officer (CEO) for help in developing and marketing telematics. Telematics is wireless communications system, designed to be delivered in an automobile, to provide drivers with personalized information, messaging, entertainment, and location-specific travel and security services. This Expeditions lasted five weeks. The youth were guided by mentors and telematics experts as they worked in small teams to develop a proposal responsive to the priorities established by the CEO.

With the exception of a 3-hour face-to-face orientation focused primarily on learning how to use the on-line iExpeditions system, the entire Expeditions was conducted through a Web environment with a coordinated set of communication and collaboration tools. The iExpeditions system provides synchronous tools, such as chat rooms, and asynchronous tools, such as a forum (a Web-based discussion board), notes (an intranet e-mail tool), and logs (electronic journals). Figure 1 captures the basic user interface associated with iExpeditions. The Web page has communication tools on the left side, the members of one's team in the middle, and a problem-solving organizational map at the bottom.

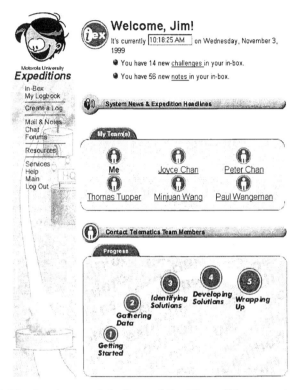

Figure 1. The basic user interface of the iExpeditions system

The organizational map established a structured procedure for carrying out problem-solving tasks in five phases: 1) getting started; 2) gathering data; 3) identifying solutions; 4) developing solutions; and 5) wrapping up. This problem-solving procedure is similar to the one that Motorola telematics experts preferred to use in their research and development activities.

The iExpeditions system was designed to facilitate and record participants' social interactions and shared problem solving. Using the communications tools visible in Figure 1, participants were able to voluntarily exchange notes messages, attend on-line chat sessions, create logs, and post questions, schedules, and other work-related messages on the forum. Did people actively communicate? Did they use the tools for communicating? Were they emotionally engaged in the problem-solving tasks? If so, to what extent? We attempted to answer these questions by examining the patterns and the nature of member communications for two Expeditions teams.

Patterns of communication

In the telematics Expeditions, 39 teenage youth and 10 on-line mentors formed six teams. We focused our analysis on teams A and E (each had 5 youth and 2 mentors) because they were the most active of the six teams. In addition, the two teams presented an interesting contrast in their formation and in their work and interaction styles. Team A was formed by self-selection by members and mentors, which resulted in stronger interpersonal and social relations. By contrast, team E's youth and mentors, who were assigned by project stakeholders, did not develop strong interpersonal and social relations. Moreover, team A augmented their on-line communications with informal face-to-face interactions. Team E relied on on-line communications only. The challenges for teams A and E were the same. Under the guidance of their on-line mentors, the five youth on each team collaborated with teammates by sending notes, holding on-line chat sessions, posting messages in forums, and distributing ideas represented in logs. Data about their participation and feelings were gathered by having the youth fill out weekly on-line self-reports.

Findings

An analysis of communication artifacts and weekly report data indicated that teams A and E had similar patterns of communications over the five weeks. The number of notes exchanged within team A decreased from week 1 (getting started) to week 4 (developing solutions) and increased in week 5 (wrapping up). The number of chat sessions increased over the five weeks. The average number of logs generated by each youth also increased. In both teams, members rarely used the forum to post questions and announcements or to hold team meetings. Similarly, the number of notes exchanged within team E decreased from week 1 (getting started) to week 3 (identifying solutions), but it increased from week 4 (developing solutions) to week 5 (wrapping up). As with team A, team E's chat sessions increased over the five weeks, and so did the average number of logs generated by each member. No member of team E used the forum.

Table 1 details team A's communications (notes, chat, logs, and forum postings) over the five weeks. Table 2 details team E's communications over the five weeks.

Figures 2 and 3 visually display the patterns of communication for the two teams. They focus attention on the quantities of notes, logs, chat sessions, and forum messages posted.

These communication patterns indicate that the beginning and the end of the Expeditions experience attracted the most interest from youth on both teams. The youth were engaged at the beginning of their Expeditions, perhaps because of novelty and curiosity, and at the close, perhaps because of a mandatory presentation that was deliverable at the end of the process. In the middle of the process, however, their attention flagged.

Table 1. Communications on Team A

Week	Notes	Chats	Youth Logs (average)	Forums	Total
week 1	39	0	0	1	40
week 2	24	1	5	1	31
week 3	14	2	5	3	24
week 4	7	2	6	1	16
week 5	41	3	12	2	58
Total	125 (89 by youth)	8 (mentors and youth)	140	8	

Notes: In the iExpeditions system, a notes message can have fewer than 50 words, but a chat conversation has no limit on length.

Table 2. Communications on Team E

Week	Notes	Chats	Youth Logs (average)	Forums	Total
week 1	10	0	5	0	15
week 2	8	2	6	0	16
week 3	5	2	7	0	14
week 4	15	2	9	0	26
week 5	32	3	9	0	44
Total	70 (15 by youth)	9 (mentors and youth)	180	0	

Pattern of Communication

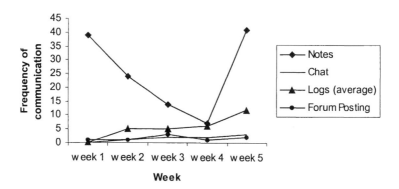

Figure 2. Pattern of communication on team A over the five weeks

Pattern of Communication

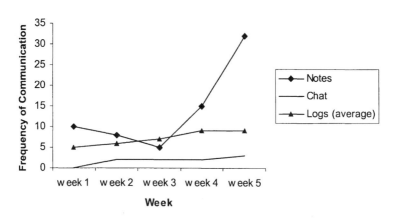

Figure 3. Pattern of communication on team E over the five weeks

Analysis of the weekly survey data showed the same pattern. Figure 4 indicates that on both teams the youths' average level of interest decreased from week 1 to week 4, and it dramatically increased in week 5.

An examination of data from both teams suggests that the on-line environment creates a new set of barriers to engagement. The weekly survey reports revealed three types of barriers: (a) institutional blocks, such as lack of technical support; (b) situational blocks, such as pre-occupation with

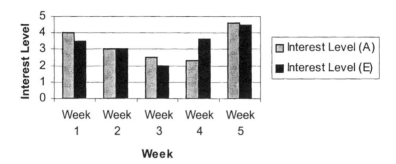

Figure 4. The youths' interest level over the five weeks

school activities or other social activities; and (c) dispositional blocks, such as loss of interest and motivation. Follow-up interviews with members of the two teams showed that situational blocks were the primary barrier for team A youth and dispositional blocks were the primary barrier for team E youth. The communications among team A members decreased from week 1 to week 4 because the two most active youth (Ya1 and Ya2) took a trip to Hawaii and were absent for a week. It then took them several days to get back on track with Expeditions. In comparison, team E youths' waning interest might be attributed to their inactive team, lack of task sharing, and the loose bonds within their team. Because participation was voluntary, individual youth were expected to muster their own motivation, set goals for work and learning, and take responsibility for their participation in the on-line teams. That they did not, as was often the case, was illustrated by their failing to efficiently complete individual readings, carry out searches for information, or complete logs. Another indicator of youth not assuming responsibility was their inconsistent participation in on-line team discussions. Teams A and E had eight to nine chat sessions over the five weeks, but only a few of the sessions were fully attended by all team members.

Desultory participation from the less active teams, not surprisingly, concerned the project's stakeholders. They tried many methods to involve youth and mentors during the first week, including the use of off-line communications. They encouraged mentors to call participants on the phone, held two warm-up chat sessions to get the youth and their mentors acquainted with each other, and established a telephone help line to solve technical problems. These efforts succeeded in reducing some of the barriers. Expeditions participants could engage if they wanted to.

The stakeholders assumed that the second week would bring a natural increase in involvement and that the on-line problem solving and the interactions would provide momenta of their own. In addition, they expected that the on-line mentors would move the effort forward. Neither occurred. For Expeditions, and perhaps for other on-line programs, other interventions must be used to boost and maintain engagement.

When they communicated, about what did they communicate?

Although social interaction from the Vygotskian (1978, 1986) perspective focuses on communications in a social context, educational researchers (e.g., Clements & Nastasi, 1988) distinguish between social interaction unrelated to work and learning and intellectual interaction focused on work and learning. Gilbert and Moore (1998) parsed interaction in distance-learning environments as social (e.g., emoticons, greetings, socializing, exchanging personal information) and instructional (e.g., content communication, exchanging information, evaluating, elaborating). Similarly, Clements and Nastasi (1988) examined the two types of interaction (social and instructional) in children's problem-solving activities in educational computer environments (e.g., Logo programming) and found they *both* contributed significantly to children's cognitive growth. Other researchers (e.g., Bearison, 1982; Mason & Kaye, 1990) also found that social and intellectual interaction could lead to the growth of cognitive and social competence and to the formation of learning communities.

Rossett and Sheldon (2001) noted that when the members of a group commit to collaborate to solve an authentic problem, some authors have begun to call their efforts action learning. Marquardt (1999) defined action learning as "...a process and a powerful program that involves a small group of people solving pressing organizational problems, while at the same time focusing on what they are learning and how it can benefit each group member and the organization" (p. 4). Action learning, which is a form of teaming, emphasizes solving real problems *and* learning *and* processing the experience, all at the same time. An example of action learning is Motorola's award-winning GOLD process. GOLD uses authentic business problems and teamwork to prepare high-potential managers to succeed in a diverse, global organization.

What happened to the Expeditions' participants as they struggled with their on-line telematics challenge? We conducted a content analysis of the chat transcripts of teams A and E. We distinguished between social interaction (social talk) and intellectual interaction (task talk). We did not attempt to explain how much each type of talk contributed to learning or to cognitive development. Rather, we focused on the effects of types of talk on members' self-reported emotional engagement and their interaction patterns (e.g., ways of talking).

Team A: Frequent social interaction

Social talk was interwoven with task talk on team A, the group with prior and place-bound ties. The five youth and the two mentors on team A were always eager to socialize! Of the 125 notes exchanged within the team, only 35 were related to Expeditions work and learning. The rest of the notes were about personal interests, school, games, and friends. In addition, the eight chat sessions all commenced with similar social interaction. Although the mentors directed participants towards discussions about the team processes and the telematics challenge, light-hearted topics emerged continuously. A representative episode to illustrate team A social talk between a mentor (Ma1) and two youth (Ya1 and Ya3) is shown in Table 3. Ya1 and her brother (Ya2) were going to Hawaii and therefore would miss one week of their Expeditions work.

The strong, pre-existing social ties that were so evident on team A had both positive and negative effects. The social network was beneficial because it encouraged participation in chat discussions and negotiations regarding members' ideas. Team members came on line more frequently to be with each other and to have fun. In particular, team A youth and the mentors used jokes and humor to build the social connections that are at the heart of high-functioning teams (Mercer, 1995). Bonk and his colleagues (1998) found that humor and social interaction shed light on the social context of the team. Mercer (1995) further advocated that both repartee and humor should be incorporated into teaching and learning because "they provide the interpersonal, emotional basis for the guided construction of knowledge" (p. 52).

In addition, team A's pre-established social network encouraged uninhibited discourse. For instance, when youth held opinions at variance with their mates, they would say so, rather than holding their opinions back. Moreover, although the mentors set the major discussion topics for each chat, team A youth frequently raised spontaneous issues. Their frank manner was itself a marker of the youths' engagement and initiative in teamwork (Harris, 1994). Mason and Kaye (1990) found that initiating

Table 3. An Example of Team A's Social Interaction

Ya1	"oh..Steward (Ma1)..next friday...the 12th Ya2 and i are leaving for Hawaii"
Ya1	"for a week"
Ma1	"Have faith, he'll come through."
Ya3	"yea yea"
Ya1	"so..we won't be here for a week"
Ma1	"Whoa, thanks for the update. We'll just work around it and catch you all up to date when you come back. :)"
Ma1	"Sounds like FUN!!"
Ya1	"oh...yes..we won the mcdonalds trip.."
Ya1	"Ya2 (my brother) won the trip."
Ya3	"errrrr"
Ya1	"im just going."
Ya1	"Ya3!! :o)"
Ya3	"hehe"
Ma1	"You guys are awesome!!"
Ya3	"really"
Ma1	"Yup!"
Ya3	"cool"

Note 1: The discussions were cited in their original format.
Note 2: Ma1 (mentor on team A) Ya1 and Ya2 (youth on team A)

communications in an on-line educational environment gives students a stronger sense of control over their learning environment, which in turn affects their motivation to participate and achieve (Reeves, 1999).

On the other hand, their ebullient social interactions appeared to reduce team efficiency, with social talk often crowding out task talk. Though team A youth exchanged a large number of notes, few of their notes were about the tasks at hand. Most youth were active in joining the chat, but they were less active in contributing asynchronously to making progress on their challenge by sending notes or making logs. The greater amount of social talk on this team appeared to build trust between members, which encouraged frankness in challenging and voicing different opinions.

Team E: Task-oriented interaction

By contrast, team E's communications were shorter and more task-oriented. Unlike the socializing that occurred on team A, team E's mentors and youth focused on problem solving. Most of the notes were sent from the mentors to the youth, and 62 of the 70 notes exchanged were related to Expeditions work. In addition, team E's chat sessions were structured like the "archetypal classroom exchange," as Mercer (1995) has defined it: The teacher asks a question, the student replies, and the teacher comments on the reply. A review of team E's chat transcripts revealed few instances where youth initiated and mentors responded.

Team E's on-line conversations appeared to be thin and not particularly substantive, with scant evidence of negotiation and argumentation. Because the youth talked more to the mentors than to each other, the mentors began to serve as filters and conduits for information and shared knowledge. This mentor mediating and filtering mimicked traditional classroom talk and became a team norm. In some cases, the youths' spontaneous contributions were ignored because the mentor followed the established interaction norm. In addition, team E's mentors were oriented more toward accomplishing team tasks than toward establishing team process or team spirit. The mentors were polite and encouraging in team chats, but rarely did they challenge the youths' understanding or engagement. We further address the influence of mentoring strategies on youth engagement in the "What made the differences?" section of this chapter.

Emotional markers

Because we lacked visible cues for assessing emotional engagement in on-line communications, we regarded exclamation marks and other characters as indicators of emotional engagement in an electronic environment. The analyses of team A and E chat transcripts support this assertion. We looked for such emotional markers as !, ?, such emoticons as -:), -;),:o), and lol; such agreeing expressions as exactly, true, OK, cool, great, and right; such disagreeing expressions as no, nope, not really, wrong, and I don't think so; such opinion words as I think, like, my opinion, your opinion; and words indicating social relationship (family members and friends).

We purposively sampled three chat sessions from each of the two teams, and we counted the emotional markers. The sample chat sessions on each team occurred in weeks 1, 3, and 5 when the teams had similar discussion topics. In addition, the lengths of the three chats (numbers of words) were similar. Table 4 compares the frequencies of each category of emotional markers by the two teams.

As Table 4 shows, team A had more exclamation marks (!) than team E. Although there were 99 such marks on team E, only a few of them were plural. We assumed that plural exclamation marks suggested even stronger emotional engagement. Similarly, team E had a high frequency of question marks (?), but only a few of them were plural. We also regarded plural

Table 4. Frequencies of Emotional Markers on Teams A and E

Category of Marks	Descriptions and Examples	Frequency of Occurrence (times)	
		Team A	Team E
!, !!, !!!, !!!!	Exclamation marks	126	99
	E: only had a few !!, !!!, or !!!!		
?, ??, ???	Question marks	213	202
	E: only had a few ?? or ???		
Friend(s)	A: The mentor called the youth as "friend."	4	4
	"Maybe a nintendo or something like that that you could play with the car next to you as you travel with a friends family." (mentor)		
	Ma1 says, "Check out the web pages so you can explain telematics to your friends."		
	Ma1 says, "goodnight my friend. ")"		
	E: used by the mentors, asking the youth to do a survey with their friends.		
I don't think so	This phase did not occur on team E. (Less disagreeing)	3	0
no, nope, not really		50	22
Wrong		3	1
Emoticon: -:), -;), ":o), lol (laugh aloud), Phew, Hehe, :nod ,and other descriptions	A: also had--laughing and grinning ear to ear	46	27
	think think think		
	smiles, laughs		
	E: Besides emoticons, it had few other emotions expressed in words.		
Wow, oh(hhh), errrr	Ya1 says, "okee dokee somkee!!"	25	11
Agree (exactly, true, Ok)		77	41
Like		40	21
Right		20	9
Cool, great		21	62
Opinion (my opinion, your opinion)	"What is your opinion?"-mentor	3	1
I think		8	18

Note: Ma1 (mentor on team A), Me1 (mentor on team E). The discussions were cited in their original format.

question marks as indicating stronger emotional engagement.

Agreement words and expressions, such as *true* and *right,* appeared more frequently on team A (137) than on team E (71). The same was true of the use of disagreement words and expressions (A: 56, E: 23). Team A used a wide variety of emoticons, including both symbol emoticons -:) and -;) and :o), and verbal emoticons lol (laugh out loud), phew, hehe, nod, laughing and grinning ear to ear, think think think, smiles, laughs. Team E used mostly symbol emoticons and few verbal emoticons.

How were participants engaged in team discussions? Did they build on each other's contributions? Did they negotiate and debate conflicting opinions? Did they get stuck in disagreements and disputes? We address these questions in the next section by examining ways of talking, or the analytical categories that researchers (Mercer, 1995; Wang, 2001) have used to parse interactions between teachers and pupils in conventional classrooms and on-line environments.

How did they talk?

Mercer (1995) described three ways of talking in the classroom environment: (a) disputational talk, which is characterized by disagreement and individualized decision-making; (b) cumulative talk, in which speakers

The high frequency of emotional markers intimate the engaging nature of exploratory talk.

build positively but uncritically on what the other has said; and (c) exploratory talk, in which speakers engage critically and constructively with each other. Ways of talking were identified by locating discourse features in each interaction episode (Mercer, 1995; Wang, 2001) in Expeditions. For instance, disputational talk is associated with assertions and counter-assertions; cumulative talk is associated with repetition, confirmation, and elaboration; and exploratory talk is associated with challenges, counter-challenges, justifications, and consensus.

Many researchers (Derry & DuRussel, 1999; Greeno, 1998, Mercer, 1995; Wang, 2001) found exploratory talk to be particularly valuable for constructing shared knowledge among discussants. Many productive communities continually engage in exploratory talk, marked by negotiation and argumentation (Derry, Gance, Gance, & Schlager, 2000). In this study, we think we may have discovered another valuable aspect of exploratory talk: emotional engagement. This comparison of ways of talking on the two teams and the high frequency of emotional markers in team A's exploratory talk intimate the engaging nature of exploratory talk.

Ways of talking on teams A and E

We randomly sampled 20 instances of notes and chat interactions, and we analyzed ways of talking by coding and locating discourse features within the interaction instances (Mercer, 1995; Wang, 2001). On team A, 10 of the 20 instances were categorized as cumulative talk, 7 of the 20 as exploratory talk. The remainder were categorized as individual discourse, or unanswered messages sent by individuals. On team E, 17 of the 20 instances were categorized as cumulative talk, 1 as exploratory talk, and the other 2 as individual discourse. Given the time constraint associated with developing an on-line presentation for their problem-solving processes and solutions, it may have been easier for participants to jump to the task than to engage in prolonged negotiation and debate.

Compared to the sparseness of exploratory talk in most of the classroom environments that Mercer (1995) studied, the abundance of negotiation, argumentation, and rational debate on team A supported the potential richness of an on-line environment. This finding corroborates Funaro and Montell's (2000) report that instructors have found that debates and mock trials worked better on line than in face-to-face classes.

Moreover, we found that certain mentoring strategies seemed to influence youths' ways of talking. The mentors on both teams appeared to encourage and reward cumulative talk, frequently giving positive feedback and uncritically accepting participants' ideas. The mentors' acceptance, no doubt, contributed strongly to the predominance of cumulative talk. Content analysis of the instances associated with cumulative and exploratory talk on team A revealed that mentors led most of the cumulative talk, but youth directed the exploratory talk. Was the exploratory talk more emotionally engaging for them? This question led us to further examine the discourse flow and the emotional markers embedded in their exploratory talk.

Exploratory discourse flow

Team A's exploratory talk was distinct from cumulative talk and individual discourse in the following three ways: First, the chats with exploratory talk were longer than the chats with cumulative talk. Second, the discourse flow in exploratory talk was more complex. The discourse flow in cumulative talk normally consisted of explaining, responding, elaborating, and confirming; but the discourse flow in exploratory talk involved conflict, challenging, counter-challenging, justifying, mediating, negotiation, and reaching consensus. During exploratory processes, mentors and youth raised ideas and debated them. They reached consensus through lengthy sessions that included negotiation and argumentation. Third, the prolonged negotiation inspired more emotional markers (!, !!, !!!, !!!!, ?, ??, ???) disagreement (I don't think so), and expressions of dislike and like.

Table 5 compares the frequency of emotional markers in a chat involving cumulative talk and a chat involving exploratory talk. A t-test (p=0.0460) indicates a significantly higher frequency of exclamations in exploratory talk than in cumulative talk.

Table 5. Comparison of Frequency of Major Emotional Markers in Cumulative Talk and Exploratory Talk—Team A

Categories	Frequency of Occurrence (times)	
	Cumulative Talk	Exploratory Talk
!, !!, !!!, !!!!	26	46
?, ??, ???	61	90
I don't think so	1	1
no, nope, not really	8	7
Wrong	1	2
Emoticon: -:), -;), ":o), lol (laugh aloud), Phew, Hehe, :nod ,and other descriptions	9	18
Wow, oh(hhh), *errrr*	5	8
Agree (exactly, true, Ok)	24	28
Like	12	15
right	6	5
Cool, great	4	7
Opinion (my opinion, your opinion)	0	2
I think	1	4
!, !!, !!!, !!!!	26	46

An episode of exploratory talk on team A

The chat episode in Table 6 illustrates the frequent occurrence of emotional markers in exploratory talk. This episode is part of a chat session held in week 5, when teams needed to identify solutions for the Expeditions problem they defined in week 1.

Table 6. Example of Emotional Markers in Exploratory Talk

Ya1, "ohhh..**i thought** it was the other one.."	[Ya1-challenging (clarifying ideas)]
Ya1, "don't they already have that one"	[Ya1-justifying: (explaining rationale)]
Ya1, "**i don't think** anyone will have the calling one."	[Ya1-justifying: (explaining rationale)]
Ya1, "where is Ya5 and Ya4..they would agree with me,"	[Ya1-justifying: (explaining rationale)]
Ya1, "im being out numbered here!!!"	[Ya1-justifying: (explaining rationale)]
Ya1, "**:o)**"	
Ma2 smiles	[Ma2- emoticons]
Ma2, "**I don't care** which one we go for -- we just need to base our decision on what customers will want most, and what will be most practical to design"	[Ma2-mentoring : rationale for decision-making]
Ya3, "the sensor one"	[Ya3-challenging-Ya1]
Ya1, "well..i am the only driver out of the teens who are here..."	[Ya1-justifying: personal experience]
Ya1, "**hehe**"	
Ya1, "I hate the sensor one!!"	[Ya1-counter-challenging-Ya3]
Ya3, "**soooo**"	[Ya3-counter-challenging-Ya1]
Ya3 has disconnected.	[technical problem]
Ma2, "do you hate it based on your own opinion, or thinking as a customer?"	[Ma2-Q-Ya1: (eliciting rationale)]
Ya1, "both."	[Ya1-input: (rationale)]
Ma2, "what is Ye2's opinion?"	[Ma2-eliciting input-Ya2]
Ya1, "since i would be a customer..."	[Ya1-justifying]
Ma2, "true"	[Ma2-consensus]
Ya1, "**he thinks** im right."	[Ya2-consensus-Ya1]
Ma2, "well let's go with that one then"	[Ma2-making decision]
Ya1, "and im not threating him or anything!!!"	[Ya1-explain ideas: Ya2 decision making]
Ya3, "**sure**"	[Ya3-consensus]
Ya1, "he says you would hear them coming anyways."	[Ya2-contribution]
Ya3, "not always"	[Ya3-challenging (disagreement)]
Ma2, "So is everyone content with the calling idea?"	Ma2-eliciting feedback: calling idea]
Ya3, "**no**"	[Ya3-challenging - disagreement]

Note: Words in bold highlight the emotional markers (exclamations).

In this chat episode, one mentor (Ma2) and three youth (Ya1, Ya2, and Ya3) went through a long process of negotiation to identify the best solutions for the team problem statement. In instance 1, Ma2 elicited contributions from the youth about their individual research activities and the ideas they liked and urged the team to make a decision. Ya1 voted for the calling system, and Ya3 chose the emergency sensor. Conflicting opinions emerged, and Ma2 mediated by explaining the principles of decision-making. "We can go with two ideas if they are both related. We just have to decide if we can handle coming up with a detailed system that incorporates both."

Ya1 and Ya2 wanted to design a system incorporating both ideas, while Ya3 preferred to go with her own idea. Ma2 encouraged the team to work together to identify a solution. Ya1 responded to this call for collaborative work and took the initiative in negotiating with Ya3 for the best solution. The team negotiated to reach consensus.

Exploratory talk requires openness to different ideas. Team A youth appeared unafraid to voice fledgling opinions. The intensive negotiation and argumentation on team A reflected the respectful and even uninhibited communicating that can transpire in an Internet-based environment, which as Walther (1996) argued could produce extensive interpersonal and social relations and facilitate a higher rate of information exchange.

We concluded from this study that the more exploratory talk, the more engagement, the better problem solving and performance. The higher frequency of exploratory talk on team A provides some support for our conclusion that A youth were more highly engaged in their Expedition.

What did they achieve?

Researchers in computer-supported collaborative work (e.g., Briggs, Reining, & Shepherd, 1998) considered idea generation to be an important part of all phases of problem solving because "the quality of ideas generated constitutes an upper limit on the quality of the problem-solving process" (p.1). In addition, the quality of the outcomes achieved was considered a major marker of team productivity (Prichard, Jones, & Roth in Briggs et al., 1998).

Team members' engagement in the teamwork affected both productivity and the caliber of team products. During the final week, each team was charged with collaboratively producing an on-line presentation describing their problem statement, solutions (marketing plans), and the process of team collaboration in completing their tasks. The presentations were delivered to a review panel of four telematics experts. The panel individually rated the team presentations by using a set of pre-defined criteria, which included the clarity of team problem statement, quality of the teamwork, data collection and analysis strategies used, team solutions, and presentation.

The experts unanimously rated team A's presentation as outstanding for the following reasons: (a) the problem statement was clearly identified and justified and linked to the CEO's charge; (b) all team members contributed to the teamwork, and they supported each other well; (c) their scientific manner of data collection and analysis; (e) the presentation was well-organized and interesting. They especially remarked upon the creativity of team A's product, which solved the problem from different perspectives and used humor and graphics to attract the panel's attention.

The experts agreed that team E did a nice job of defining the target market and collecting and analyzing data. Their product ideas were well conceived, and their presentation was organized. However, they noted that team E's solutions could have been improved with more innovative ideas. The reviewers also noted that team E's presentation could have been longer, and they could have included humor and effective graphics.

What made the differences on teams A and E?

We believe that the higher frequency of social interaction and exploratory talk and the complex negotiating process on team A probably were connected with their pre-existent social network. Team A youth, already close through relationships that predated Expeditions, manifested warm and collaborative bonds on line. We also believe that mentoring strategy was a critical factor in differentiating team A from team E.

Human touch and mentoring strategies

On-line mentors were expected to influence the success of the Expeditions programs. Their role was defined as leading the youth to complete unfamiliar tasks in a short time period with a new set of tools. Their responsibilities included team building, communication, problem solving, artifacts-generation, and reflective thinking. In particular, they were responsible for team building and engagement. The mentors for teams A and E used different strategies with their respective teams. Table 7 compares their mentoring strategies.

Table 7. A Comparison of Mentoring Strategies on Teams A and E

Attributes	Mentoring On line	
	Team A	Team E
Quantity of asynchronous contact (notes)	49	55
Personalization	More friends-like	More teacher-like
Task directions	Less	More
Implementing problem-solving procedures	More efforts	Less efforts

Quantity of asynchronous contact

Team E mentors consistently encouraged the youth to contribute to teamwork by writing notes and creating logs. They provided prompt feedback to the youths' logs by making appends, which are documents added to the logs through hyperlinks. Although there was still a lack of active participation from team E members, this mentoring strategy facilitated the youths' use of notes and logs in communicating and completing team tasks and their engagement in individual activities. By contrast, team A's mentors did not specifically encourage the youth to create logs or to send notes. They were therefore less successful in engaging the youth in their individual reading of the learning materials, the chat agendas, and other supportive materials. In many cases, team A youth had not completed their individual preparatory work when they logged on for a synchronous chat session.

Task direction

The stronger mentor involvement on team E resulted, not surprisingly, in a mentor-driven milieu. Although team E youth were better prepared than team A youth to give input during chat sessions, they engaged in teacher-centered talk. Although team A youth appeared to be less prepared to participate, they manifested creativity, imagination, and brainstorming during team discussions. Their interactions were livelier. Because team A's mentors were less directive, the youth had more leeway in leading the discussion themselves.

Mediating exploratory talk

Our analysis of ways of talking revealed that the mentoring strategies appeared to affect occurrences of exploratory talk. Team A mentors were frank in initiating negotiation or argumentation in team discussion, and they consciously facilitated the development of exploratory talk. They said, "Feel free to criticize!" when new ideas were proposed and "How do you guys propose we resolve this?" when conflicting opinions arose. Team E mentors could best be described as "polite" in team discussions. They tended to uncritically accept all opinions. In some cases, they discouraged diverse opinions, perhaps because of their eagerness to complete tasks. They frequently said, "You are right" or "That is very true" as feedback to the youths' ideas. Team E mentors did not follow up the youths' statements of disagreement, such as "I don't think" and "not really," to encourage more conversation, substantiation, or negotiation.

Learning problem-solving procedures

Mercer (1995) argued that many schools and other institutions take the establishment of rationales for granted; they fail to provide clear indications of the reasons for doing things, the expectations for achievement, and the evaluation criteria. As a result, children in collaborative activities "learned to follow practical procedures without ever coming to understand the underlying principles involved" (Mercer, 1995, p. 93). We think this issue probably applies to adult activities as well, which include those of the Expeditions mentors. Experiencing on-line mentoring and problem solving for the first time, the mentors were expected to actively engage in exploring problem solving and mentoring strategies. Because Expeditions was a structured program, it was easier for the mentors to follow the organizational map in guiding their team activities than to adapt it in creative ways.

The rationale for Expeditions included understanding the phases associated with problem solving, how the phases linked to each other, and why each phase was important. We traced occurrences of discussion about problem solving in the chat sessions of the two teams. Interaction evidence suggested that the Expeditions problem-solving procedures were more frequently discussed on team A than on team E. We observed six instances of discussion of the Expeditions procedures on team A: one youth note with one log attachment and four instances of chats in Weeks 2, 3, 4, and 5.

One of team A's mentors (Ma1) situated the weekly teamwork in the context of the Expeditions problem-solving phases and then set sub-goals each week. Ma1 also frequently informed the youth about past and upcoming discussions and tasks in an apparent effort to establish shared knowledge and affirm work status. These ongoing statements about procedures and rationales provided team A youth with a better understanding of the underlying principles of Expeditions, which appeared to facilitate individual and team performance in gathering data and identifying solutions. According to an e-mail survey of team A youth after a discussion of Expeditions procedures, the youth reported more interest and promised to do their best in achieving team goals. As an indicator of their engagement, several team A youth applied their knowledge of the Expeditions procedures to individual activity and teamwork. Ya1 especially took the initiative in using procedural knowledge in generating the *Log of Team Accomplishment*. She also led negotiations when identifying the best team solutions.

By contrast, team E's discussion of Expeditions procedures was limited to revisiting milestones and noting their progress from one milestone to another. It was also rare. Team E's discussions included only two instances of procedure talk—one mentor note and one communication instance in the first team chat. Although the mentors for team E were well organized in furthering team tasks, they rarely mentioned *why* the team needed to complete assigned activities. Facing time constraints, team E (and to some extent team A) mentors did not help the youth understand thoroughly the rationale underlying the problem-solving activities. As a consequence, the youth on team E lacked knowledge about what they were doing and why they were doing it. This finding conforms to Mercer's (1995) argument that knowing the underpinnings for rules and expectations is a motivating factor in collaborative activity. He posits, and this study seems to support, that participants were more committed when they had an earlier and better understanding of larger purposes and processes.

Recommendations

Although on-line interaction is a popular mode for learning and collaborative work today, it will not remain so without study, planning, and systematic interventions by human resources professionals. What can we learn from the literature review and from this exploratory study? What follows are the key lessons associated with promoting learner engagement in on-line activities. We start with recommendations for preparing mentors for their roles and move to recommendations regarding strategies for motivating participants.

Preparing on-line mentors

On-line mentors in the Expeditions program did not receive systematic training about how to lead teams with an emphasis on teaming, conversing, and processing the experience. Performance expectations were not clearly articulated for mentors. From our analysis of the teams' interactions and the mentors' activities, we derived the following suggestions for better preparing on-line mentors so they can improve participation and increase commitment to the activities.

Explain the importance of building a more intimate team

A strong social network seems to be associated with greater engagement in on-line activities. Social ties and interpersonal relationships within a team appear to keep team members more consistently engaged. In addition, members are more likely to work as a team when they form the team on their own initiative. After team formation, mentors should strengthen the social network by organizing social chats or electronic "parties" that are unrelated to task work. Social networks appear to serve as foundations for exploratory talk. In parallel with typical team behavior on terra firma, on-line team members are more prone to be frank when they are better acquainted. The mentor's role is to encourage and deepen that acquaintanceship, no matter the location.

Encourage exploratory ways of talking

Sloffer, Dueber, and Duffy (1999) encouraged embedding in on-line tools various supports for different types of interactions, primarily exploration, analysis, and decision-making. They also emphasized the importance of the human factor in supporting interactions. For example, in order to support exploration in Web-based problem-solving activities, groups must develop a sense of community, build trust in each other, and engage in unstructured conversational communication (Sloffer et al., 1999). Recent research on on-line professional development and mentoring (Williams, Goldman, Gabella, Kinzer, & Risko in Sloffer et al., 1999) pointed to the creation of an undemanding and unstructured environment as a critical factor in the success of collaborative work over the Web.

In addition to using team-building strategies, on-line mentors should facilitate the creation of an open and collaborative climate where diverse views can be freely expressed. Mentors are encouraged to nurture negotiations and diverse opinions in these sessions. In these Expeditions, some mentors were agenda driven, polite, and uncritical. Their taking such a stance was understandable, given the time constraints and task expectations. But perhaps teaming would have been more interesting and engaging for the youth if they had explored ideas together and used statements like "I don't think so" and questions like "Why do you think...?" Furthermore, by encouraging exploratory talk, mentors create opportunities to discover appropriate strategies, to clarify confusions, and to reconcile conflicts. This too is a critical mentoring role, as manifested by such mentoring language as "Feel free to criticize constructively."

Practice good mentoring

Previous research (Cobb, 1994; Collins et al., 1990; Mercer, 1995) identified good mentoring as flexible guidance and support that changes in response to learner needs. Poor mentoring can be either a lack of mentor-apprentice interaction or an overly frequent mentoring dialogue (Derry et al., 2000). However, Derry and her colleagues found that still unknown, in a quantitative sense, is what is too much or too little mentoring. As an alternative, they proposed analyzing mentoring practices from a situative perspective; that is, they proposed assessing the quality of mentoring in the context within which it occurs.

We took a situated approach in this small study and found several occurrences of adjustment on teams A and E when the mentors consciously withdrew their support. For instance, mentors reduced their communications in order to prompt students' initiatives and critical thinking. Sometimes, however, mentors appeared to provide too many explanations and elaborations, which may have slowed the collective discussion and discovery. According to Derry and Schlager (2000), frequent dialogue might indicate the leaders' dominance, the ineffectiveness of mentorship, or the establishment of tasks that are too difficult for participants. Mentors, therefore, need to be encouraged to collect and examine examples of their mentoring, to reflect on what worked and what didn't work, and to self-assess using archived samples of their efforts.

Explain problem-solving procedures to participants

An on-line mentor commented on the positive effects associated with participants' understanding of the larger efforts: "It's like a 'click' in their mind, all of a sudden they knew why we had to complete some of the tasks. They were charged to go forward!" The association between team A youths' understanding of the problem-solving procedures and their engagement confirmed how important it is that participants grasp the strategies that fortify their problem-solving efforts. In particular, the youth needed to understand the final goal and the sub-goals of their teamwork, what they were expected to achieve, and what the desired products or outcomes of an activity would be. As one youth suggested in a weekly survey of ideas for improvement, "I think that if we got through all the team-building work and onto understanding what to do and then doing it more quickly, it would be more enjoyable."

Motivating on-line participants

Besides preparing on-line mentors, project stakeholders should better rivet youths' and others' attention to on-line problem-solving activities. The strategies we recommend include building social bonds, seeking external motivators, encouraging team competitions, and increasing participants' control of their activities.

Build social bonds on teams and beyond

Human resource professionals should act to assure greater engagement in on-line programs by building social networks within and across teams. As Mason and Kaye (1990) discovered, face-to-face meetings provide contextualizing cues that enable participants to communicate on-line. Where possible, professionals should encourage both face-to-face and on-line interactions—the definite advantage experienced by team A.

Internet "field trips" are a promising means to connect people with each other. Expeditions provides an example. In Week 2 (gathering data), the Expeditions teams divided into sub-teams to explore the features and functions of telematics and to survey customers' preferences. Participants charged with similar tasks across teams should be encouraged to attend cross-team chat sessions and share and exchange information, resources, and strategies.

Seek external motivators

Although an on-line program can be intrinsically motivating and engaging, perhaps HR professionals should create organizational systems that honor on-line team efforts. How will managers and supervisors support the effort? How will job descriptions reflect the expectation of collaborating with mates from afar? In Expeditions, many youth were attracted to the program because of its novelty, but a few of them soon lost interest. Although the Expeditions program was stimulating, it had to compete with many other engaging activities going on in the lives of participants. One youth requested in a weekly survey, "to receive something in return for our help!"

Motivate adult workers

Unlike the volunteer youth in this study, employees might be asked to participate in on-line teams as part of their job responsibilities. We propose instituting other engagement incentives, such as team competitions and greater participant control of activities. We also advocate implementing on-line mentoring as an inducement for participation by employees. On-line mentoring offers a beneficial way for busy professionals and students to learn from each other across geographic boundaries (Raths, 2001). NursingNet, MentorNet, and TAPPED IN™ are examples. Raths noted that few of the face-to-face mentoring programs in corporate America now have an on-line component.

An on-line leader or mentor with a soft touch should be available to boost confidence and to remind participants why they're on line. In addition, we agree with Raths (2001) that on-line mentoring will be especially critical in high-tech firms that wish to transfer knowledge from long-time employees to rookies.

Needs for future research

This chapter describes an exploratory study. It is a beginning effort based on a dissertation. Because the study involved a small number of participants and only two teams, we have made many leaps of faith in our comments and recommendations. In addition, the study focused on the communication patterns of youth. We therefore call for future studies, especially of adult experiences on line, to confirm these findings about emotional engagement in on-line problem-solving activities. Mentor practices and the training of mentors for on-line programs is another area for study. Finding the proper balance of freedom and direction when working on line with youth and adults in different countries and cultures intrigues us. We are also interested in research on the relationship between self-selected and assigned teams, emotional engagement, and performance. Besides, we noted in this study that organizations are no longer focusing solely on employee learning and contributions. Instead, Expeditions creates a community of youth to support Motorola. Traditionally, the word *development* in human resource development focused on the growth of employees. What it means when companies extend development to those outside the firm will be another intriguing topic for research.

Conclusion

From the two Expeditions teams, we learned that on-line problem solving could be engaging, as indicated by differences in the quantities of communication artifacts, the variety and number of emotional markers, and the frequencies of exploratory talk. Exploratory talk appeared to be particularly engaging when participants attempted to resolve dissonance and reach consensus, and it appeared to occur more readily in the presence of a strong social network. Moreover, an engaged team, in this case team A, produced a higher quality team product.

Although we do not intend to generalize findings from this study to other on-line programs, we see implications for human resource professionals interested in encouraging individuals to bond, to participate, and to persist in on-line learning and work activities. Most important, we note that participation is by no means automatic. The resources and strategies of mentors and organizations must be devoted to the task of cultivating on line problem-solving processes. Such understanding will facilitate continuous, habitual member participation in on-line teams and enhance team contributions to organizational challenges.

References

Barnes, D. (1976). Language in the secondary classroom. In D. Barnes, J. Britton, & H. Rosen (Eds.), *Language, the learner and the school*. Harmondsworth: Penguin.

Bearison, D. J. (1982). New directions in studies of social interaction and cognitive growth. In F. C. Serafica (Ed.), *Social-cognitive development in context*. New York: Guilford Press.

Briggs, R. O., Reinig, B. A., Shepherd, M., Yen, J., & Nunamaker, J. F., Jr. (1997). *Quality as a function of quantity in electronic brainstorming*. Proceedings of the Hawaii International Conference on System Sciences.

Brown, J. S. & Duguid, P. (May-June, 2000). Balancing act: How to capture knowledge without killing it. *Harvard Business Review, 78*(3), p. 73-80.

Bonk, C. J., & King, K. S. (Ed.). (1998). Electronic collaborators: Learner-centered technologies for literacy, apprenticeship, and discourse. Mahwah, N.J.: L. Erlbuam Associates.

Chapman, P., Selvarajah, S., & Webster, J. (1999). *Engagement in multimedia training systems*. Proceedings of the 32nd Hawaii International Conference on System Sciences.

Clements, D., & Nastasi, B. (1988). Social and cognitive interaction in educational computer environments. *American Educational Research Journal, 25*, 87-106.

Collins, B., Andernach, T., & Van Diepen, N. (1996). *The Web as process tool and product environment for group-based project work in higher education*. Paper presented at the WebNet'96 Technical Program, San Francisco.

Derry, S. J., & DuRussel, L. A. (July 1999). *Assessing knowledge construction processes in on-line learning communities.* Paper presented at the AIED99, Conference of the International Society for Artificial Intelligence, Lemans France.

Derry, S. J., Gance, S., Gance, L. L., & Schlager, M. (2000). Toward assessment of knowledge building practices in technology-mediated work group interactions. In S. P. Lajoie (Ed.), *No more walls: Theory change, paradigm shifts and their Influence on the use of computers for instructional purposes* (Vol. II). Mahwah, NJ: Erlbaum.

Edwards, A. D., & Furlong, V. J. (1978). *The language of teaching.* London: Heinemann.

Edwards, D., & Mercer, N. (1987). Common knowledge: The development of understanding in the classroom. London: Muthuen.

Edwards, A. D., & Westgate, D. P. G. (1987). *Investigating classroom talk* (2nd ed.). Washington, D.C.: Falmer Press.

Ernest, P. (1995). The one and the many. In L. P. Steffe & J. Gale (Eds.), *Constructivism in education* (pp. 459-486). Hillsdale, NJ: Lawrence Erlbaum Associates.

Feenberg, A., & Bellman, B. (1990). Social factors research in computer-mediated communications. In L. M. Harasim (Ed.), *Online education: Perspectives on a new environment* (pp. 229-64). New York: Praeger.

Funaro, G. M., & Montell, F. (2000). Pedagogical roles and implementation guidelines for online communication tools. *Asynchronous Learning Network, 3*(2).

Gilbert, L., & Moore, D. (1998). Building interactivity into web courses: tools for social and instructional interaction. *Educational Technology, 38,* 39-25.

Greeno, J. G. (1998). The Situativity of knowing, learning, and research. *American Psychologist, 53*(1), 5-26.

Harasim, L. (Ed.). (1990). Online education: Perspectives on a new environment. New York: Praeger.

Harasim, L., Hiltz, S.R., Teles, L., & Turoff, M. (1995). *Learning networks: A field guide to teaching and learning online.* Cambridge, MA: The MIT Press.

Harris, R. C. (1994). *CERI/Motorola active learning*: A case study report (Motorola Internal Report). Provo: Brigham Young University.

Koschmann, T. (Ed.). (1996). CSCL: *Theory and practice of an emerging paradigm.* Mahwah: Lawrence Erlbaum Associates, Publishers.

Laurel, B. (1991). *Computers as theatre.* Addison-Wesley, Reading, MA.

Lowell, N. O., & Persichitte, K. A. (2000). A virtual ropes course: Creating online community. *Asynchronous Learning Network, 4*(1).

Mason, R. (1994). Using communication media in open and flexible learning. London: Kogan Page.

Mason, R., & Kaye, T. (1990b). Toward a new paradigm of distance education. In L. M. Marquardt, M.(1999). *Action learning in action.* Palo Alto: American Society for Training and Development.

Miller, S. M., & Miller, K. L. (1999). Using instructional theory to facilitate communication in Web-based courses. *Educational Technology and Society, 2*(3).

Mercer, N. (1995). The guided construction of knowledge: Talk amongst teachers and learners. Philadelphia: Multilingual Matters LTD.

Mehan, H. (1979). *Learning lessons: Social organization in the classroom.* Cambridge, MA: Harvard University Press.

Prahalad, C. K. & Hamel, G. (1990, May-June). The core competence of the corporation. *Harvard Business Review, 68,* 79-87.

Raths, D. (January 2001). *Make me a match.* Available: http://www.onlinelearningmag.com/new/jan01/feature1.htm.

Reeves, T. (1999). *A model of the effective dimensions of interactive learning on the World Wide Web.* Available: http://itech1.coe.uga.edu/Faculty/treeves/WebPaper.pdf (1999).

Rogoff, B. (1990). Apprenticeship in thinking: Cognitive development in social context. New York: Oxford University Press.

Rossett, A. & Sheldon, K. (2001). Beyond the podium: delivering training and performance to a digital world. SF: Jossey Bass.

Rossett, A. (August, 2000). Confessions of a web dropout. *Training Magazine, 37*(8), 100-99.

Roschelle, J., & Pea, R. (June-July 1999). Trajectories from today's WWW to a powerful educational infrastructure. *Educational Researcher, 28*(5), 22-25.

Sloffer, S. J., Dueber, B., & Duffy, T. M. (1999). *Using asynchronous conferencing to promote critical thinking: Two implementations in higher education.* Proceedings of the 32nd Hawaii International Conference on System Sciences.

Souder, W. E. (1993). The effectiveness of traditional vs. satellite delivery in three management of technology master's degree programs. *The American Journal of Distance Education, 7*(1), 37-53.

Vygotsky, L. S. (1978). *Mind in society: The development of higher psychological processes* (M. Cole, V. John-Steiner, S. Scribner, & E. Souberman, Eds. and Trans.). Cambridge, MA: Harvard University Press.

Vygotsky, L. S. (1986). *Thought and language.* Cambridge: MIT Press.

Walther, J. (1996). Computer-mediated communication: Impersonal, interpersonal, and hyperpersonal interaction. *Communication Research, 23*(1), 3-43.

Wang, M. J. (2001). The construction of shared knowledge in an Internet-based shared environment for expeditions (iExpeditions): A study of external factors implying knowledge construction. Unpublished doctoral dissertation, University of Missouri, Columbia.

Webb, N. M. (1982a). Student interaction and learning in small groups. *Review of Educational Research, 52*(3), 421-45.

Webb, N. M. (1982b). Group composition, group interaction, and achievement in cooperative small groups. *Journal of Educational Psychology, 74*(4), 475-84.

A CONCEPTUAL FRAMEWORK FOR COMPUTER SUPPORTED COLLABORATIVE LEARNING REQUIRING IMMEDIATE PRESENCE (CSCLIP)

Ramesh Sharda
Oklahoma State University

Nicholas C. Romano, Jr.
Oklahoma State University

Joyce A. Lucca
Oklahoma State University

Abstract

Recent dramatic increases in enrollment in distance learning are likely to continue. Billions of dollars are being poured into extending and expanding electronic learning (e-learning). However, currently available technologies are insufficient for educational program modules that typically require hands-on experience with equipment. Therefore, laboratory (lab) coursework will become the limiting factor in the growth of educational opportunities that are available at a distance. We now need to explore the potential combination of high bandwidth, hardware, software, and human-computer interaction principles to make virtual simulations of lab modules both realistic and effective learning experiences. Current initiatives will have to operate in a specific lab domain, but the principles may be generalizable to any lab domain. This chapter defines and develops a framework to enable computer-supported collaborative learning requiring immediate presence (CSCLIP). Immediate presence (IP) may be characterized in at least two ways. First, it allows same-time/different-place interaction among learners, instructors, equipment and Information Technology (IT). Second, it implies IP that is typical in the lab environment. We believe that the right mix of learning theory, group dynamics, IT, and high bandwidth will enable a new level of interactivity to support CSCLIP. The goal is to enable learners to fully experience all relevant activities of a lab through remote interactions. Activities include interacting simultaneously with peers who are located at remote sites and with peers who are located in the physical lab. They also include interacting with lab hardware and software. All technical and social interactions will be remotely supported. This chapter proposes a functional description of CSCLIP, identifies the underlying theoretical constructs that will be important in further studies, and concludes with a glimpse of a research program to further develop CSCLIP.

Introduction

Given today's volatile, complex global environment and the fact that knowledge rapidly becomes obsolete, learning has become an ongoing activity for almost everyone. Researchers from business, education, and psychology have cited several factors that contribute to the demand for geographically distributed delivery of education services, including the increased demand for knowledge and skills, the increased knowledge content of all types of work, the larger proportion of workers who are knowledge workers, the shortened half-life of acquired knowledge, the increased costs

The next generation of distance learning should emphasize bringing the laboratory to the remote learner.

of education, and the geographically dispersed populations of learners (students, adults, trainees, employees) (Hämäläinen, 1996; Purser, 1995; Stewart, 1998). IT can enhance and structure on-line education by providing interactive learning systems that enable anyone to learn anything from anywhere at any time (Cornish, 2000).

Current distance-learning technologies, sometimes called digital learning or e-learning, emphasize bringing the classroom to the remote learner. The next generation of distance learning should, however, emphasize bringing the laboratory (lab) to the remote learner. Virtual Reality (VR) systems are being developed to engage local and remote users as fully as possible within a computer-aided environment. Emerging technologies with gigabit, and in the near future terabit, speed telecommunications are enabling the fusion of distance learning and VR, which could provide a cost-effective and convenient way to educate learners in same-time/different-place learning environments. This chapter describes a framework for the development of a virtual lab (VL), where learners no longer are required to be physically present to conduct experiments and operate equipment.

Many of the ideas for the next generation of distance-learning technologies are based on several bodies of related research known as computer-supported collaborative learning (CSCL), computer-mediated communication systems (CMCS), and computer-aided instruction (CAI). These technologies gained popularity in the 1980s, when the use of personal computers first became widespread in homes, schools, and offices (Hiltz,

1994). Until recently CSCL was text-based. E-mail and bulletin board technologies have been widely used to support group learning projects and group discussions. These technologies, although useful, are best at supporting asynchronous activities, not at facilitating tasks in which immediate presence (IP) is required, such as in a lab setting. Our goal is to support virtual lab activities that require IP by creating an architecture for an effective virtual lab environment that incorporates CSCL and IP to create CSCLIP.

The purpose of this chapter is to integrate learning theory, learning processes, interactive technologies, and human computer interaction principles that will make it possible for learners to take a lab course without having to be physically present in the lab. This chapter integrates current knowledge from the domains of learning theory, interactive technologies, and human-computer interaction. We begin by extending the group work model to include lab experiences. Then we propose adapting learning objectives for a lab course, and we examine the research in the computer supported collaborative learning literature relative to the topic. At that point, we are able to propose a CSCLIP architecture and a framework for CSCLIP Research.

Collaborative learning requiring immediate presence: Virtual laboratories

The growth of IT in general and the World Wide Web in particular has spawned exciting developments in technology-supported learning. However, these developments have not focused on learning that typically requires co-location of instructor and learners. The primary reason is that learning modules requiring interaction with lab equipment also typically required learners and instructors to be present in the lab (same-time/same-place).

A typology of learning technology

DeSanctis and Gallupe's (1987) 2 by 2 framework for categorizing group support systems has been applied to understanding the uses of IT in learning environments (Alavi, 1995; Reinig, 1997b; Tyran, 1997). While this framework enables us to classify learning settings by the dimensions of space and time, it does little to improve our understanding of the technologies required in lab settings. We extend the framework by adding a third dimension, IP, to explain the technological and behavioral requirements for a lab environment. Figure 1 presents our framework for categorizing learning technologies by three dimensions—temporal, spatial,

Typology of Learning Technologies

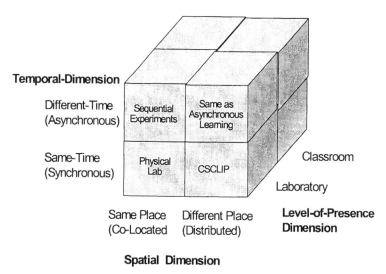

Figure 1. A typology of learning technologies

and level of presence—and helps explain differences in requirements for learner presence in classroom and lab settings. For example, a physical lab setting requires same-time/same-place interactions. We propose using IT to extend lab settings to support same-time/different-place interactions in the classroom and in the lab. The focus of CSCLIP is to support lab courses that require group collaboration through same-time/different-place interactions. Lab activities could also be conducted in a different-time/same-place setting through the use of sequential experiments. As technologies and communications bandwidths continue to improve, certain lab experiences can be offered using different-time/different-place interactions, asynchronous learning, that rely on the use of such technologies as videotapes, computer models, and simulations.

CSCLIP learning

CSCLIP effectively will raise the bar of distance learning by providing face-to-face (F2F) and learner-to-equipment interactive support. The goal of most traditional lab activities is to have learners interact in small groups to solve real-world problems such that they learn by doing. Puntambekar (1999) contends that real-world problems are helpful for the learner who is attempting to make the connection between theoretical knowledge and problems in the real world. The benefits of using real-world problems include the following:

- Real-world problems are complex and ill structured, with possible multiple solutions and methods for solving them (Jonassen, 1999). The advantage of using real-world problems over contrived problems is that learners gain realistic experience and a better sense of the issues, which they can generalize to future situations.
- Real-world problems are complex and under-specified. Thus they require learners to develop several hypotheses and seek additional information to solve them.
- Real-world problems provide opportunities for collaborative learning and developing shared meanings.

In lab settings, guided discovery is a useful method of instruction for aiding learners in developing expert-like abilities. Guided instruction provides learners with actual problems as the basis for learning (Clark, 1998). Although learning groups are flexible in terms of how they solve problems, they often require the type of instructional help that is referred to as scaffolding. Scaffolding is an interactive learning process in which learners are assisted by others (teachers, tutors, peers) to acquire knowledge or skills that they could not acquire without immediate assistance. Scaffolding, which is temporary and task oriented, aids the learner in developing domain knowledge.

In addition to scaffolding, instructors can use learning objectives to guide learners. Groups that lack explicit learning objectives and clearly established procedures to follow may remain at undeveloped levels, or worse, become bogged down with personality issues and dysfunctional group dynamics (Hiltz, 1989; Kettlehut, 1994; Nunamaker, 1996-97; Reinig, 1997a; Reinig, in press). Additionally, having explicit learning objectives may help learners avoid information overload (Phillips, 1990; Rodden, 1993; Romano, 1998).

Bloom's (1956) definition of learning objectives includes the cognitive, affective and psychomotor domains. Researchers have developed hierarchical taxonomies for each area: Bloom's Taxonomy of Cognitive Behaviors (Bloom, 1956), Krathwohl's Taxonomy of Affective Behaviors (Krathwol, 1964), and Simpson's Taxonomy of Psychomotor Behaviors (Simpson, 1966). The cognitive domain refers to intellectual learning and problem solving. The cognitive levels of learning are as follows: knowledge, comprehension, application, analysis, synthesis, and evaluation (Krathwol, 1964). The affective domain refers to emotional learning and developing one's value system. The affective levels of learning are as follows: receiving, responding, valuing, organizing, and characterizing by a value. The affective levels of learning are associated with emotions, feelings, being, relationships, and the ability to deal with situations. The psychomotor domain refers to movement characteristics and physical capabilities (Simpson, 1966). Based on a combination of these taxonomies, Table 1 presents the learning objectives for a CSCLIP environment and its associated lexicon.

Research in computer-supported collaborative learning

The 1990s saw an explosion in innovation and technology as much of the world migrated toward a knowledge- and service-based economy. The integration of work processes and electronic network infrastructures rapidly changed the dynamics and structure of organizations, how workgroups were defined, and how workers communicated. As Christie points out in his chapter, "HR to the Power of e: Internet-Powered Transformation of Human Resources," a consequence is that university programs and organization training departments are under increasing pressure to produce technically trained knowledge workers who are capable of adapting to change. Including on-line collaborative courses in the curriculum is a way of providing learners with valuable experiences that will prepare them for new and changing careers (Brandon, 1999) in current and future organizations. We believe that those who have experienced working in CSCL environments will more easily assimilate into virtual work groups than those who have not. Increasingly, employers seek to hire and promote people who are equipped with such skills and experiences.

An initial review of the literature on learning theory in general and technology-supported learning in particular revealed no single theory that adequately explains how people learn, how an instructional system should be designed, how social interaction effects learning, or how people and technologies function best together (Koschmann, 1994).

However, effective learning processes and cognitive learning theory can provide useful insights. Alavi (1995) identified three characteristics of effective learning processes:

- Active learning and construction of knowledge
- Cooperation and teamwork in learning
- Learning through problem solving

Table 1. The Levels of Learning Objectives for the CSCLIP Domain

Taxonomy classification	Action verbs that represent intellectual activity/learning tasks on this level
1: Identification Awareness of and familiarity with the physical qualities and visual appearance of the laboratory equipment /technology by way of senses.	*Recognize* and *identify* various types of laboratory equipment. *Scan* or *inspect* a piece of laboratory equipment and, based on its qualities, correctly associate it with the class of equipment to which it belongs. *Notice* specific features associated with different classes of laboratory equipment. *Inspect* and *compare* various pieces of laboratory equipment and *select* or *locate* one of a particular type or class. *Name* or *label* specific types of laboratory equipment based on their appearance and physical qualities. *Describe* various pieces of laboratory equipment in terms of their appearance. *Classify* a piece of laboratory equipment as belonging to a specific class or type.
2: Environmental perspective Awareness of and familiarity with the laboratory infrastructure and equipment in terms of its location or position within the laboratory context as a whole and in relation to other pieces of equipment.	*Place, position, situate* or *arrange* equipment appropriately within the milieu of the laboratory. *Move about* within the laboratory environment. *Locate* or *find* equipment and tools within the laboratory setting.
3: Manipulation Ability to manipulate equipment controls (buttons, switches, knobs, etc.) to achieve a desired outcome.	Proactive–practical with a specific outcome in mind. *Turn* knobs, *throw* switches, or *push* buttons to make specific outcomes occur.
4: Regulation Ability to manipulate equipment controls (buttons, switches, knobs, etc.) in response to an emergent situation.	Reactive–responsive to a particular situation. *Monitor* and *correct* problems as they arise. (Amend, adjust, fix, rectify, remedy, tweak, tune, synchronize, change, manage, coordinate)
5: Configuration/ integration	*Connect, link up, configure, integrate* or *arrange* multiple pieces of laboratory equipment together to accomplish a goal or purpose.

According to the cognitive learning theory perspective, individuals learn by processing information through their existing mental models to construct meaning. Vygtosky (1978) and Piaget (1967) consider learning to be a social process that takes place through cooperative interactions. The activity of considering alternative points of view can enhance the learner's understanding, which may further motivate learning (Glaser, 1989). Anderson (1983; 1987) addresses the issue of problem solving with a knowledge compilation theory: Initially, a novice's domain knowledge is sketchy and might include principles, rules, or vocabulary without knowing how to apply them (Glaser, 1989; 1990). Declarative knowledge is traditionally received from texts and lectures. As proficiency in knowing what develops, this declarative knowledge is more easily retrieved and in larger chunks. Procedural, or use-oriented, knowledge is the process of converting knowing what into knowing how. The compilation theory holds that effective procedural knowledge can be acquired only by using declarative knowledge in problem solving. Experts apply knowledge by quickly accessing information based on well-developed rules of applicability.

Converting knowledge gained in the classroom into hands-on, real-world problem solving is the major learning goal of a lab. However, in the lab setting that we propose, we will look at collaborative learning theory as well. CSCL is a broad area of research. It is continuously evolving in the direction of developing a complete theory that includes many pedagogical and theoretical issues. In the next section, we focus on these issues.

Collaborative interaction for computer-mediated instruction (CMI)

Collaborative Interaction (CI) offers great promise for lab learning experiences. The fields of psychology, education, business, and management information systems (MIS) offer a vast amount of literature that addresses CI from a variety of perspectives. Some of this literature is based solely on theory and conceptual notions. Some is based on empirical observations, such as courses, case studies, and experiments. We present next a summary of the key findings from empirical observations. First, we define CI for CMI, the types of technologies, and motivations for use. Finally, we discuss CI from the perspective of CMI in terms of educational support and the design and development guidelines to be derived from empirical research and practice.

Defining and understanding collaborative interaction

CI within the context of CMI can be described as learning that involves information, computing, and communications technology in more than one location (Alavi, 1995). Empirical and conceptual research have been undertaken on this topic in many disciplines. Before we discuss CI and how it may best be employed within CMI, we briefly define it within the scope of this chapter in terms of collaboration and interactivity.

Collaboration includes many behaviors, but generally it means that two or more persons work on a given task (Roschelle, 1995). From a computer-mediated perspective, the term *groupware* (GW), coined by MIS researchers (Johnson-Lenz, 1980), refers to computer-mediated communication to support interaction and collaborative work among group members regardless of their location (Johansen, 1991). The objective of GW is to provide a multi-user environment in which group members share information, evaluate all contributions, and through a structured, collaborative learning process of focused activities and communication, generate and develop ideas, make decisions, and accomplish work together (DeSanctis, 1985; Dickson, 1992; Huber, 1984; Nunamaker, 1991; Theirauf, 1989; Valacich, 1991a).

Types of collaborative support

Literally hundreds of technologies have been designed to support group collaboration, from e-mail systems to group support systems. David Woolley's Web roster of the synchronous and asynchronous communication and collaboration systems available for use over the Internet lists 146 products as of August 1999 (Woolley, 2001). It is available on-line at http://thinkofit.com/webconf/.

These technologies vary greatly along a number of dimensions, but not all of them support the type of collaboration that we are suggesting here. Coleman (1999) offers a GW taxonomy of twelve functional categories:

- Electronic mail and messaging
- Group calendaring and scheduling
- Electronic meeting systems
- Desktop video and real-time data conferencing (synchronous)
- Non-real-time data conferencing (asynchronous)
- Group document handling
- Workflow
- Workgroup utilities and development tools
- Groupware services
- Groupware and knowledge management frameworks
- Groupware applications
- Collaborative Internet-based applications and products

While this taxonomy includes all possible GW applications, it does little to explain the relationships among them, the overlap within the categories, or the types of support they offer. Nunamaker, Romano, and Briggs (2001a; 2001b) and Nunamaker, Briggs, and de Vreede (2001) propose a hierarchical framework for collaboration with three levels: collective, coordinative, and concerted (see Table 2). The concerted level of collaboration will add real value to CMI courses and applications.

Table 2. Levels of Collaborative Support

Collaborative Level	Efforts	Processes	Productivity	Metaphor
Collective	Individual uncoordinated	Individualized – start to finish	Simple sum of individual efforts	Sprinters
Coordinative	Ad hoc team uncoordinated Team coordinated	Ad hoc, unstructured, coordinated	Simple sum of individual efforts applied to team efforts	Relay
Concerted	Concerted team efforts	Clearly established procedures for structured, customized, repeatable e-learning processes	More than sum of individual efforts applied to concerted team effort through synergy	Crew

Adapted from (Nunamaker , Romano, and Briggs, 2001a; Nunamaker, Romano, and Briggs 2001b; Nunamaker, Briggs, and de Vreede, 2001).

CI and CMI learning researchers (Anderson, 1995; Brandon, 1999; Hiltz, 1989; Kettlehut, 1994; Nunamaker, 1996-97; Reinig, 1997a; Reinig, 1997b; Rogoff, 1990; Tyran, 1997; Webb, 1996) have made distinctions among these three levels of collaborative support. CSCL researchers have distinguished between cooperation-based groups (coordinative level), wherein the members share the workload by addressing separate problem components, and collaboration-based groups (concerted level), wherein the members develop shared meanings about their work and work jointly as a unit on the problem, learning together and from one another. (Anderson, 1995; Brandon, 1999; Webb, 1996).

For example, in a coordinative-based learning group, members would independently write four separate sections of a paper and perhaps work more closely together to write an introduction and a conclusion. In a collaboration-based learning group, members would develop a single unified paper to represent their shared reasoning and conclusions (Brandon, 1999).

Researchers have also found that important aspects of the concerted level of collaborative support are important for CMI groups to achieve positive learning outcomes. Clearly established procedures with explicit goals have been found to be critical to the success of CMI collaborations (Hiltz, 1989; Kettlehut, 1994; Nunamaker, 1996-97; Reinig, 1997a; Reinig, in press; Rogoff, 1990) because without them groups may stagnate in terms of learning process, or they may adopt dysfunctional dynamics.

While all three levels of support are important to the success of CMI, greater gains in productivity, participation, learning, and assimilation have been found in groups that employed the concerted level of collaborative support (Brandt, 1995; Brandt, 1996; Kwok, 1997; Leidner, 1996; Reinig, 1997b; Scalia, 1996b; Tyran, 1997; Walsh, 1996). The key point is that concerted level (collaboration-based learning) groups achieve through mutual efforts a synergy that leads to positive learning outcomes.

A CSCLIP architecture

Based on our learning objectives and the learning theories to be applied in the CSCLIP environment, we identified key technical components of the CSCLIP architecture. Technology issues deal with hardware and software in terms of their robustness, usability, and richness. Research on asynchronous text-based environments provided insights. Important issues include the communication medium, VR, and collaborative learning tools.

Communication medium

As we developed the concept of CSCLIP, we considered several communication media, including e-mail, audio, desktop videoconferencing, and traditional electronic meeting systems (EMS). In F2F communication, important information is conveyed through eye contact, body language, and facial expressions. In particular, Isaacs and Tang (Issacs, 1994) found that desktop video conferencing increases the ability to acknowledge understanding, provide nonverbal cues, improve verbal explanations, deal with pauses, and articulate attitudes. Although desktop video conferencing is considered a *leaner* medium than F2F communication because of the latencies in audio and video technologies, videoconferencing is considered a *richer* medium than other forms of electronic media because it includes tone of voice through audio and IP through video (Daft, 1986).

Traditional electronic meeting systems (EMS) were built to support collaborative decision-making processes. They have been shown to be beneficial in organizational settings; however, they may not be the best solution for small groups in educational settings. EMS has been shown to be very effective when tested in the business community. EMS improved the productivity of project work by reducing labor costs up to 70 percent and project cycle times by up to 90 percent (Nunamaker, 1997). However, EMS requires expensive hardware and software, extensive human or embedded facilitation, complex tools and structures, and heavy reliance on text-based communication.

Because many education and training departments cannot afford to supply EMS technology to every participant in every lab, the communication medium proposed for CSCLIP is desktop video conferencing. The equipment requirements for the end user are inexpensive and widely available. They are an audio/video card attached to the bus of the PC, a small video camera, which is usually mounted on the monitor, a microphone, and speakers.

Virtual reality

Another important component of CSCLIP is the development of a VR application for interaction with existing hardware located in the lab. In the past, VR applications were primarily visual in nature rather than interactive. Ferrero and Piuri (Ferrero, 1999) developed lab components using an off-the-shelf product, LabView by National Instruments. On the client's initial contact with the server, the simulation engine automatically downloads. Learners then select equipment from an extensive workbench of components. The workbench consists of virtual signal generators that can simulate real systems. Learners can measure physical quantities from their simulations using virtual instruments that reproduce the measurement operations of real instruments on the physical quantities.

Argonne's Cave Automatic Virtual Environment (CAVE) advanced basic VR technology by allowing scientists to see, touch, hear, and manipulate data (www.anl.gov:80/OPA/frontiers96/cave.html). In a 10-foot square room containing projection screens, designers can use CAVE technology to develop a range of equipment. In the CAVE, using a headset and joystick-like computer wand controls, university and industry researchers equipped with stereoscopic glasses turn projections into hologram-like images. A super computer collects and analyzes data from the simulation.

Leigh, Rajlich, Stein, Johnson, and Defanti (2000) at the National Center for Supercomputing Applications have attempted to improve upon existing VR applications through Tele-Immersion, which they define as the integration of audio and video conferencing with collaborative VR. CAVE5D expands on the previous work, which was in the area of weather modeling. VR systems simulate wind trajectory tracings in a 3-D grid that can rotate and animate the images in real time. CAVE6D, allows the use of multiple remotely located CAVEs and desktop workstations for collaborating within VR simulations.

Collaborative learning tools

To facilitate learner familiarity with the lab environment and the equipment, we propose using archived videotaped footage of the lab. Learners will preview the rooms and the equipment and consider how best to approach their lab assignments prior to the class sessions. We have already seen the use of such applications as NetMeeting and Web-Board technologies. These technologies are important components in computer-mediated learning and can reinforce reality-based experiences by providing continuous support for group task completion. Applications like NetMeeting allow synchronous document sharing that aids learners working on group projects. Schreiber and Berge (1998) and Scalia and Sackmary (1996a) assert that distance learning is enhanced when off-line experiences are part of the learning processes. Asynchronous Web-Board technology allows learners from all groups to interact and share their learning experiences. These asynchronous learning tools supplement the synchronous learning tools envisaged under the CSCLIP framework.

A research framework for CSCLIP

Having specified the major goals of a lab setting, we can now address the issues and identify the technologies that will enhance research efforts in the virtual lab environment. We start our research by investigating how application-sharing programs, such as NetMeeting and Web Board technology, may enhance interactions among learners and instructors before, during, and after lab sessions.

In Figure 2 we expand on Hiltz and Turoff (1992) and Nunamaker (1997) to present a research framework that accounts for the variables we posit will affect the learning process and the outcomes. Both types of outcomes—achievement and non-achievement—are important. Non-achievement outcomes may have significant negative or positive impacts on achievement outcomes, much as they have been shown to affect outcomes in group support system (GSS) research (Fjermestad, 1998-99).

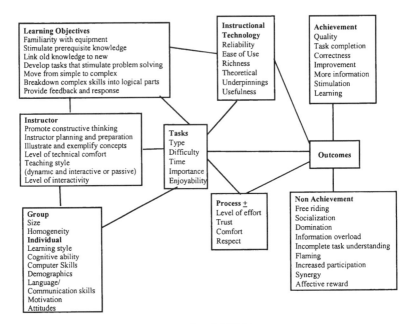

Figure 2. A research framework for CSCLIP

Figure 2 shows categories of variables that can impact the outcomes and the learning process. Key variables from the figure are discussed in the following sections. The goals that a particular instructor sets are affected by a number of the instructor's characteristics, for example, how dynamic and interactive the instructor's teaching style is or the instructor's attitudes toward the subject matter and the learners. These and other variables may or may not affect the outcomes of CSCLIP.

Learning objectives

The learning objectives listed in Figure 2 represent some of the specific CSCLIP lab variables we hope to measure. Lab participants are expected to gain knowledge, skills and, behavior in three areas: Cognitive, Affective, and Psychomotor. Table 3 presents some examples of specific learning objectives for each overall objective.

Although similar learning objectives have been studied in virtual learning environments, little is known about interactions requiring IP. Questions we hope to answer include the following: Which learning objectives can be achieved satisfactorily within a CSCLIP environment? Which cannot? What learning objectives are actually achieved? Are learners

Table 3. Specific CSCLIP Learning Objectives in Terms of Objectives

Specific Objective	Cognitive	Affective	Psychomotor
Familiarity with equipment	Learn terminology and appearance	Increase comfort level	Manipulate and control equipment
Stimulate prerequisite knowledge	Concept mapping	Gain appreciation	Trial-and-error testing based on previous experience
Link old knowledge to new	Develop and refine mental models	Develop positive attitudes and beliefs	Combine and extend manipulation and control sequences
Develop tasks that stimulate problem solving	Consider alternatives and plan ahead	Enjoy the process as well as the result	Carry out procedures effectively
Move from simple to complex	Generalization /specialization	Organize the concepts learned	Assemble and connect components
Breakdown complex skills into logical parts	Decomposition		Disassemble components
Provide feedback and response	Think through questions and statements fully before taking action	Provide and accept positive and negative feedback constructively	Communicate effectively with others through various mediums

able to complete the tasks necessary to achieve the learning objectives? Are learners able to interact effectively and complete tasks in a timely fashion? Do they interact more or less effectively or the same as groups that are co-located? Are learners using the system in ways we expect?

Instructor variables

Empirical research suggests that instructors and learners must accept certain responsibilities in order to make CI-supported CMI a success. The instructor variables in Figure 2 are based on our literature review and reflect lessons learned from experience.

First and foremost, instructor planning and preparation are essential for effective CI in general (Dennis, 1996; Desantics, 1995; Nunamaker, 1989a;

Nunamaker, 1991; Nunamaker, 1996-97; Vogel, 1989) and may be even more essential for CI-supported CMI [(Hantula, 1998; Pychyl, 1999; Webster, 1997). It is important not to underestimate the planning costs in terms of time and effort. Empirical studies have illustrated a number of points that should be addressed before starting the on-line interactions with learners in a CI-supported CMI course. One critical planning and ongoing instructor activity is the development of scaffolding that provides students with an initial structure within which to learn concepts.

Second, lab instructors must have a high level of technical comfort with all of the equipment, including how to use it and control it and how to help learners overcome technical and procedural problems in real time. Researchers (Hantula, 1998; Webster, 1997) have found that the instructor's level of technical proficiency and comfort, in terms of having the ability to control the technology and having a positive attitude toward it, affects positive outcomes and learner ratings of instructors. Also important is the instructor's attitude toward distance learning and the perceptions of the relative advantages of distance learning (Webster, 1997). In their study of the use of GSS to support distributed experiential learning, Vogel et al. (2000) found that the "focus in virtual teamwork must be less on the technology and more on the human aspects." Pychyl (1999) pointed out that instructors must consider the time constraints imposed on learners by learning and applying the technology. Hantula (1998) learned from his experiences that it is critical to adapt text material to promote active participation on the part of the learners.

Instructors must employ dynamic and interactive teaching styles that promote constructive thinking on the part of the students. During real-time broadcasts remote learners must be able to easily access the instructor to ask questions and request help during the various exercises. Neale et al. (2000) mounted a miniaturized camera to a pair of clear-lens eyeglasses to provide a flexible visual approach. Instructors may require feedback from remote learners in order to assess the degree to which they have understood and completed lab exercises (Hankins, 2000). Instructors may desire archiving capabilities so they can review the sessions and learner queries and respond more fully to questions. They may then choose to broadcast answers and clarifications to all learners. Instructors need to be highly interactive to motivate students, to promote constructive thinking, to provide feedback, and to illustrate and exemplify concepts.

That the instructor's level of involvement and participation becomes extremely important in CSCL, CI, and CMI interactions has been demonstrated in many studies. We hope to learn which of these variables will also be important in environments requiring IP. At the outset, we will have to observe instructors working in this new environment to gain insights as to which variables apply and perhaps discover new ones that are unique to this new domain.

Group and individual variables

Relevant group variables include group size and homogeneity. The ideal group size has been shown to be different in computer-supported environments from that in F2F environments (Dennis, 1990; Gallupe, 1992; Jessup, 1989; Jessup, 1990; Nunamaker, 1989b; Valacich, 1991b; Valacich, 1992). We will explore if these findings hold true when IP is required. Group composition poses such concerns as homogeneity, distribution, and history. We will explore how and if such concerns are relevant in a CSCLIP environment and how best to control or manipulate such variables for the best learning outcomes.

Individuals have specific characteristics that may affect how they learn, such as preferred learning style, cognitive ability, and computer skills. For example, Ghost Bear and Conti identify three learning strategies in their "Using Adult Learning in HRD Programs to Bridge the Digital Divide" chapter. These strategies, which are specific to Engagers, Navigators, and Problem Solvers, can be used to study Internet-based learning. Additionally, as Russ-Eft et al. described in their chapter, "Web-based leadership training: Determining success factors and effectiveness," individuals have such personal and cultural characteristics as age, gender, language, communication skills, motivation, and attitudes—all of which can affect their learning experience and interactions with the instructor, fellow students, and the CSCLIP environment.

Instructional technology

Technology will play a key enabler role in implementing CSCLIP. Based on theoretical underpinnings, the reliability, ease of use, richness, and usefulness of the technology are important concerns. However, the effects of alternative technologies on learning outcomes and their potential application to CSCCLIP remain to be studied. For example, how can artificial intelligence techniques, such as semantic analysis and neural networks, be exploited to develop CSCLIP? What new knowledge representations and specifications will arise in CSCLIP? Will such models as Davis's Technology Acceptance Model fit CSCLIP applications (Davis, 1989)? Will voice become the preferred method of interaction for CSCLIP, as Keen predicts (Keen, 1999)? Which new devices will provide usable interfaces for CSCLIP? Will the richness of the medium (i.e., richness of video vs. leanness of text) play a role in CSCLIP as it has in other CSCL studies?

Tasks

All four previously discussed categories of variables influence task selection. Different types of tasks require different support from the instructor and the technology. Task variables include the nature of the task itself (or the task type), the individual's perception of the task, and the instructor's expectations. For example, it will be important for both the learner and the instructor to perceive a particular task as being important. Also, individual differences will play a role in both task difficulty and enjoyability. Time is another important consideration in task selection. Will the learners have unlimited time, or will they be under a time constraint for task completion? Can CSCLIP support certain tasks better than F2F interactions? Are there tasks that CSCLIP cannot support and that require F2F interactions? Does level of task difficulty or complexity affect the effectiveness of the CSCLIP environment?

Learning process

The learning process is directly impacted by the task, which mediates instructional technology, the learning objectives, group and individual differences and comfort level, and chosen instructional technology. The learning process can be positive or negative and can be affected by the level of effort put forth by individual group members, the level of trust among group members, as well as mutual respect. The process must be comfortable enough for learners that they can focus their attention on the task and not be distracted or confused due to discomfort with the process. Process pre-planning as well as flexibility and willingness of the instructor to alter the process as needed can help ensure that learners are comfortable with the process.

The process category of variables is influenced by the sequential nature of the tasks, the necessity for instructor scaffolding, the ability to determine level of completion, which is a function of the task-time limitation, and the nature of the communication between group members. What characteristics of the CSCLIP environment improve task completion? Does CSCLIP enhance or hinder group communication when compared to a traditional lab environment? Do CSCLIP groups require significantly greater amounts of scaffolding than F2F groups?

Outcomes

All the variables we identified can influence the quality and quantity of achievement and non-achievement outcomes. Achievement outcomes are related to how well the tasks were completed, improved skill levels, and learning. Non-achievement outcomes can be both positive and negative. Positive outcomes include increased participation, group synergy, and affective rewards. Negative social outcomes include free riding (loafing), excessive socializing, domination by certain group members, and flaming. Negative learning outcomes include information overload and incomplete task understanding. The research questions posed for each category of variables are illustrative rather than exhaustive. Our ultimate research goal would be to explore the relationships among the different variables and determine how their interaction can be used to improve the outcomes for learners working in a CSCLIP environment. One challenge will be to reliably and validly measure outcomes; therefore, we anticipate developing new metrics to assess the performance of virtual lab groups. Is there some best equation for mixing voice, video, and data interaction with personal contact? Under what conditions is one mix better than the others? What organizational factors are involved? What new applications and interfaces will be required? How will CSCLIP build long-term commitments to relationships among learners?

A case study under development

Our specific application is a telecommunications lab. A single course is required of all students in our Master of Telecommunications Management Program. This course is offered on campus and by live video and streaming video to students in Oklahoma and several adjoining states. It is considered one of the most innovative inter-disciplinary telecommunications management programs in the nation, and it has attracted enrollees from around the world. The lab course (see a description of the course at http://faculty.mstm.okstate.edu/~weiser/tcom5012) currently entails considerable travel and inconvenience for part-time students. The limited availability of the course constrains the potential expansion and reach of the program.

Members of our extended research team (George Scheets, Mark Weiser, and J-M Chung) will employ a same-time/different-place approach to extend the IP of a lab course experience around the world. The goal of the study is to capture all the relevant activities of a lab experience, including synchronous interactions with peers in remote locations and in the local lab setting and synchronous interactions with lab hardware and software. All interactions will be remotely supported. The efficacy of the prototype lab will be validated through rigorous empirical research methodologies. Learning achievement, satisfaction with the learning process and the outcomes, and the efficiency and effectiveness of the knowledge delivery process will all be assessed. This project is described further in the next chapter.

Conclusions

Technology does not make learning easier, but when it is used effectively, it can improve achievement and non-achievement outcomes. Multimedia tools can enable instructors to improve the quality of instruction and make the learning process more creative, more interactive, and more collaborative. CSCLIP may also be used to improve communication between experts in many fields, and it may lead to better, more efficient collaborative systems. Collaborating and networking skills are important career success factors. We live in a world where work groups constantly change and the members continually update their knowledge. Giving learners an abundance of alternative technologies from which to choose how they will collaborate is important. Not everyone learns or communicates in the same way, and providing options allows individuals to participate and learn in the modes they find most effective and efficient. The CSCLIP environment provides learners with the skills necessary to learn efficiently and effectively through using emerging multimedia and collaborative technologies.

References

Alavi, M., Wheeler, B. C., and Valacich, J. S. (1995). Using IT to reengineer business education: An exploratory investigation of collaborative telelearning. *MIS Quarterly, 19,* 293-312.

Anderson, A., Mayes, J. T., and Kibby, M. R. (1995). Small group collaborative discovery learning from hypertext. In C. O'Malley (Ed.), *Computer supported collaborative learning* (pp. 23-38). Berlin: Springer Verlag.

Anderson, J. R. (1983). *The architecture of cognition.* Cambridge, MA: Harvard University Press.

Anderson, J. R. (1987). Methodologies for studying human knowledge. *Behav. Brain Sci., 10,* 467-77.

Bloom, B. S. (1956). *Taxonomy of Educational Objectives: The Classification of Educational Goals,* handbook 1: Cognitive Domain. New York: McKay.

Brandon, D. P., and Hollingshead, A. B. (1999, April). Collaborative learning and computer-supported groups. *Communication Education, 48*(2), 109-126.

Brandt, S., and Briggs, R. O. (1995). *Exploring the use of EMS in the classroom: two field studies.* Paper presented at the Proceedings of the Twenty Eighth Hawaii International Conference on Systems Sciences, Maui, HI.

Brandt, S. A., and Lonsdale, M. (1996). *Technology supported cooperative learning in secondary education*. Paper presented at the Proceedings of the Twenty Ninth Hawaii International Conference on Systems Sciences, Maui, HI.

Clark, R. (1998). *Building expertise*. USA: International Society for Performance Improvement.

Coleman, D. (1999). Groupware: Collaboration and knowledge sharing. In J. Liebowitz (Ed.), *Knowledge management handbook* . Boca Raton, FL: CRC Press.

Cornish, E. (Ed.). (2000). *Exploring your future: Living, learning, and working in the information age*. Bethesda, MD: World Future Society.

Daft, R. L., and Lengel, R.H. (1986). Organizational information requirements, media richness and structural design. *Management Science, 32*, 554-571.

Davis, F. (1989, September). Perceived usefulness, perceived ease of use, and user acceptance of information technology. *MIS Quarterly*.

Dennis, A. R., Valacich, J. S., and Nunamaker, J. F. ,Jr.,. (1990). An experimental investigation of the effects of group size in an electronic meeting system environment. *IEEE Transactions of Systems, Man, and Cybernetics, 20*(5), 1049-1057.

Dennis, A. R. (1996). Information exchange and use in group decision making: you can lead a group to information, but you can't make It think. *Management Information Systems Quarterly, 20*(4).

DeSanctis, G., and Gallupe, B. R. (1985). Group decision support systems: A new frontier. *Database*, 190-201.

DeSanctis, G., and Gallupe, R. B,. (1987). A foundation for the study of group decision support systems. *Management Science, 33*,(22), 589-609.

Desantics, G., and Jackson, B. (1995). Coordination of information technology management: team-based structures and computer-based communication systems. *Journal of Management Information Systems, 10*(4), 85-110.

Dickson, G. W., Poole, M. S., and DeSanctis, G. (1992). An overview of the GDSS research project and the SAMM system. In R. P. Bostrom, Watson, R. T. and Kinney, S. T. (Ed.), *Computer augmented teamwork: A guided tour* . New York: Van Nostrand Reinhold.

Ferrero, A., and Piuri, V. (1999). A simulation tool for virtual laboratory experiments in a WWW environment. *IEEE Transactions on Instrumentation and Measurement, 48*, 741-746.

Fjermestad, J., and Hiltz, S.R. (1998-99). An assessment of group support systems experimental research: Methodology and results. *Journal of Management Information Systems, 15*(3), 7-150.

Gallupe, B. D., A. Cooper, Valacich, J. Bastianutti, and Nunamaker, J.F. Jr. (1992). Electronic brainstorming and group size. *Academy of Management Journal, 35*(2), 350-369.

Glaser, R., and Bassok, M. (1989). Learning theory and the study of instruction. American *Review of Psychology, 40*, 631-666.

Glaser, R. (1990). The reemergence of learning theory within instructional research. *American Psychologist, 45*, 29-39.

Hämäläinen, M., Whinston, A. B., and Vishik, S. (1996). Electronic markets for learning: education brokerages on the Internet. *Communications of the ACM, 39*(6), 51-58.

Hankins, M. L. (2000). Distance learning providers do their own homework. *Signal*, *54*, 23-26.

Hantula, A. (1998). The virtual industrial/organizational class: Learning and teaching in cyberspace in three iterations. *Behavior Research Methods, Instruments & Computers*, *30*(2), 205-216.

Hiltz, S. R., Turoff, M., and Johnson, K. (1989). Experiments in group decision making, 3: disinhibition, deindividuation, and group process in pen name and real name computer conferences. *Decision Support Systems*, *5*, 217-232.

Hiltz, S. R., and Turoff, M. (1992). Virtual meetings: computer conferencing and distributed group support. In R. P. Bostrom, Watson, R. T., and Kinney, S. T. (Ed.), *Computer augmented teamwork* (pp. 67-85). New York, NY: Van Nostrand Reinhold.

Hiltz, S. R. (1994). *The virtual classroom. learning without limits via computer networks*. Norwood, NJ: Ablex Publishing Corporation.

Huber, G. P. (1984). Issues in the design of group decision support systems. *Management Information Systems Quarterly*, *8*(3), 195-204.

Issacs, E. A., and Tang, J.C. (1994). What video can and cannot do for collaboration. *Multimedia Systems*, *2*, 63-73.

Jessup, L. M., Connolly, T., Galegher, J. (1989). The effects of anonymity on GDSS group process with an idea-generating task. *Management Information Systems Quarterly*, *14*(3), 313-321.

Jessup, L. M., and Valacich, J. S.,. (1990). Effects of anonymity and evaluative tone on idea generation in computer-mediated groups. *Management Science*, *36*(2), 689-703.

Johansen, R., Martin, A., Mittman, R., Saffo, P. I., Sibbit, D., and Benson, S. (1991). *Leading Business Teams*. Reading, MA: Addison Wesley.

Johnson-Lenz, P., and Johnson-Lenz, T. (1980). *Groupware: The emerging art of orchestrating collective intelligence*. Paper presented at the First Global Conference on the Future, Toronto, Canada.

Jonassen, D. H., Peck, K. L., and Wilson, B. G. (1999). *Learning with technology A constructivist perspective*. Upper Saddle River, NJ: Prentice Hall.

Keen, P. G. W. (1999). *Competing in chapter 2 of Internet business* . Delft, The Netherlands: Eburon Publishers.

Kettlehut, M. (1994). How to avoid misusing electronic meeting support. *Planning Review*, *22*(4), 34-38.

Koschmann, T. D., Myers, A.C., Feltovich, P.J., & Barrows, H.S. (1994). Using technology to assist in realizing effective learning and instruction: A principled approach to the use of computers in collaborative learning. *The Journal of the Learning Sciences*, *3*, 227-264.

Krathwol, D. R. (1964). *Taxonomy of educational objectives: The classification of educational goals* (Handbook 2). New York: McKay.

Kwok, R. C. W., and Khalifa, M. (1997). *Effect of GSS on meaningful learning*. Paper presented at the Thirtieth Annual Hawaii International Conference on Systems Science, Maui, HI.

Leidner, D. E., and Fuller, M. (1996). *Improving student processing and assimilation of conceptual information: GSS-supported collaborative learning vs. individual constructive learning*. Paper presented at the Proceedings of the twenty Ninth Annual Hawaii International Conference on system Sciences, Maui, HI.

Leigh, J., Rajlich, P., Stein, R., Johnson A., and Defanti, T. (2000). *LIMBO/VTK: A tool for rapid tele-immersive visualization*. Available: http://www.evl.uic.edu/spiff.

Neale, D. C., McGee, M.K., Amento, B., and Brooks, P. (2000). *Making media spaces useful: Video support and telepresence*. Available: http://citeseer.nj.nec.com/262942.html.

Nunamaker, J. (1997). Future research in group support systems: Needs, some questions and possible directions. *International Journal Human-Computer Studies, 47*, 235-385.

Nunamaker, J. F., Jr., Vogel, D. R., Heminger, A., Martz, W. B., Jr., Grohowski, R., and McGoff, C. (1989a). *Group support systems in practice; experience at IBM*. Paper presented at the Proceedings of the Twenty-Second Hawaii International Conference on System Sciences.

Nunamaker, J. F., Jr., Dennis, A. R., Valacich, J. S., Vogel, D. R., and George, J. F. (1991). Electronic meeting systems to support group work: Theory and practice at Arizona. *Communications of the ACM, 34*(7), 40-61.

Nunamaker, J. F., Jr., Briggs, R. O., Mittleman, D. D., and Balthazard, P. B. (1996-97). Lessons from a dozen years of group support systems research: a discussion of lab and field findings. *Journal of Management Information Systems, 13*(3), 163-207.

Nunamaker, J. F., Jr., Romano, N. C., Jr., and Briggs R. O. (2001a). *A framework for collaboration and knowledge management*. Paper presented at the Proceedings of the Thirty-Third Annual Hawaii International Conference on System Sciences, Maui, HI.

Nunamaker, J. F., Jr., Romano, N. C., Jr., and Briggs, R. O. (2001b). *Increasing intellectual bandwidth: An integrated framework of KMST And CST*. Paper presented at the Proceedings of the 2nd Annual Group Decision and Negotiation Conference. La Rochelle France: Faculty of Technology, Policy and Management.

Nunamaker, J. F. J., Vogel, D. R., and Konsynski, B. (1989b). Interaction of task and technology to support large groups. *Decision Support Systems, 5*(2), 139-152.

Nunamaker, J. F. J., Briggs, Robert O., and de Vreede, Gert-Jan (Ed.). (2001). *Value creation technology: Changing the focus to the group*. Harlow, Essex, UK: Pearson Education: Edinburgh Gate.

Phillips, G., and Santoro, G. (1990). Teaching group discussion via computer-mediated communication. In G. Phillips (Ed.), *Teaching how to work in groups* (pp. 115-129). Norwood, NJ: Ablex Publishing Company.

Piaget, J. (1967). *Bilogie et connaissance [Biology and knowledge]*. Paris, France: Gallimard.

Puntambekar, S. (1999). *An integrated approach to individual and collaborative learning in a web-based learning environment*. Paper presented at the Proceedings of the Computer Support for Collaborative Learning (CSCL) 1999 Conference, Paolo Alto, CA.

Purser, R. E., and Montuori, A. (1995, June). Varieties of knowledge work experience: a critical systems inquiry into epistemologies and mindscapes of knowledge production. In D. A. J. Michael M. Beyerlein (Ed.), *Advances in Interdisciplinary Studies of Work Teams : Theories of Self-Managing Work Teams 1994* . Greenwich, CT: JAI Press.

Pychyl, T. A., Clarke, D. , and Abarbanel, T. (1999). Computer-mediated group projects: Facilitating collaborative learning with the World Wide Web. *Teaching of Psychology, 26*(2), 138-141.

Reinig, B. A., Briggs, R. O., Brandt, S. A., and Nunamaker, J. F., Jr. (1997a). *The electronic classroom on fire: why it happens and how to put out the flames*. Paper presented at the Proceedings of the Thirtieth Hawaii International Conference on System Sciences, Maui, HI.

Reinig, B. A. (1997b). *An empirical investigation of the electronic classroom*. Paper presented at the 1997 Pacific Asian Conference on Information Systems.

Reinig, B. A., Briggs, R. O., and Nunamaker, J. F., Jr. (in press). Flaming in the electronic classroom. *Journal of Management Information Systems*.

Rodden, T. (1993). Technical support for cooperation. In D. Diaper, and C. Sanger (Eds.), *CSCW in practice: An introduction and case studies* (pp. 1-22). London, UK: Springer-Verlag.

Rogoff, B. (1990). *Apprenticeship in thinking : cognitive development in social context*. Oxford, UK: Oxford University Press.

Romano, N. C., Jr., Nunamaker, J. F., Jr., Briggs, R. O., and Vogel, D. R. (1998). Architecture, design, and development of an HTML/Javascript web-based group support system. *Journal of the American Society for Information Science* (JASIS): Special Topic Issue: Artificial Intelligence Techniques for Emerging Information Systems Applications, *49*(7), 649-667.

Roschelle, J., and Teasley, S. D. (1995). The construction of shared knowledge in collaborative problem-solving. In C. O'Malley (Ed.), *Computer supported collaborative learning* (pp. 69-97). Berlin: Springer Verlag.

Russ-Eft, D. (2001). *Using technology to develop management and leadership skills*. Paper presented at the Academy of Human Resource Development, Tulsa, OK.

Scalia, L., and Sackmary, B. (1996a). Groupware and computer-supported cooperative work in the college classroom. *Business Communication Quarterly, 98*.

Scalia, L. M., and Sackmary, B. (1996b). Groupware in the classroom: Applications and guidelines. *Computers in the Schools, 12*(4), 39-53.

Schreiber, D., and Berge, A. (1998). *Distance training: How innovative organizations are using technology to maximize learning and meet business objectives*. San Francisco, CA: Jossey-Bass.

Simpson, J. S. (1966). *The classification of educational objectives, psychomotor domain*. Urbana, IL: University of Illinois.

Stewart, T. A. (1998). *Intellectual capital: The new wealth of organizations*. (1st Currrent ed.). New York, NY: Bantam Books.

Theirauf, R. (1989). *Group decision support systems for effective decision making: a guide for MIS practitioners and end users*. New York, NY: Quorum Books.

Tyran, C. K. (1997). *GSS to support classroom discussion: Opportunities and pitfalls*. Paper presented at the Thirtieth Annual Hawaii International Conference on Systems Science, Maui, HI.

Valacich, J. S., Dennis, A. R., and Nunamaker, J. F., Jr. (1991a). Electronic meeting support: the group systems concept. *International Journal of Man-Machine Studies, 34*(2), 261-282.

Valacich, J. S., Dennis, A. R., and Nunamaker, J. F., Jr. (1991b). *Group size and anonymity effects on computer mediated idea generation*. Paper presented at the Proceedings of Academy of Management Meeting.

Valacich, J. S., Dennis, A. R., and Nunamaker, J. F., Jr.,. (1992). Group size and anonymity effects in an electronic meeting systems environment. *Small Group Research, 23*(1), 49-73.

Vogel, D. R., Lagumdzija, Z., and Nunamaker, J. R., Jr. (1989). Session management for collaborative work. *Transactions on Decision Support Systems*, 227-238.

Vogel, D. R., Lou, D., van Eekhout, M., van Genuchten, M., Verveen, S., and Adams, T. (2000, Jan 4-7). *Distributed experiential learning: The Hong Kong -Netherlands project.* Paper presented at the Proceedings of the Thirty-Third Annual Hawai'i International Conference on System Sciences, Maui, HI.

Vygotsky, L. S. (1978). *Mind in society: The development of higher psychological processes.* Cambridge, MA: Harvard University Press.

Walsh, K. R., Briggs, R.O., Ayoub, J., Vanderboom, C., and Glynn, M. (1996). *Learning with GSS: a case study.* Paper presented at the Proceedings of the Twenty Ninth Annual Hawaii International Conference on System Sciences, Maui, HI.

Webb, N. M., and Palincsar, A. S. (1996). Group processes in the classroom. In R. C. D. C. Berliner (Ed.), *Handbook of educational psychology* (pp. 841-873). New York, NY: Macmilian.

Webster, J., and Hackley, P. (1997). Teaching effectiveness in technology-mediated distance learning. *Academy of Management Journal, 40*(6), 1282-1309.

Woolley, D. R. (2001). *Conferencing software for the web.* Available on-line at http://thinkofit.com/webconf/.

IMPLEMENTING A REMOTE AND COLLABORATIVE "HANDS-ON" LEARNING ENVIRONMENT[1]

George Scheets
Oklahoma State University

Mark Weiser
Oklahoma State University

Abstract

The need to train the knowledge workers of the future is evident, and so is the need to continuously re-train current employees in the latest advanced technologies. These dual needs have led many organizations to use distance-learning technologies for course work. Although it is currently possible to deliver most traditional course content through a combination of Web and video technologies, most students still travel to a common location for significant hands-on application with technical equipment. This chapter describes an ongoing implementation of a laboratory (lab) environment that allows remote interaction with equipment and with other students. We employ same-time/different-place and different–time/different-place approaches to extend the reach of a technical lab class to students around the world. We apply current and emerging technologies and will develop new software and equipment to create a virtual lab experience that is as good as or better than that of the traditional physical lab course, while we simultaneously provide local students with access to students in remote sites.

Introduction

This chapter describes an ongoing implementation of a remote laboratory (lab) environment that allows real-time interaction with the equipment and with other students in a manner that previously required co-location. This lab

---

[1] The work discussed here is funded in part by a grant from SBC.

employs a combination of same-time/different-place and different-time/different-place Internet-based technologies. Our goal is to develop a remote lab learning experience that will capture *all* of the social and technical interactions that take place in the traditional, same-time/same-place lab course.

We begin with an overview of the impetus behind this lab at Oklahoma State University (OSU), the Master of Science in Telecommunications Management (MSTM) degree program. We describe the lab. We provide specific details of remote lab implementations. We close with an examination of several issues that remain to be considered.

Background

In the fall of 1995, OSU-Stillwater instituted a Master of Science in Telecommunications Management (MSTM) program to serve the growing telecommunication industry in Oklahoma and the surrounding area. Twenty-three hours of management and technically oriented telecommunication courses, an industry practicum, and a hands-on lab comprise the required core curriculum. Twelve hours of electives round out the curriculum (MSTM, 2001). Interest in the program has surpassed our expectations, and enrollment has ballooned beyond our most optimistic projections.

Current enrollment caps are slowly being eased as additional faculty are hired. We presently limit the number of MSTM students to about 200, of which approximately half are traditional, full-time students on the main

Our goal is a remote lab that captures all the social and technical interactions of the traditional, same-time/same-place lab course.

campus, and half are professionals who work full-time in the telecommunications industry. The non-traditional students are chiefly concentrated in the Tulsa and Oklahoma City areas, but a significant number are in the Dallas-Fort Worth area and in states serviced by Southwestern Bell. Most recently, we have added several students who are based at UUNET headquarters in Virginia.

The program has relied heavily on distance-learning techniques since its inception. Fortunately, OSU's Educational TV Services has been a leader in distance learning for years and has the resources and the technical know-how to support multiple delivery methods (ETS, 2001).

Oklahoma owns a large network of fiber optic cabling that extends throughout the state. Live, interactive, two-way video classes are delivered to the OSU-Tulsa and OSU-Oklahoma City branch campuses over this network. Such corporate sites as Seagate Technologies in Oklahoma City and Halliburton Industries in Duncan have elected to tie into the network. Oklahoma's Network for Education, ONENET, manages much of the network, which today includes high schools and vocational technology schools scattered around the state (ONENET, 2001). MSTM uses ONENET for students who are located in parts of the state other than Tulsa and Oklahoma City to provide live interactive two-way video directly to their sites.

Some out-of-state students link to the program in a different manner. Southwestern Bell and UUNET typically have 384 Kbps Integrated Service Digital Network (ISDN) connections to their sites, which allow two-way interactive video. At the time of this writing, OSU's Educational TV Services is evaluating the possibility of supporting interactive Internet-based video conferencing using H.323.

Other out-of-state students are served asynchronously. Corporate sites that elect not to connect to the live classes via ISDN are sent videotapes of the lectures, which typically arrive for viewing by the remote students anywhere from a week to ten days after the actual class. Pioneered at OSU by the Telecom Management program and one of the authors (Mark Weiser), non-interactive, after-the-fact, Internet-based video streaming is now offered for many courses (ETSVideo, 2001). Off- and on-campus students can watch or review classes at their convenience. Streamed video classes are usually finished with post-production and available for viewing from a video server two to three days after the actual class. The quality of the streamed production is reasonably good at the high bandwidths provided by campus or corporate networks and by newer home connectivity options, such as digital subscriber lines and cable modems. When streamed video must be viewed via an analog modem running at 28.8 or 56 Kbps, however, the experience leaves a lot to be desired. The minimum video play-back rate of a typical home PC exceeds the speeds that many older modem-based systems are capable of providing. This means that the video and the audio cycle between playing back smoothly for several seconds and freezing for several seconds while the delivery system seeks to catch up. Despite this stop-and-go encounter, Internet-based streaming has proved to be very popular with home-based students. The inconvenience of substandard quality is outweighed by the convenience of any-time/any-place availability. Instructor interaction with asynchronous remote students relies wholly on telephone calls, e-mail exchanges, and on-line discussion groups and bulletin boards.

A hands-on telecommunications lab course is required for the MSTM degree. This lab course covers various aspects of voice, video, and data networking. The goal is not to train students to be experts on specific hardware, but to ground the learning previously obtained in several theory-based lecture courses, to familiarize students with the telecommunications equipment they may become involved with in the future, and to enlighten them about many of the processes technicians deal with. To minimize inconvenience for off-campus students, the lab course is currently a 4-day, 8 hours-a-day experience that concludes with a take-home design problem. The course may be offered over four consecutive weekdays or two Friday/Saturday weekends. Proposals to replace this lab with alternative labs to be implemented at certain remote corporate sites (provided the experience meets with the approval of MSTM faculty) have never been implemented. As a consequence, all on- and off-campus students are required to travel to a common location to attend the lab. Despite this inconvenience, post-graduation surveys reveal that most students consider the lab to be one of the most beneficial courses in the program.

The necessary travel to Stillwater by the non-traditional, off-campus students for this single class receives mixed reviews. Some students enjoy it. They view campus living as an opportunity to relax from the pressures of their jobs, to stay in a dorm, and to relive some of their college experiences. Other students view the travel as a nuisance, and they treat it as such. Though we have never surveyed the students to verify the correlation, we believe that to some extent students' views of a trip to Stillwater are related to the attitudes of their employers. At one extreme is the company that views the lab course as equivalent to corporate training. Such a company allows employees to attend on company time, and pays for all associated expenses.

Post-graduation surveys reveal that most students consider the lab one of the most beneficial courses.

At the other extreme is the company that views university graduate education as benefiting the employee more than the company and requires the student to pay for all expenses and to use vacation time to attend.

Although evaluations of the lab experience are almost entirely favorable, requiring students to travel to a common site is not the optimum solution. Techniques to circumvent this requirement have frequently been proposed by faculty, students, and industry partners, including allowing remote students to substitute equivalent experience at corporate sites in their area. Although remote experiences are a reasonable alternative, they have never been pursued because of the time and expense that would be required to develop equivalent learning laboratories at alternate sites. During the early days of the program, there was some discussion of outfitting a large tractor trailer with a portable lab and using it to bring the lab to the students, as opposed to bringing the students to the lab. This proposal was quickly rejected due to problems with providing power and telecommunications connectivity, not to mention the added expense of outfitting and maintaining a second lab.

Continued advances in wide-area and last-mile communications have now opened a third possibility—a virtual lab (VL). Our pursuit of this option is described in this chapter. In the discussion that follows, the term *local* will refer to anything physically located in the Telecommunications Lab on the OSU campus. The term *remote* will refer to anything physically located at the remote student's site.

Virtual lab

Different-time/different-place is one approach to delivering a lab experience virtually. The remote student might log onto a server using Web-based browser technology, and use software to *virtually* interact with equipment in order to perform an experiment. Or the remote student may *actually* interact with the lab equipment over the Internet. Unlike conventional on-campus labs in which a large number of students converge on a specific location to execute their lab experiments during a scheduled lab period, a remote student can execute the lab at his or her convenience from a location where limited equipment is physically available. With this methodology, students do not have to be at the same location to take the lab (different place), nor do they have to take it at the same time (different time).

This latter type of lab is becoming reasonably common. Examples include Cisco Systems' E-Learning Remote Labs, Mentor Technologies' vLab System, and Rice University's Virtual Lab in Statistics (Cisco, 2001; MentorLabs, 2001; Lane, 2001).

Although this type of lab does provide training that may otherwise be unobtainable, it does not provide the rich learning environment of the traditional same-time/same-place lab. Sharda, Romano, and Lucca, in the chapter, "A Conceptual Framework for Computer supported Collaborative Learning Requiring Immediate Presence (CSCLIP)," make the following point: Gone is the chance to interact with a lab mate or other lab teams and discuss problem-solving techniques or one's current experimental results. Gone is the chance to interact with and draw on the experience of a live lab instructor. And gone is the opportunity to learn by interactive observation.

An alternative, or complementary, methodology might be a same-time/different-place experience, in which all students take the lab and perform the experiments, but they all do not have to be physically located in the on-campus lab. Some students may be performing the lab experiment on campus; some may be performing the lab experiment from remote sites. Regardless of their location, students can utilize the equipment, interact with the instructors, and interact with other students. If executed properly, this type of lab should capture the essence of and offer essentially the same learning experience as a same-time/same-place classroom environment. Furthermore, because the subject of our curriculum is telecommunications, extending the system to the remote sites provides additional learning components. This methodology currently appears to be very rare. Perhaps non-existent.

Immediate presence (IP) implies the marriage of same-time/different place interactions among learners, instructors, equipment, information technology, and the lab equipment. The proposed lab's learning objectives and technological requirements exactly fit the notion of IP. We will support IP with computing and conferencing technology, using computer-supported collaborative learning requiring immediate presence (CSCLIP), as presented by Sharda et al. in the chapter that immediately precedes this one. In this chapter we describe and explain the proposed implementation of an actual lab that will employ many of the concepts of CSCLIP.

Physical lab course overview

The lab is located in what was formerly an office complex on the OSU-Stillwater campus. The equipment includes a Nortel DMS-10 telephone switch, smaller telephone switches known as private branch exchanges (PBX), routers, ethernet hubs and switches, asynchronous transfer mode (ATM) switches, stand-alone and PC-based video conferencing gear, OPNET and COMNET simulation software, and a plethora of PCs. Students form 2- or 3-person groups. Generally, each group is assigned one of the offices, works on the equipment therein, and is not allowed to communicate with the other groups until the group has successfully installed a telephone or a data network between offices.

Although the exact sequence of experiments can vary from time to time at the instructor's option, experiments are generally structured to mimic the order in which communications might be installed in a small company. The groups first install telephone services using the DMS-10 and PBXs. Then the groups in their respective offices use Microsoft Windows to establish peer-to-peer ethernet local area networks and to enable file sharing and e-mail services. The groups experiment with PC-based video conferencing. They then connect their individual office local area networks (LAN) via a backbone packet or ATM network, and connect the resulting network to the rest of the world. They conduct experiments to better understand the intricacies of Internet protocol- based networking, client-server networking, Web-server hosting, and circuit- and packet-switched voice and video. They also investigate carrier-type, wide area network issues using simulation software. In a following section, we will discuss selected experiments and provide details about implementing them virtually.

The MSTM Lab, more than many other lab-based courses, is an excellent candidate for implementing the same-time/different-place methodology, because student interactions with the majority of functions in the hardware that are used in the experiments are accessed via a personal computer. Given today's technology, there is no reason for PCs to be physically located in the lab. Provided that adequate Internet connectivity exists and can be accessed, the PCs used to perform the experiments can easily be several states away.

To enable most of the interactions that normally occur in a same-time/same-place lab, good quality audio and video communications between the lab and the remote students' sites are mandatory. Several interrelated technological advances have recently occurred that in combination can facilitate this requirement.

The ongoing deployment of improved high-speed, last-mile telecommunication systems, such as cable modems and Digital Subscriber Lines, which offer 1.5 Mbps of connectivity to the home or small company office, are promising steps toward a networking nirvana of high-speed connectivity

The MSTM Laboratory is an excellent candidate for experimental implementation of the same-time/different-place methodology.

for all. Improved last-mile connectivity, when it is coupled with continued increases in the speeds of Internet service provider (ISP) backbone networks, will bring decent quality audio and video over the Internet to the home and to small company users.

Today, most large corporations have high bandwidth pipes to the commodity Internet. When their connectivity is coupled with OSU's 155 Mbps connectivity, sufficient resources will usually exist between OSU and corporate sites to support the remote communications necessary for a media-rich virtual lab (VL).

Remote students could also enroll in the lab from those college campuses that are connected to Internet2, which typically offers better end-to-end performance than the commodity Internet. Interactive video conferences that both authors have experienced recently over Internet2 have been smoother and have had fewer disruptions than video conferences over the commodity Internet.

Continued improvements in end-to-end Internet transport have reached a point where it is capable of supporting the interactions necessary for a same-time/different-place lab. Unfortunately for our purposes, Internet traffic is generally processed on a first-come, first-served basis. The only widely deployed technique to guarantee good quality of service (QoS) is to keep the network lightly loaded. As anyone who has accessed the commodity Internet is aware, good QoS is sometimes hard to come by. The ability to reserve resources and prioritize traffic on the Internet is still several years away. Until that change occurs, video and audio will have to compete for resources on the same basis as less time-sensitive exchanges, such as e-mail and normal Web traffic. Note, however, that at times the poor performance one experiences on the Internet is *not* due to ISP backbone bandwidth problems, but to server overload at the information source; that is, the server just isn't powerful enough to handle smoothly all the requests for information. Insufficient bandwidth between the local server and the ISP backbone, because of over-economizing on the last-mile connectivity, is also a common source of delays.

In addition to recent improvements in the transport system, audio-visual equipment, which until recently used proprietary hardware and software, is now largely available based on open standards, such as H.323, a protocol for audio and video delivery over packet-based networks. Overall product quality and the abilities of products from one vendor to interact with products from other vendors continue to improve dramatically. At the same time, prices continue to fall.

All things considered, the time appears ripe to begin investigating and overcoming the difficulties associated with a VL, and to develop an experience that will give remote students the option of not traveling to Stillwater. Ideally, we will develop a general technique that could be applied by academicians to laboratories in other disciplines, and by practitioners to laboratories in workplace settings.

Virtual lab: Implementation

Our goal is to capture in remote desktop interactions all the relevant activities of a lab experience, including interacting simultaneously with other remote students, with students in the physical lab, and with lab hardware. All interactions will be supported remotely. In addition to implementing the obvious requirement that remote students be able to manipulate the equipment associated with a particular experiment and to interact with their lab mates, wherever they may be, we intend to implement other facets of a typical lab experience. We plan to include a capability that will allow remote students to virtually stick their heads out in the hall and holler for an instructor or stroll down the hall, walk into an adjacent room, and interact with the people in the room.

To meet these goals, we envision making extensive use of video, audio, and networking technologies. We will include real-time access to the instructor lab hardware, software, and media. Successful implementation of this project will involve research and development in learning theory, networking hardware, communications, electrical and computer engineering of new hardware, and human-computer interfaces.

Typically, lab experiments in any discipline involve learning that must be completed before attending class. Students are expected to review materials and complete specific tasks. Prelabs for the VL will be implemented through independent study and through the use of different-time/different-place technologies, such as taking a virtual tour of a telephone switch.

The actual lab experiments will be implemented same-time-different-place. Implementation will proceed in three phases. Phase I involves

The lab experiments will be implemented same-time-different-place.

experimenting with off-the-shelf hardware and software. Phase II involves developing the hardware and software that is not available commercially and must be built or coded specially for our purposes. Phase III involves making the discrete parts of the lab function as a seamless whole.

Key components used in Phase I include the following:

- Microsoft's NetMeeting (Microsoft, 2001), which enables such applications as video and audio conferencing, white boarding, application sharing, and desktop sharing over the Internet.
- Stand-alone camera packages based on Polycom's View Station (Polycom, 2001). Packages consist of a camera, a monitor, and an audio device. These will be wall mounted in selected rooms. Remote students will connect with the camera via the Internet and will see and talk with people in the vicinity. Video from the remote student will be displayed on a local monitor allowing local students to see who is virtually in the room. These camera packages will be always on and will serve as key components in giving remote students the ability to see what is going on in the actual lab and to communicate with local students and the instructors. Proper placement of cameras and ease of access will insure their successful virtual presence in the lab.
- Quick Time Virtual Reality, which allows the generation of 360 degree, high-fidelity images (QT, 2001). This software package will be used to generate interactive videos for pre-lab study, as well as a virtual walk-through of the lab.

- Final Cut Pro, a MacIntosh-based software package, which will be used to edit and produce video segments suitable for streaming over the Internet.

Phase II of VL construction will commence when we've gone as far as we can with off-the-shelf hardware and software. We will focus on developing special-purpose hardware and software to address the unresolved issues from Phase I, and we will automate and make seamless many lab processes. Key components of Phase II include the following:

- Developing the software that allows remote students to simulate some of the cable installations required in the actual lab. This project is discussed in greater detail in the Peer-to-Peer LAN Lab section below.
- Developing for the instructor a wireless camera and audio system capable of transmitting and receiving audio and video from any location in the lab and capable of lasting a minimum of three to four hours on a single battery charge. This system will allow remote students to contact the instructor anywhere in the local lab. It will also allow the instructor to select his or her personal camera as the video source so the remote student(s) sees what the instructor is looking at, enabling virtual 'over-the-shoulder' discussions and explanations. The instructor and the teaching assistant will each wear a unit.
- Developing software to allow the remote students to virtually walk down the hall and visit the various rooms in the lab will insure ease-of-use. This project will require generating software to switch automatically from one stand-alone camera package to another, depending on where the remote student wants to go. To prevent a feeling among the local students that they are being watched by unknown persons, the software should announce when a remote student has virtually entered a room.

In addition to addressing the many unforeseen issues that will arise as the VL construction proceeds, we will focus on hardware and software to allow lab groups to have more than one remote lab mate and to allow totally virtual lab groups.

We are currently in the midst of Phase I.

To gain a better understanding of some of the issues and potential solutions involved in developing a same-time/different-place VL, it is informative to explore in greater detail the steps we are taking to implement specific lab experiments. We examine three experiments below.

Implementing the telephony lab

Current same-time/same-place methodology

The curriculum follows the order normally taken in setting up a communications system for a growing business. Therefore, the first lab experience requires that telephone service be established. We anticipate that MSTM graduates will be placed with employers who are providers or consumers of telephone service. Therefore, local students will perform the functions of both the Central Office DMS-10 provider and the internal technician who is responsible for acquiring and manipulating telephone service within a company. This work includes establishing a client-side PBX telephone switch.

Students enter the class with knowledge of basic telephony, including requirements analysis, which they obtained in a required core course. This pre-existing knowledge is supplemented with a pre-lab lecture, which covers the many different ways that communication providers install lines and trunk bandwidth to companies that require voice service. We then explain the structure of the Central Office DMS-10 telephone switch and the PBXs that we use in each "corporate office" in our campus building. The pre-lab continues with an instructor-led tour of the DMS switch, the control interface, the power plant, and the cabling structure.

At this point, the small groups establish physical connectivity by running appropriate cables from the DMS to their assigned office spaces. They accomplish the appropriate line settings and complete other exercises through a dedicated dumb-terminal connection attached to the DMS. Finally, the groups accomplish PBX settings through a PC-based Windows interface, which requires attaching a PC to the PBX with an RS-232 direct connection.

Different-time/different-place pre-lab

Typically, about two hours of this pre-lab is spent in classroom lecture followed by a cursory physical tour of the switch and other components. This exposure is necessary because of the diverse backgrounds of the

The lecture materials are being captured with full audio and video in a format that can be streamed to students.

students. It ensures that students understand the functions they will implement. An alternative would have the students simply read and follow instructions on how to physically complete the task. To implement this process virtually, the lecture materials are being captured with full audio and video in a format that can be streamed to students. The lectures will be accompanied by detailed graphics and digital images of the DMS switch, power plant, interface, and cabling structure. Students will be able to preview both the functions they will implement and the equipment configurations they will interact with.

This on-line lecture may be reviewed as an independent-study assignment any time prior to the class meeting. Following this prepatory step, students will continue with a pre-lab exercise. They will be able to virtually walk around the switch, remove covers, and click on "hot spots" associated with major system components. These clicks will replay relevant portions of the lecture or will offer an electronic guided tour of that part of the switch, much like the live tour of past pre-labs. Clicking on an individual component of the switch, such as a processor or a line card, will virtually remove that component and provide a VR view of the component as it is rotated by the student. Clicking on specific areas of a component will link students to technical documentation pertinent to that component. Finally, students can trace a call through the switch using a narrated demonstration of the internal components and the functions of the switch.

Students will then complete a short assignment that uses information from the on-line lecture and from their exploration of the VR version of the equipment. The assignment is designed to reinforce the learning and to serve as a guide during the actual lab experiment. Upon completion of the assignment, the students will download a pre-lab reading that describes the actual processes the groups will undertake. It should be read prior to executing the actual lab experiments.

Same-time/different-place voice experiments

The DMS switch structure allows two serial interfaces. A staffed office typically uses one interface for a local dumb terminal to control the switch, and the other interface for a local printer to record alarm notifications and other information generated automatically by the switch. An unstaffed office typically controls the switch through a modem rather than a dumb terminal. By using a terminal emulator, a remote technician can use a PC to dial into the switch and modify the settings. The remote interface looks identical to that of the local terminal.

We modify the structure (see Figure 1) to incorporate a Linux workstation, which is connected to the second serial port via a RS-232 cable. The workstation is connected to the Internet and is made accessible to remote students with user name and password provided. Access is currently being configured to allow either local or remote students to manipulate the switch. That is, the local students' terminal mirrors the actions of the remote

PCs. If all students were co-located with the switch, they would take turns physically moving to the seat in front of the terminal. In the VL configuration, local students will still move as before, and control will pass to remote students to allow them to perform portions of the lab experiments.

Additionally, two H.323 cameras will be mounted with views of the switch and the students at the local terminal. One camera can be controlled remotely, to allow viewing the activities of the local students. A microphone beside the terminal will provide audio to the remote students who are viewing the controllable camera. Video and audio from the remote students is fed to a standard television monitor that is placed just above the local terminal. This combination will provide the immediacy that allows remote students to be an active part of the group. They will be able to participate in discussion questions posed during the lab.

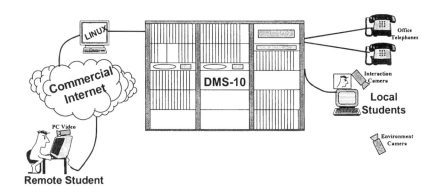

Figure 1. DMS switch structure

After the students configure the DMS, they will establish the wiring. This is a physical process that must be accomplished between the DMS switch and the telephone in the group's assigned office. The physical process can be actively followed from the remote locations via controllable cameras placed throughout the lab. Additionally, as local students complete various physical processes, remote students can check via their Linux terminal connections to see if the DMS recognizes a proper connection. This exercise mimics the real-world processes of field technicians, who implement a connection to the consumer site and test that connection with the help of a switch technician at the central office.

After the lines from the DMS switch and their features have been tested, the groups will move to the client-side PBX setup. They will manipulate the telephone switching equipment used in the offices via a Windows interface on a PC that is directly connected to the PBX. The PCs that will be used to configure the PBX are running remote-access software that allows control of the local PC to be passed back and forth between the local site and the remote sites via the Internet. Each office will have a controllable camera and audio. Figure 2 illustrates the configuration of a client room for the telephone PBX configuration.

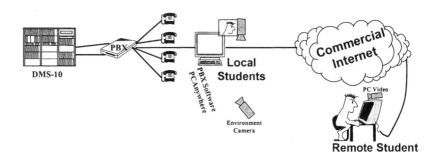

Figure 2. PBX structure

Implementing the peer-to-peer LAN lab

Current same-time/same-place methodology

To begin building a network for a small company, a simple hub-based peer-to-peer local area network is required. This exercise requires that students connect three to four PCs to a common hub to provide communication between computer systems. Once established, a Microsoft Windows e-mail system is configured, and portions of each system's hard drives are accessed by the other computers.

Same-time/different-place peer-to-peer network experiments

Extending remote sites to allow peer-to-peer LAN exercises is particularly challenging, because until a network is established, it is difficult to logically justify interactive connections to the remote students. Recall that in the local lab, a lab group cannot communicate with students outside their assigned office until they have set up an inter-office telecommunications system and enabled either telephony or video conferencing. To ensure that remote students can meet the learning objectives, communications with their local lab mates will utilize a pre-configured, always-on audio and video system that is externally connected to the OSU Campus network. This system will not be manipulated during the regular lab exercises. The independence of this system is made obvious by its physical separation from the other systems. Note also that this system was previously mentioned as a stand-alone H.323 video package. It enables the remote students' virtual presence in their respective lab groups.

Figure 3 shows the LAN hub structure. The setup includes a local PC for every on-campus and off-campus student. The local students' PCs will be running Microsoft Windows. The local PC assigned to the remote student will be running Linux. The remote students' local PC has two network interfaces. One interface is assigned to the Internet via the OSU campus network and provides a path that will allow the remote student to communicate with his or her local PC. The other interface is assigned and connected via a known good cable to the office hub that will be shared with the local lab mates. The local students are supplied a cable that they will eventually connect to their hub (shown by dotted lines).

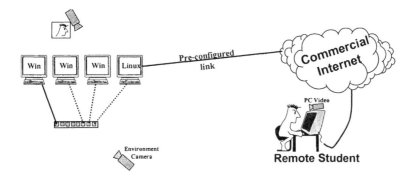

Figure 3. LAN hub structure

Connecting cables from the local PC to the LAN hub in each office, confirming a good electrical and logical connection between each system and hub, and testing it with data are important parts of the lab experience. Because remote students cannot make the physical connection, our plan for Phase II of the VL includes developing special-purpose software for use on the remote system. This software will show a facsimile of the physical hub and the group's local PC. The remote student virtually connects his or her system to the hub by selecting the proper cable from a list of possibilities and drawing a line between two representative images on the screen. "Errors" with the cable are set to occur randomly in the software. If an "error" occurs, the student must troubleshoot it appropriately. If no "error" is assigned by the software, the light on the virtual hub will come on. At the same time, a Simple Network Management Protocol (SNMP) message will be sent to the actual hub to activate the port. The interface to the remote student's PC will let him or her see, in the form of representative lines on the screen, that the connections were made by the local users. They can follow the troubleshooting process by monitoring the progress on their VL software and the video system, which will be continuously updated by SNMP.

After having virtually established a physical connection between the local Linux system and the hub, the remote user can connect to the local Linux system via Telnet through the Internet. From that point on, the remote user is effectively on the local LAN. After the local students have properly established connections and configured basic transmission control protocol/Internet protocol (TCP/IP), all the connections can be tested via Packet Internet Groper (PING).

A benefit to be realized by this configuration is including Linux as part of the peer-to-peer LAN. Previously, students established a Microsoft LAN-based e-mail solution, which is not easily extended to a wide area network, as would be required in most company environments. Under this new configuration, the remote student will be assigned the task of configuring a Unix-based mail server, including Simple Message Transfer Protocol (SMTP) and Post Office Protocol (POP). The remote student can test the configuration by sending mail to herself on the local Linux system.

While the mail server is being established, local users can establish POP-3 clients on their Windows systems and configure them to send and receive mail through the local Linux system. Each local student connects to the local Linux system, configures an account for himself, and reviews the server configuration that has been completed. At this point, the only outside connection is through the Internet, by which the remote student accesses the Linux system. Each group member can then test the functionality of the mail system by exchanging e-mail with attachments with all other members of their group.

The last major component of the peer-to-peer networking lab is installing the capability to share folders over Microsoft's LAN-based file-sharing system. This method of transferring folders and files was originally intended to be used only by Microsoft systems running Server Message Block (SMB). Fortunately, Linux now supports file and print sharing over SMB through a package called Samba (2001). Samba will be pre-configured on the local Linux system prior to the beginning of the lab exercises. Each student (local and remote) sets up directories on his or her local hard drive that may be accessed by the other team members. Each team member then connects to each of the other shared folders that have been made available. The connection is tested by copying and using files. To make the remote user more comfortable with the interface, a Samba connection through the commodity Internet will also be established, thereby allowing remote users to directly access their teammates' hard drives from their remote systems.

The remote extensions provide added learning elements for all students. All students are exposed to the two operating systems most used in corporate environments. They will create a peer-to-peer environment across multiple systems, and they will establish seamless sharing of information across the computers of their lab group.

Implementing the interconnected networks lab

Current same-time/same-place methodology

This exercise takes network implementation to the next level, in which the small isolated LAN's established by each 2- or 3-person group are connected with each other, creating a lab-based Internet with a coordinated address space. The physical lab allows for up to nine local groups, each of which may be configured as an isolated peer-to-peer network. In this interconnected networks lab, students design and implement a lab-wide network that supports the small Internet Protocol subnets created by all groups. They then connect this lab-wide network to the campus network, which in turn provides connection to the Internet and the rest of the world.

An in-class review of previous course material covering the Internet Protocol routing allows students to independently complete a homework assignment, in which each designs a structure that could support the network to be implemented. Because there are multiple correct answers to this exercise, it is not uncommon for students to generate many viable alternatives. In a classroom session immediately prior to entering this lab, a final implementation plan is derived through a guided discussion. The intended architecture is transcribed by a lab assistant onto a centrally located whiteboard, which allows each group to ensure that their portion of the final network is implemented as agreed.

Each group configures and tests its local LAN, using the new Internet protocol address space. After ensuring local functionality, a physical connection to a router is made. Additional connections between routers may be assigned to individual groups to ensure that the required physical connectivity exists to support the overall target network. Each group then configures its portion of the network via a laptop computer that directly connects to a router through an RS-232 port. Finally, the network is tested between groups by using both PING and file sharing.

Same-time/different-place interconnected network experiments

The lecture that directly relates to the required homework exercise is available via video streaming, with coordinated diagrams and simple reinforcing exercises. Additionally, a discussion forum of student questions and responses is maintained across class sessions and is available asynchronously through a Web page. As a rule, all student questions can be answered by a review of this system, which serves as a continuously refined file of frequently asked questions (FAQ) on the topic of network routing.

Developing a consensus for an appropriate network structure is well suited to an interactive classroom environment, in which discussion is possible between all students and the instructor. H.323 video will connect all remote students with the classroom discussion, via real-time, two-way video and audio. Frequent captures of the contents of the classroom whiteboard will be sent to remote students, showing them the design changes in a size that they may easily view and digitally save.

The lab-group structure remains unchanged after completion of the peer-to-peer lab exercises. Remote students will still access their respective local LANs via a local Linux workstation and will still have video views from controllable student and environment cameras. Additionally, cameras will be available at the router locations, and a router port will be pre-configured to allow remote access to the router via an Internet connection that is separate from the constructed network (See Figure 4).

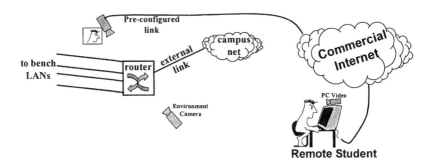

Figure 4. Router structure

While the local students are physically connecting their bench hub to the router, the remote students will complete a series of cabling exercises that simulate connecting to a router, including the application of different supporting devices, such as transceivers. The progress of the local group members can be observed remotely via the lab video network. Once a physical connection has been established, the remote student will log onto the router via the external connection and begin the configuration. Local students will connect to the router through a serial connection and complete the configuration.

Testing the Internetwork configuration is accomplished via an expansion of the e-mail system. To this point, e-mail could only be transmitted within a single LAN. Once connections between the networks are established and tested with PING, configuration changes to the mail server will be implemented by both remote and local students. E-mail is then transmitted to at least one other destination within the lab and to a known e-mail address external to the lab. Ideally, this destination would be the remote student's personal e-mail account so that immediate feedback about successful action could be obtained from within the project group.

Conclusion

This chapter has described an in-progress implementation of a same-time/different-place remote teaching lab employing Internet-based technologies to enable remote student participation.

To date, we have focused on installing as much off-the-shelf equipment as possible, saving the development of special-purpose hardware and software for Phase II. Many areas associated with a reliable VL remain to be investigated, including the following:

- Security issues. Given a university budget, how will we authenticate remote users to insure that only authorized personnel are able to connect to and manipulate lab equipment?
- Resource contention. How will we seamlessly allocate video and audio resources when two or more remote students decide to virtually walk down the hall at the same time? How can we seamlessly allocate experimental resources? What steps will be necessary to prevent resource hijacking?
- Effectiveness evaluation. To what extent does the application of CSCLIP in this environment assist or detract from attaining the five levels of learning that are described by Sharda et al. in their chapter? What changes could make it more beneficial? How effective is the

experience for the local students? Does having remote lab students significantly impact the learning of local lab students?

- Framework development. How can the lessons learned from developing this lab be incorporated into a general framework applicable to developing *any* same-time/different-place lab?

The virtual lab described herein is an initial step toward developing a truly interactive hands-on remote lab experience. Quality of service of the Internet must continue to improve, and the questions above must be addressed and satisfactorily answered before same-time/different-place laboratories can become common within the training and instructional environment.

References

Cisco. (2001). 'Cisco Remote Labs' [On-line]. Available:
    http://www.cisco.com/warp/public/10/wwtraining/demos/vlab_demo/

ETS. (2001). *OSU Television Services* [On-line]. Available: http://www.osutv.org/

ETSVideo. (2001). *OSU Videostreaming Resources* [On-line]. Available:
    http://web.ets.okstate.edu/

Lane, D. M. (2000). *Rice Virtual lab in Statistics*. [On-line]. Available:
    http://www.ruf.rice.edu/~lane/rvls.html

MentorLabs. (2001). *Welcome to the VLab System* [On-line]. Available:
    http://www.mentorlabs.com/vlab/access

Microsoft. (2001). *Windows NetMeeting* [On-line]. Available:
    http://www.microsoft.com/windows/netmeeting/features/

MSTM. (2001). *Master of Science Degree in Telecommunications Management* [On-line].
    Available: http://www.mstm.okstate.edu

ONENET, (2001). *OneNet: Oklahoma's Telecommunications Network* [On-line]. Available:
    http://nic.onenet.net/

Polycom. (2001). *Polycom Products* [On-line]. Available:
    http://www.polycom.com/products/video_family.html

QT (2001). [On-line]. Available: http://www.apple.com/quicktime/

Samba. (2001). *Quicktime* [On-line]. Available: http://www.samba.org

USING ADULT LEARNING IN HRD PROGRAMS TO BRIDGE THE DIGITAL DIVIDE

Anne A. Ghost Bear
Oklahoma State University

Gary J. Conti
Oklahoma State University

Abstract

While many people around the world enjoy using computers and the Internet, many more are excluded due to lack of access. This phenomenon is commonly known as the *digital divide*. The digital divide is a powerful force that threatens to continue dividing the world population into "haves" and "have nots." The divide can be bridged by the skillful application of adult learning principles if those who design and implement HRD programs understand how these principles apply to people in particular life situations with particular approaches to learning.

Millions of people are experiencing the benefits of increased access to computers and the Internet, but such access eludes vast numbers of people. This phenomenon is commonly referred to as the *digital divide*, which is the gap between those with access to computers and the Internet and those without it. Some see using advanced computer technology as a means to improve the lives of those who are marginalized and oppressed, while others view using computer technology as irrelevant, as long as issues of economic access go unaddressed (Holt, 1998). Information technology has "demonstrated the power to include and exclude, to assimilate and isolate" (p. 67). In the Information Age, new technology does not stand isolated, Rather, it is "linked to transformations in real groups of people's lives, jobs, hopes, and dreams" (Apple, 1991, p. 77). These transformations are enhanced by computer literacy efforts that may be as important as traditional literacy efforts. This "digital literacy" (Gilster, 1997, p. 31) concerns an "awareness of other people and our expanded ability to contact them to discuss issues and to get help" (p. 31) and an "awareness of the way the Internet blends older forms of communication to create a different kind of content" (p. 31).

U.S. access to technology

In early 1995 Vice President Al Gore commissioned the National Telecommunications and Information Administration (NTIA) to analyze telephone, computer, and Internet access in the United States. The NTIA's findings were reported in July 1995. They were later updated, and re-released in February 1998 (National Telecommunications and Information Administration, 1998). The NTIA report, which is cited more often than any other report addressing the digital divide, provided information about computer and Internet access based on geographic location, level of income, race, and educational level. The report described a divide in computer ownership in the United States by level of income, race, ethnicity, and level of education. The report found that

- People with higher incomes were more likely to own computers.
- White American households were more than twice as likely to own a computer as African American, Hispanic American, or Native American households.
- College-educated people were 10 times more likely to own a computer than those without a high school education.
- The NTIA reported findings that showed a marked lack of access to the Internet in various geographic, income, racial, and educational groups.
- Internet access for people in urban and inner cities was comparable, but people in rural areas were less likely to be on line.
- Households earning between $5,000 and $10,000 annually were almost 10 times less likely to have Internet access than households earning over $75,000 per year.
- Internet access of Anglo Americans was nearly three times greater than that of African Americans, Native Americans, or Hispanic Americans.
- People with college degrees were 20 times more likely to have access to the Internet than those without a high school education.

In general, the NTIA report showed educational level to be the basis for the most pronounced disparity in computer use and Internet access.

Global access to technology

People in many countries have low or no access to computer and Internet technology. While tens of millions of people in the United States have computer and Internet access, the number of people with access "is only in the thousands in most African countries" (Godlee, Horton, & Smith, 2000, p. 1129). An extensive report on computer and Internet access by the Organisation for Economic Co-operation and Development (OECD) revealed that North America and Europe have 89 percent of all Internet hosts worldwide, while Africa has less than one-half a percent. And its share of all Internet hosts is decreasing (OECD, 2001). Table 1 summarizes additional information from the report.

Other geographic areas have similar disparities in access. For example, in Saudi Arabia, Internet service providers have been in operation only since 1998, and a mere 1.4 percent of the population has access to the Internet (Hill, 2000, p. xxii). In India, the proportion of on-line users is even lower at 0.5 percent (p. xxii).

Table 1. Global Computer and Internet Access

Internet Hosts in 2000 (per 1000 inhabitants)			
United States	Europe	Central/South America	Africa
168.8	20.22	2.53	.31

Personal Computer Penetration by Household Income				
	Australia	France	Japan	Netherlands
Low-Income Households	32%	10%	13%	20%
High-Income Households	69%	72%	68%	99%

Personal Computer and Internet Penetration by Ethnic Group				
	Pacific Islander/Asian American	White	Hispanic	Black
Computer Penetration	65%	58%	35%	34%
Internet Access	56%	46%	23%	23%

As with the NTIA report, the OECD (2001) report showed differences by age (younger people have more access than older people) and by gender (men have more access than women). However, the most pronounced disparity in computer use and Internet access was based on educational level. Among people with the same income level, "those with higher educational attainment will have higher rates of access" (OECD, 2001, p. 19).

The digital divide

When 65 percent of the world's population have never used a telephone and 40 percent have no electricity, the divide takes on a more cataclysmic breadth (Rifkin, 2000). This digital divide is more startling than any other injustice of health or income (Godlee, Horton, & Smith, 2000). The worldwide economy continues to be plagued by great disparities where "over 10 percent of the people living in rich countries are still below the poverty line" (Brown, et al., 2001, p.7). Over 10 percent of people worldwide are homeless or live in unsanitary or unsafe housing. These

The most pronounced disparity in computer use and Internet access was based on educational level.

people are at risk of being pushed even farther behind as those with computer and Internet access communicate with each other, build common commercial and social networks, and leave the less fortunate isolated (Rifkin, 2000).

Could the digital divide be eliminated by providing universal access to computers and the Internet? Unfortunately, the availability of hardware and software is only one barrier to full participation in the digital society. In his chapter, "HR to the Power of ^{e}: Internet-Powered Transformation of Human Resources," Christie discusses how human resource managers are using IT to empower their constituents. Employees can use the technology to obtain information and can participate in updating their personal information. The evolution in HR through the information, automation, and transformation stages will give new power to employees and their managers. Christie discussed the need for employees to have access to Intranet-connected computers. Employees also need the requisite knowledge, skills, and capabilities to search, access, and process information on line.

The many barriers to participating in the new technology include the lack of pertinent local information, literacy and language, and cultural diversity (Revenaugh, 2000). Those individuals thus barred are being forced farther to the edges of society because of their inability to access telecommunications technology (Apple, 1991; Kornblum & Julian, 1995; Rifkin, 2000; Schiller, 1999).

The phenomenon of the digital divide has tremendous implications for all educators, and it places special burdens on the professionals who are responsible for human resource development (HRD). HRD managers must assess the degree to which the digital divide affects their organizations and take steps to address it. In the chapter titled "Building a Competitive Workforce for the New Economy," Meeder and Cude present a model that addresses the need for ongoing education and development of the current and future workforce. Their model describes collaboration among business, education, employee organizations, and policy makers. HRD managers who are sensitive to the digital divide as it affects their international partners, employees, and customers can take actions to include disadvantaged segments of the workforce and the customer base. The findings from a recent study of learning on the Internet suggest factors that could influence the actions of HRD managers as they seek to implement new technologies.

Learning on the Internet

A study (Ghost Bear, 2001) that investigated how adults learn when they are engaged in the auction process on eBay confirmed the existence of the digital divide in electronic commerce. The digital divide was revealed in the data about who accessed the eBay Website and how they went about learning when they were on the Internet.

Background

EBay, which is an Internet Web site that sponsors auctions for its members, was born on Labor Day 1995. EBay's popularity has since grown swiftly, to where it is the world's largest person-to-person on-line trading community (http://www. ebay.com). By October 2000, there were more than 12 million registered users on eBay's Website (http://www.ebay.com). The present user population is roughly the same size as the population of Illinois (http://census.gov/population), more than the population of Cuba, and more than the populations of Singapore and Switzerland combined (http://www.population.com). In January 2000 the average daily number of visitors to eBay's Website set a new Internet record of 1.782 million (http://www.ebay.com). Each day, 6.5 percent of all Internet users across the world visit eBay's Website to buy, sell, browse, or chat with other members (http://www.ebay.com).

Thus, it is clear that a large number of adults around the world have learned how to access eBay's Website and how to participate in its interactive features. Who are these learners and how did they voluntarily go about this real-world, self-directed learning process?

Research questions

The study posed the following research questions:

- What are the demographic characteristics of eBay users?
- What are the identified learning strategy preferences of adult learners using eBay?
- How do adult learners describe their learning experiences related to the eBay auction process?
- How do they feel about their computer skills and self-confidence as a result of participating in the eBay auction process?

Method

Rather than use traditional forms of data collection, this study used the Internet to collect data about how adults learn. eBay posts the results of each auction after the auction is completed. This information includes a list of all the people who bid on an item, along with their eBay user-identification names. These names are linked to the users' e-mail addresses and their histories with eBay. A representative sample of 380 eBay users was identified by electronically downloading the e-mail addresses of auction participants who completed sales between August 15, 1999, and January 30, 2000. The auction data were stratified according to the 12 categories of eBay. During the sample-identification process, eBay added a new category, which was included in the study. Several subgroups exist within each category. A single subgroup with a high volume of auctions was selected from each category for the study. Within that subgroup, high-volume auctions were selected in which the final sale price of the item was under $10, between $11 and $100, and over $100. These price ranges were selected to ensure that the data would reflect the fact that eBay's auctions were accessible to people of various income levels.

Each participant's e-mail address was captured electronically from the public domain areas of the eBay Website and used to solicit participation in the study. The consenting participants clicked on the Internet address in the e-mail message, which took them directly to the questionnaire. They typed their responses into scroll boxes that permitted entering as much information as they desired. Submitted forms were sent to the researchers in an e-mail message. For purposes of analysis, each response was tagged with the participant's learning strategy and demographic information.

Findings: Demographic characteristics

The sample of 380 participants approximated the 384 required for a statistical 95 percent confidence level in a study with a population the size of eBay's on-line membership (Mitchell & Jolley, 1988, p. 302). Fifteen responses were received from eight countries in addition to the United States: Australia (2), Canada (6), Germany (2), Denmark (1), Finland (1), Mexico (1), Russia (1), and United Kingdom (1). Table 2 shows ethnic groups, gender, education level, and type of Internet service provider for the respondents.

Table 2: EBay Study: Demographic Characteristics

Ethnic Groups		
	White	93.3%
	Hispanic	1.7%
	Asian	1.0%
	Native American	1.0%
	African	3.0%
	Other	7.0%
Gender		
	Male	50.1%
	Female	49.9%
Education		
	No high school diploma	1.4%
	High school diploma	23.0%
	Post-secondary degree/certificate	20.0%
	Bachelor's degree	30.5%
	Graduate degree	25.1%
ISP Type		
	.com	58.7%
	.net	34.5%
	.edu	3.6%
	.org	1.5%
	.us	1.5%
	.gov	0.3%

As shown in the table, the demographic profiles of the participants in this study were that of the "haves." These findings support the issues of access revealed in digital-divide statistics. Although the sample was balanced in gender, the participants were much better educated than the general population of either the United States or the world. The sample in the eBay study was overwhelmingly White. As with digital divide statistics, almost all of the study participants were from the United States. Because so much of the traffic on the Internet accesses the eBay site and because the sampling procedures for this study were congruent with both established research practices and the real-life operation of eBay, it can be assumed that these demographic findings are representative of the users of eBay. As such, they confirm that the digital divide should concern not only societies, but also organizations. HRD professionals who plan to use technology must deal with this fact.

Findings: Learning differences on the Internet

This study found that the respondents used various learning strategies while on eBay. As part of the study, the participants completed an instrument called Assessing The Learning Strategies of AdultS (ATLAS). This instrument is a valid means of identifying a person's learning strategy preferences (Conti & Kolody, 1999). Learning strategies are "the techniques or skills that an individual elects to use in order to accomplish a learning task" (Fellenz & Conti, 1989, p. 7).

ATLAS places learners in the categories of Navigators, Problem Solvers, or Engagers (Conti & Kolody, 1999). Navigators are "focused learners who chart a course for learning and follow it" (p. 9). They are high achievers who tend to concentrate on external learning processes. Problem Solvers rely heavily on strategies that are associated with the process of critical thinking. They "rely on a reflective thinking process which utilizes higher order thinking skills" (p. 11). Engagers are "passionate learners who love to learn, learn with feeling, and learn best when they are actively engaged in a meaningful manner" (p. 13). They thrive on the learning process and the enjoyment gained while interacting with other people. Table 3 depicts the learning strategy, source of motivation, preferred learning environment, descriptive learning phrase, and descriptive name for the three learning categories. It also shows the distribution of respondents in this study.

The findings of this study revealed that a disproportionately large number of Problem Solvers use eBay (χ^2=30.3, $\underline{df}$=2, $\underline{p}$=.001). This finding is of interest because the three learning preference groups identified by

ATLAS exist in nearly equal portions in the general adult population and because such demographic variables as age and gender are not good predictors of learning strategy preferences (Gallagher, 1998). However, recent ATLAS studies have determined that the nature of the organization tends to attract a certain type of learner (Goodwin, 2001; James, 2000; Massey, 2001; Willyard, 2000). This finding is consistent with Spencer's (2000) study of self-directed learners on the Internet.

Table 3: ATLAS Groups

	Navigators	Problem Solvers	Engagers
Learning strategies used	Planning; attention; identification; critical use of resources	Critical thinking; testing assumptions; generating alternatives; conditional acceptance	Confidence; reward/enjoyment; memory application
Source of motivation	External	External	Internal
Preferred learning environment	Orderly; structured; efficient	Experimentation; hands-on activities	Actively engaged with other people
Descriptive learning phrase	Plan the work and work the plan	Ask them what time it is, and they will build you a clock	It's fun!
Descriptive Name	Strivers	Storytellers	Stimulants
Distribution of participants in the study	28.5%	45.2%	26.3%

Source: Conti & Kolody, 1999; Ghost Bear, 2001

To uncover how people learned about eBay once they had accessed the Internet, we asked the participants in this study a series of open-ended questions related to their learning. It is interesting to note that each category of participants had a unique approach to answering the questions and distinctive responses. Table 4 summarizes the differences found among users based on their learning categories.

In summary, eBay users approached learning tasks differently based upon their learning strategies. These differences are reflected in (a) cognitive processes in approaching the task, (b) language and concepts in describing the task, and (c) motivations and desires related to the task. Even when individuals used a similar approach, such as in their bidding strategy, they went about it differently. The examination of learning strategies in this study revealed marked differences in initial learning patterns and in the descriptive language used by Navigators, Problem Solvers, and Engagers.

Table 4: Differences among Navigators', Problem Solvers', and Engagers' responses to survey questions

	Navigators	Problem Solvers	Engagers
General approaches to answering the survey questions	Bulleted answers or lists	Lengthy, detailed answers	Emotional, brief answers
How they learned about eBay	Advertisements, other collectors	Co-workers, Internet activities	Friends
How they opened an account	Search engine	Combination of techniques with examples	Began bidding
How they learned about eBay Web site	Personal logic	Combination of sources; trial-and-error method	Search engine
How they described a typical eBay session	Predetermined plan	Variety of techniques; detailed methods	Current auction sites
How they learned about the items to be auctioned	External references	Personal knowledge; detailed examples	Item descriptions/ pictures; other people
How they learned about other eBay members	Used feedback forum	Combination; detailed methods	Intuition
How they learned about other aspects	eBay Web site; item descriptions	Combination; detailed methods	Declined to answer; used other people

Source: Ghost Bear, 2001

Implications for HRD programs

The integration of new technologies, such as the Internet, in HRD programs is a necessity if organizations wish to remain competitive. Incorporating the findings of adult learning research related to individual differences and learning strategy preferences can increase the effectiveness of internal and external HRD programs. These findings can be a means for bridging the differences among learners and the differences that result from the digital divide.

Technology has changed the work environment. More information is processed than ever before and with greater speed. The barriers of distance and time have evaporated. Work sites have multiplied. And making global contacts during the workday is commonplace for many employees. In this atmosphere, it is easy for those who have become accustomed to using the technology to forget the difficulties they may have experienced or the anxieties they may have felt when they first learned to use IT applications. HRD managers must be aware of the intimidation factor and the digital divide when dealing with learners and others inside and outside the organization.

The findings of this research that profiled the users of eBay are consistent with the findings of earlier surveys that uncovered the digital divide, and they further demonstrates its breadth. As HRD managers seek to extend training and organization communications through distance education or on-line information services, they must be keenly aware that they may be reaching out to a narrow population. The users who are able to access their services may be only those who are privileged to have higher education and the disposable income to purchase the necessary equipment and Internet connections. HRD managers are challenged to test their assumptions concerning the users of a technology before they initiate activities that are dependent upon it. For example, it is easy to assume, incorrectly, that a technology, such as e-mail, is pervasive. Likewise, it is easy to assume that some potential participants are laggards in adopting a new technology (Houle, 1980), when in reality they lack access to it or they need a support structure or handholding while they learn to use it (Solomon, 2000).

Because the United States is the center of much current technological development and implementation, HRD managers in the U.S. may easily

Organizations in the Information Age can succeed by facilitating learning and interaction among all their partners, employees, and customers.

forget about user's needs and the conditions in other countries. For example, one Australian respondent in the eBay study complained about the difficulty of participating in eBay's auction process because auction times are pegged to behavior patterns in the U.S., the auctions are conducted in U.S. dollars, and the exchange of sold items and payments is dependent upon having a reliable mail service. All of these factors make it difficult for many users in countries outside of the U.S. to participate in the auction process.

While issues of language, culture, and currency may be too complex for the current technology or their solutions too expensive to develop and implement, raising awareness of the diversity of user needs around the globe is an inexpensive tool that could yield high benefits. HRD managers in the U.S. who are aware of these factors can identify if and how such factors affect their organizations' global interactions. They can then take actions to improve the situation. HRD managers who are unaware of learning diversity and global differences may cause their organizations to project an image of arrogance and unconcern that further contributes to the digital divide.

Programs internal to organizations that use new technology or teach about it may also be affected by factors related to the digital divide. Employees may lack access to the technology at their work sites, and many may lack access to it at home. Furthermore, they may not have the resources to purchase the technology and thus become more familiar with it (Solomon, 2000). In addition, all learners may not be equally receptive to using the new technology. The task of generating alternatives and exploring options on the Internet may appeal to Problem Solvers (Ghost Bear, 2001; Spencer, 2000), may frustrate Navigators, and may intimidate Engagers. These factors should be taken into consideration before implementing training related to using the technology. Navigators could feel disgruntled with the lack of opportunities to strive for excellence. Problem Solvers could feel annoyed with the lack of opportunities to explore. Engagers could feel dissatisfied with the limited opportunities for meaningful interaction with others and enjoyment while learning. These difficulties can be avoided by structuring programs to meet the needs of various learners. Given a learner-centered approach, the emphasis will be placed upon the process of learning how to learn (Smith, 1982) so that learners will be better able to effectively apply the technology in real-world conditions, and they will also be better prepared to learn other technologies in the future when the current technology is inevitably replaced.

Conclusion

The Information Age is bringing people throughout the world together in ways they never imagined. "Now, in the ever more complex world, we need to accept and apply this basic truth: that we are all in this together, like a family, interconnected and interdependent" (Cuomo, 1995, p. 12). People half way around the globe can be as close as next door neighbors with the click of a mouse on a computer with Internet access. However, as Taulbert poignantly captures in the chapter titled "Touch & Technology: The Look of Sensory Contact in the New Millennium," the same technologies that have the power to bring people together have the potential to isolate people from each other. The digital divide is a powerful force that threatens to continue dividing the world into "haves" and "have nots." The digital divide can be bridged by the skillful application of adult learning principles, especially if those who design and implement HRD programs understand how these principles apply to people in particular life situations with particular approaches to learning. When HRD managers enter collaborations with international partners, employees, and customers, they must consider how to overcome the issues of computer and Internet access. When they do, they will be able to welcome and include vast numbers of people who previously may have been excluded.

HRD managers can learn from the models provided by eBay and other on-line enterprises how different types of learners adapt and successfully use the required on-line tools. Imagine the costs if eBay were obliged to provide formal training on how to access its auctions for each of its 12 million users. This study demonstrates that self-evident applications can replace traditional training programs. To be most effective, applications should address the learning strategies of Navigators, Problem Solvers, and Engagers. Skillfully designed computer applications will encourage self-directed learning and will avoid the traditional training costs associated with teaching employees and customers how to use on-line applications.

Organizations in the Information Age can better succeed by facilitating learning and interaction among *all* their partners, employees, and customers. Skilled HRD managers are crucial in achieving this success!

References

Apple, M. W. (1991). The new technology: Is it part of the solution or part of the problem in education? *Computers in the Schools, 8*, 59-81.

Brown, et al., (2001). *State of the world 2001*. New York: W. W. Norton & Company.

Conti, G. J. & Kolody, R. C. (1999). *Guide for using ATLAS*. Stillwater, OK: Oklahoma State University.

Cuomo, M. (1995). *Reason to believe*. New York: Simon & Schuster.

Fellenz, R. A., & Conti, G. J. (1989). *Learning and reality: Reflections on trends in adult learning*. Columbus: The Ohio State University (ERIC Clearinghouse on Adult, Career, and Vocational Training, Information Series No. 336).

Ghost Bear, A. A. (2001). *Adult learning on the Internet: Engaging the eBay auction process*. Unpublished doctoral dissertation. Stillwater, OK: Oklahoma State University.

Gilster, P. (1997). *Digital literacy*. New York: John Wiley & Sons.

Godlee, F., Horton, R., & Smith, R. (2000). *Lancet, 356*(9236), 1129-30.

Goodwin, S. K. (2001). *Learning strategies in the workplace to create effective employees*. Unpublished doctoral dissertation. Stillwater, OK: Oklahoma State University.

Harris Interactive (2000). The Harris Poll #60. October 11, 2000. *Internet Access continues to grow but at a slower pace*. Available: http://harrisinteractive.com. Retrieved from the World Wide Web October 24, 2000.

Hill, S. (2000, July 10). The global view. *New Statesman*, xxii-xxiii.

Hoffman, D. L. & Novak, T. P. (1998). *Bridging the digital divide: The impact of race on computer access and Internet use*. (Eric Document Reproduction Service, ED No. 421 563).

Holt, M. E. (1998). Ethical considerations in Internet-based adult education. In B. Cahoon (Ed.), *Adult learning and the Internet. New Directions for Adult and Continuing Education*, p. 70. San Francisco, CA: Jossey-Bass.

Houle, C. O. (1980). *Continuing learning in the professions*. San Francisco: Jossey-Bass.

James, C. B. (2000). *Learning strategy preferences of high school noncompleters*. Unpublished doctoral dissertation. Stillwater, OK: Oklahoma State University.

Kornblum, W. & Julian, J. (1995). *Social problems* (8th ed.). Englewood Cliffs, NJ: Prentice Hall.

Massey, S. M. (2001). *Learning styles and learning strategies of OSU-Okmulgee Students*. Unpublished doctoral dissertation. Stillwater, OK: Oklahoma State University.

Mitchell, M. & Jolley, J. (1988). *Research design explained*. New York: Holt, Rinehart, and Winston.

National Telecommunications and Information Administration (1998). *Falling through the Net II: New data on the digital divide*. (ERIC Document Reproduction Service No. ED 421 968).

Organisation for Economic Co-operation and Development (2001). *Understanding the Digital Divide*. (www.occd.org).

Revenaugh, M.(2000). Beyond the digital divide: Pathways to equity. *Technology and Learning, 20*(10), 38-44.

Rifkin, J. (2000). *The age of access: The new culture of hypercapitalism where all of life is a paid-for experience*. New York: Tarcher/Putnam.

Smith, R. M. (1982). *Learning how to learn: Applied theory for adults*. Great Britain: Open University Press.

Smith, R. M. (1991). How people become effective learners. *Adult Learning, 2*(6), 11-13.

Spencer, R. G.(2000). *Self-directed learning on the Information Superhighway*. Unpublished doctoral dissertation. Stillwater, OK: Oklahoma State University.

Solomon, B. S.(2000). *Computer assisted technology transfer: Understanding technology diffusion in Oklahoma small-to-medium sized manufacturers*. Unpublished doctoral dissertation. Stillwater, OK: Oklahoma State University.

Willyard, P. (2000). *Learning strategies of first-generation community college students*. Unpublished doctoral dissertation. Stillwater, OK: Oklahoma State University.

TOUCH & TECHNOLOGY

The Look of Sensory Contact in the New Millennium

Clifton L. Taulbert
Author of "Eight Habits of the Heart"

The 21st Century emerges as a time of great paradoxes, which are driven by the presence of new technologies in our workplace. Because of the efficiency, speed, and accuracy that are achievable with these new technologies, the people in our workplaces are having to pause and refocus on the role of building community—a set of emotionally satisfying relationships.

Can building community be a high priority in a world that is now being defined by bits, bytes, and Pentium chips? The question looms as we realize that many of our modern conveniences are making our workplace lives more complicated and more cluttered. Cell phones bring quicker communication more often, but fewer face-to-face interactions. Our ever present access to others through cell phones, pagers, palm pilots and other time-saving gadgets is giving us less time to be reflective, all the while increasing our stress and our need to be quicker and faster. Where are the people in our workplaces? We hear their voices. We get their faxes. We are overrun by their e-mails. But where are the real people we used to know? As technology continues to advance, we are slowly being romanced away from *touch* and its importance to business profit and personal fulfillment. The lure of technology as a workplace panacea is all but overwhelming. Today's speed of communication is modeled after the launching of rockets into space. On the receiving end, we have been hit so quickly from all sides that we are ready to turn over our workplace lives to the technological wonders of the modern world.

While our organizations are quick to embrace the new technology, many of us in the workplaces are unable to speak the required language. Hard, cold, and loaded with blinking lights, technology requires conversation, but not the conversation of laughter and relationships that has always been the basis for getting things done at work. Technology, the new wonder, is logical. It only needs the information that its designers have specified—no more, no less. Thus, in time, a new breed of interveners was born: women and men who not only know technology's strange language, but also understand its temperament. Together, they promise us that this new space-age technology will reshape our business strategy and take us where no workplace has gone before. Like them, we too can learn to "beam" the world down to our desktops quicker and more accurately than ever.

All around us, the technology of the last years of the 20th Century will continue to play a major role in achieving outcomes in our personal and professional lives, but at what price? The Aristotle-like thinkers of our time have observed that our amassing of technical skills has left us hungry for the *touch* we used to know. We are hungry for community. Our conversations around the water cooler and in the car pool on the way home, when the technology experts are not listening, tend to highlight our need for human touch. "We work right down the hall from you, but we haven't seen you in days." "I didn't know your son received a scholarship to Harvard." "I should have asked you about the report we did together last year. It would have made writing this report so much easier." It seems that at the end of the day we still need the *touch* of others to feel respected, affirmed, and included.

Marla Donata (1999), a Chicago Tribune staff writer, compared technology to a cancer that is consuming our humanity with sense-dulling conveniences: "The very things that are supposed to simplify our lives and allow us to stay in touch with each other are putting us further out of reach with sense-dulling 'conveniences.' Just what good is all this easy living if you remove sensory contact?" (p. B1). In the midst of the technological revolution, we are challenged to keep in mind and to value our personal role in building community. We are the practical antidote to a potentially all-consuming technological cancer. During the initial euphoria brought by the new frontier, it seemed that many of us were willing to abdicate the role of personal involvement and rely on the information generated by technology. The convenience of the mouse and the mouse pad was slowly replacing "handshakes and thank-yous."

We are challenged to remember that the complement of technology's value is community. Both technology and community are needed and, from my perspective, they both can co-exist. Just as gravel roads and super highways need the sound and the presence of wheels, so does the Information Superhighway of the 21st Century need the sound and the presence of human communication. The Information Superhighway has little or no value without human relationships, which are best sustained when community—a set of emotionally satisfying relationships—is cultivated and maintained. If our focus is totally on the outcomes of science and technology, how will we account for the maintenance of emotional relationships in the new millennium?

A brief detour from the Information Superhighway

With your permission, I would like you to join me in taking a detour from the Information Superhighway to visit another place and another time where "specialists" were needed to build, maintain, and sustain community against great odds. Building community was their high-technology activity, their total focus. In that time and place, they raised *touch* to an art form of immense proportions. Oh, I know that for many of you, Silicon Valley and its counterparts throughout the world are the places where the future lives and where the past pays homage. However, there are other places where the past continues to provide for the future, where the timeless and universal ideals needed to build relationships and to sustain them can be located. The builders I speak of used materials that were not held captive by race, gender, or geography. These builders of community used the "Eight Habits of the Heart": Nurturing Attitude, Responsibility, Dependability, Friendship, Brotherhood, High Expectations, Courage, and Hope (Taulbert, 1997).

You will not need your computer or your palm pilot on this detour, just your observant attention.

৶ ৶ ৶

Though my professional journey has taken me around the world, I know this place best, Glen Allan, Mississippi. My hometown was a small agrarian community in the heart of the Mississippi Delta. I grew up in and experienced the benefits of building community during the final days of legal segregation, which was an obvious and very real obstacle to that activity. My elders, however, ignored the reality of segregation and focused on building the relationships that continue to nourish my life. It is the nourishment of unselfish acts that keeps people at the center of my living. While you are on the detour with me, you will meet the people who became the "Eight Habits of the Heart" and validated the role of *touch* in our community. Their actions reveal the timeless and universal look and feel of what is needed to address the challenge of attending to the people within our workplace lives.

Forget your computer chip and the great speed of your technology, both of which may be required to maximize a technical strategy. To attend to the needs of people, we must slow our pace and get to know them. Slowing our pace to really know those who share our workplaces is the first rule of building and maintaining community in our lives. I first saw this attention to people lived out by my great-grandfather, who in his 1949 Buick would take 2½ hours to make a 28-mile trip. Poppa stopped to visit with the families who were seated on their front porches. We might not need to "slow down" to build and improve our technologies, but we must slow down if we are to build relationships with people. We call this Habit of the Heart, Nurturing Attitude. Within our workplaces, Nurturing Attitude means being supportive of others, being willing to share one's time, and caring unselfishly. Dilbert reminded us of this need, when he overheard it at the water fountain.

Once we have slowed our lives enough to nurture and build relationships, we are apt to demonstrate to others our personal commitment to task. Cleve Morman, the ice man of Glen Allan, was the embodiment of commitment to task. He took the time to show me personally how he tackled the task of cutting a 300-pound block of ice into the desired sizes. His total involvement in the task and in instructing me had outcomes for me that an e-mailed message of instruction could never have. We call this Habit, Responsibility. We cannot build solid relationships without it.

The next Habit of the Heart is called Dependability. It too is essential to building relationships, and it does not stand alone. Not so surprising, Dependability is more than a mere word or the habit we chide others for not having. It is a person. I remember seeing Dependability standing on the front porch of a frame house in the Mississippi Delta every school day for four years. Dependability was my great aunt, who raised me. On her front porch wearing a flannel gown, her hair tightly tucked under a head rag, my great aunt every day for four consecutive years pulled the light string so that Mr. Murray, the bus driver, would know that I was indeed going to school that day. Legal segregation required that I travel 100 miles round trip to school each day. I never missed a day of school and graduated valedictorian of my class. This positive outcome happened for me because of the *touch* of her dependable unselfishness. Our workplaces and our lives are better lived in the presence of Dependability. Rob Lebow (1990) defined what he called "people values." He reviewed thousands of tests given to employees in many types of organizations over a long period of time and found the eight values that people most often seek. One of Lebow's eight values is actually an inside look at Dependability, putting the interests of others above one's own. Unselfishness cannot be e-mailed. Dependability is required to balance the depersonalization in our workplaces brought on by advancing technology.

Ensuring community within our workplaces will not happen without the presence of the next Habit of the Heart, Friendship. I often ask workshop participants to travel mentally with me to a discount store, where some version of everything we need is in stock. After I have the participants emotionally walking down the aisles, I ask them to put in their baskets at least one gallon of Friendship. We all laugh because Friendship cannot be found as an item to purchase, store, and dispense at will. Friendship does not exist apart from our efforts to give it life. When we become this Habit of the Heart by our relationship acts in our workplaces, we encourage the *touch* that I recall. In Glen Allen, Friendship looked like the people who prepared for the annual visit of Blind Birta. Blind Birta came to town to experience life and laughter on the front porches of the Mississippi Delta. Her friends anticipated her coming. They made room for her, cut her meat, and shared their lives. Their Friendship became her vision. Anticipation and vision are key components of ensuring sensory contact in all the places of our lives. Anticipating the needs of others becomes easier as we get to know them, their names, their responsibilities, and their visions. When we anticipate the needs of others and provide the assistance they will need, we extend their vision. We create the dynamics from which the *touch* of Friendship will emerge.

When segregation was the law of the land, to reach beyond being comfortable, to extend a welcome to people different from oneself, was a challenging opportunity. Building relationships in the age of technology requires the same of us now. Though technology and science have opened up the world, we are still challenged to live beyond earlier learning that

My computer requires no accolades, no lunches, and no notes of thanks. But I do.

could preclude our taking advantage of universal opportunities to reach out to others. I know that we can reach beyond comfortable, having seen it lived out in the Mississippi Delta. Reaching beyond comfortable is much easier to do now, but no less challenging. As a kid who raked fig leaves for an older white lady, I benefited by the actions of someone who reached beyond comfortable and 'stretched her table' for me. We ate together in her home at a time when it was socially unacceptable. We call this Habit of the Heart Brotherhood. We were together in our workplace where we each had a job to do, and the unselfish act of stretching her dining room table became the reality of a *touch* I experienced yesterday that still affects me today.

My computer requires no accolades, no lunches, and no notes of thanks. But I do. Most of us will do our jobs better when we feel appreciated and are expected to do well. Yes, I enjoy the messages of encouragement that I can download to my computer on a moment's notice, but I still need to hear the voices of those with whom I share my life telling me that they believe in me, expect me to do well, and admire my accomplishments. In Glen Allen, this *touch* was called High Expectations...and it looked like many of the people I knew. In Glen Allen, people saw their visions for life extended through us, their children, grandchildren, and great-grand children. The voice of the old, stuttering man who lived in a small shotgun house in Issaquena County was this Habit of the Heart for many of us. Through his stutters, he told us boys —we were shooting marbles, the computer game of my time—that he had read all about us and in spite of what anyone thought, he knew that we were marked for good. He had read the books that showed the growth and strength of the "colored" communities. In our workplaces, it is important that we do not abdicate to the daily routines of getting the job done our role in giving voice to High Expectations.

Surrounded by the latest in high tech gear, it almost seems as though a note written with a pen will become like a painting on the wall of a cave, an art form to discover and ponder. In this century, when the paradoxes of modern conveniences do not support building relationships, it takes Courage, the next Habit of the Heart to bring into our workplaces proven acts of unselfishness. Courage is not an abstraction. It takes a person to stand up and do what is right, to speak out on behalf of others, and to do so even in the absence of support. Courage always involves risk. Courage rewards not only those who practice it, but those who witness it. I saw an overlooked people struggle courageously against the reach of segregation into their lives. Their daily Courage and unselfish acts wounded the tentacles of legal segregation and limited its reach. Our 21st Century workplaces will need this same Courage on a daily basis.

Slowing down and taking the time to get to know people gives us the opportunity to become the last Habit of the Heart, Hope. We can plan strategically for tomorrow because we see where we are today and we can extrapolate into the future. When we reflect on snapshots of the relationships we have made and the projects we have completed, we see a tomorrow that goes beyond today because of what we believe in our hearts. When I was growing up in the 50s and 60s, life really was an unwritten plan lived out in the presence of the children. It was "fessor White" teaching my parent's generation as if the whole world could hardly wait to embrace their achievements, when in fact their mental capacity was a matter of intellectual debate. Hope as it was personified by "fessor White," looked beyond that real-world challenge because of what he believed in his heart. When we bring the Habit of Hope into our workplaces, we ensure the quality of life that will drive the success of the people and the organization.

ન્હ ન્હ ન્હ

You may not have expected to take a detour to the American South to find life lessons. Thank you for coming with me. Now, you might ask how these life lessons can be applied in today's organizations.

New forms of mass communication based on advancing technology will bring either widespread alienation or closer integration among human beings. Without question, they will alienate if we abdicate our community-building opportunities. Without question, they can connect us to the world. To build a real community, we must sustain connection through human interaction. And no one is more aware of both alienation and connection than are we in our own workplaces. We have sensed a movement away from the norm of community. However, we know that norms are continually being established, and we are smart enough to question the direction of the change and provide our input.

In our workplaces we are driven by the requirements and the rewards associated with contributing to the organization and to the strategic plan, which often specifies technology as essential. Driven by the plan and by 21st Century technologies, the requirement to build in *touch* seems to have lost ground. However, we must not accept the current status. Instead, we must act to build community. Our workplaces will be more productive as a result.

Strategies for building communities

I want to share with you some data from ten of our national Building Community Workshops, several of which were held in Europe and in Central America. These workshops are guided by the Eight Habits of the Heart. They include activities that allow participants to reflect on what is required to build community in their ideal workplaces and to leave their voices as proof of their support. Over 1000 participants have written responses to the following survey question: *In order to ensure a productive work environment, list at least (5) unselfish acts that you'd like to see on a daily basis from your executive management team, immediate supervisor, and fellow employees and from department to department.* Nearly 100% of the responses indicated the need to put into place practices that focus on building sensory contact. Workshop participants have ranged from scientists to engineers to military leaders to educators and non-profit professionals. Though they hailed from different professional backgrounds, their responses to the question were similar. These 21st Century professionals understood and embraced the value of technology in their lives and in their work. They also recognized that in their workplaces, they were missing the empowerment that comes, not from technology, but from the human touch.

A community of touch does not happen automatically. It is totally dependent upon the unselfish commitment of those with whom we share our lives. In contrast to the materials required to build missile systems, wireless communication empires, and the Information Superhighway, the materials needed to build *touch* do not require extensive strategizing and research. The materials of *touch* are easily found and quickly applied, but they require daily attention by us in our workplaces. The following wisdom was abstracted from the responses of the managers of a science and technology Fortune 500 company. We sorted their answers into four broad strategies for building a community of *touch* in their workplaces:

I.   Manage visible moments: Be on site and be seen

    Talk to us in person, rather than by e-mail
    Get out of the office, visit employees
    Walk around, informal one-on-ones
    Walk around, get to know your employees
    Join us for lunch in the cafeteria
    Personally attend lower level staff meetings
    Walk the floor and talk to day-to-day workers

II. Value employees at all levels

    Know people's names and roles
    Praise at all levels—drop dual standards
    Ask if I have questions and listen
    Take a chance and act on our suggestions
    Spend time in the workplace, observe working conditions
    Say "Good Morning, Hello" when walking the halls
    Provide better means of communication with lower level employees

III. Provide personal touch in the professional environment

    Meet face-to-face on an unexpected basis
    Get together outside the workplace
    Learn about our personal lives
    Make eye contact with employees
    Have lunchtime opportunities for team growth through sharing
    Keep an open-door policy
    Make time to walk the halls and listen more passionately
    Create less e-mail
    Take time to work with people, and do not just assign work

IV. Model the values

Be a better listener
Do not show favoritism
Provide more honest communication
Always ask, "Can I help?"
Ignore the telephone when I am in your office
Respond truthfully to questions
Do not tolerate intimidating behavior
Provide positive greetings with a smile
Compliment each other on a job well done
Allow others to speak their minds

Based on the reflections of these manager-professionals, we have a practical picture of what is required of people who will build the desired workplaces where sensory touch is not abandoned. The euphoric notion that technology is an elixir for the workplace has had its moment. Technology will not determine our destiny, nor will it be allowed to run unbridled. Technology must be used to help build community. Participant responses in our workshop have given us a definite look at sensory contact and at the important role of the "Eight Habits of the Heart" in empowering us to create workplaces where *touch* and *technology* are of equal value. In the Mississippi Delta, I observed the gardeners (the professionals) as they threw their care and concern (their commitment to community) across fences while at the same time they raised a good stand of vegetables (their jobs). We can follow their lead. We can build technologically advanced 21st Century workplaces. At the same time, we can throw our care and concern across our professional fences.

References

Donata, M. (1999, January 17). Technology is consuming our humanity. (Albany, NY) *Times Union*, p. B1.

Lebow, R. (1990). *A journey into the heroic environment: 8 principles that lead to greater productivity, quality, job satisfaction, and profits*. Rocklin, CA: Prima Publications.

Taulbert, C. (1997). *Eight habits of the heart*. New York: Penguin Books.

REFLECTING ON OUR JOURNEY THROUGH HRD IN THE E-WORKPLACE

Catherine M. Sleezer
Oklahoma State University

Linda K. Lawson
Williams Companies

Roger L. Cude
McLeod USA

Tim L. Wentling
University of Illinois

> *Oh, the Places we've gone!*
> *—Adapted from Dr. Seuss*

We used the metaphor of safari to describe our journey to discover how individuals, teams, and organizations integrate information technology applications in the e-workplace. We invited experts from various disciplines to join us on the journey, expecting that cross-disciplinary collaboration would help us discover cutting-edge thinking and practice. As it turned out, we underestimated the insights we would gain by roaming the e-workplace terrain in the company of these experts.

To begin our safari, the experts produced papers that depicted their unique knowledge of the territory. The ensuing dialogue among the travelers benefited from their collective acumen, their wealth of practical experiences, and their in-depth understanding of research. En route, we reviewed and revised the papers to capture insights that we could not have imagined when we set out to explore the territory. We've likened the resulting chapters to expert snapshots of our safari through the e-workplace. In this final chapter we summarize our collective insights and suggest topics for future exploration.

Insights

The ecosystems that we observed on this safari proved fascinating. We learned that the IT applications that change work processes, customer and employee relationships, and organizational structures are ubiquitous. Everywhere we looked, we saw examples of people using IT applications to connect information and people and to create communities.

Along the way we observed that the networked world is comprised of many local "ecologies." Ghost Bear and Conti and Meeder and Cude revealed the uneven distribution of network connections and IT applications across geographic areas. Some areas have many strong links. Others have few weak links. Lawson and Sleezer, Christie, and Van Buren highlighted the great diversity of IT applications within organizations.

We learned that IT decisions are shaped by human visions, needs, and relationships. We learned that any attempt to understand what is happening in the e-workplace by looking at IT applications alone can be misleading. Rather, IT applications can best be understood within individual, group, and organizational contexts.

We gained insights by comparing our observations to traditional Human Resource Development (HRD) models. HRD professionals generally apply concepts from such disciplines as training, management, organization development, and human performance technology (HPT) to solve real-world problems in organizations. Indeed, Wentling, Waight, and King described these concepts and how HRD has advanced to meet organization needs. The IT applications described by the authors in this book do not fit easily into the traditional HRD concepts. Rather, they provide a glimpse of what the future will be like. Consider, for example, the Knowledge Development Networks described by Meeder and Cude and the Motorola Expeditions Program described by Wang, Rossett, and Wangeman. These IT applications meet the traditional HRD purpose of developing people to meet the strategic goals of the organization. However, rather than enabling the development of employees, these applications enabled the development of people who may some day be employed by organizations. Consider Christie's description of IT applications that empower HR's customers. These IT applications focus on customers and processes, concepts that can readily be found in HPT models. Less explicitly evident in Christie's description were aspects of

HPT's general process model—analyze, design, develop, implement, and evaluate (Rosenberg, 1999).

Indeed, it is particularly informative to review the citations at the end of each chapter. Note that the authors in this book did not reference many of the works and the concepts that are foundational to HRD, for example, performance problems, their causes, and their solutions, and cost-benefit evaluation (e.g., Mager and Pipe, 1984; Gilbert, 1975; Rossett, 1999; Swanson and Gradous, 1988). In a similar vein, important organization development works and management concepts were not specifically referenced, for example organization design (e.g., Nadler & Tushman, 1997), organization transformation (e.g., Dean, 1999), leadership (e.g., DePree, 1998), team building (e.g., Thiagarajan, 1999), strategic planning (e.g., Kaufman, 1997), and performance management (e.g., Cummings & Feyerherm, 1995).

Three explanations for the absence of references to core HRD concepts come to mind. First, the particular aspects of the networked world that the experts chose to describe influenced their citations. For example, no chapter explicitly focused on using IT to build teams. Therefore, the lack of team-building citations comes as no surprise, despite the discussions in several chapters about IT applications that enhanced teamwork. Second, the citations reflect the cross-disciplinary interests of the authors. Most authors cited literature from their own disciplines and from a broad range of other disciplines. A third possibility exists. The absence of references to core HRD concepts appears to reflect the need to develop tools and models for today's e-workplaces.

Paradoxes

We were intrigued by two inconsistencies that emerged.

In the e-workplace, people are the most important resource...or are they?

Some chapter authors observed that the most important resource in today's organizations is the people who create and provide the knowledge that enables the organization to be competitive. Van Buren and Ardichivilli especially described the importance of managing and measuring knowledge.

On the other hand, it appears that individual workers and their contributions to the e-workplace can be easily overlooked. With good IT solutions, end users are able to directly access desired information. The "hands-on" laboratory for distance learning described in this book is an example. The theoretical work reported by Sharda, Romano, and Lucca and the practical work reported by Weiser and Sheets will likely provide a new foundation for learning and performance in the e-workplace. The end users of the IT applications that will result from their work are unlikely to know of the expertise, the hard thinking, and the hours of effort that were devoted to developing the virtual learning laboratory. It seems that when IT applications work as expected, individual contributors to those applications become invisible.

The paradox between the intrinsic value of individuals (human capital) and the value of their contributions (intellectual capital) and how both are viewed in the e- workplace is highlighted in Taulbert's chapter "Touch and Technology: The Look of Sensory Contact in the New Millennium." Community provides an important balance to technology.

IT applications empower people...or IT applications control people

Several authors described how IT applications enable people to access timely information for decision making. Panelists in the Lawson and Sleezer chapter described as expected and unexpected benefits of IT, increased sharing of knowledge, wide-ranging inputs, and democratic participation in decision making. The Web-based leadership training described by Russ-Eft et al. provided yet another example of empowerment based on IT. The trainees' expectations of Web-based leadership training included improved effectiveness, better communication, and maximized employee potentials.

However, we also noted that many chapter authors described IT applications, especially centralized data systems, which succeed only when all the parts of the system conform to a single prescribed architecture. For example, an HR department that configured its IT applications to share information limited users to accessing only the information allowed by the system.

The paradox of empowerment and control is informed by considering power issues. Ghost Bear and Conti argued that the digital divide is perpetuated when the technology enables only some people to be users and to gain from the power. Lawson and Sleezer's study also revealed power issues in the ways typical organizations use IT.

Topics for future research and action

Clearly, our journey pointed to many new directions for future research and action in the e-workplace. Here we present several research needs based on the insights and paradoxes.

Research is needed to describe and classify the changes that are occurring in today's e-workplace. Specifically, the use of IT applications within various contexts should be explored and described. Such research could map new terrain for practitioners and scholars. Research is also needed to examine the empowerment of employees and customers that results from IT applications in the e-workplace and to identify and compare the IT and HRD concepts that organization decision makers actually use with the concepts that experts from these fields and others say they should use. Finally, research studies are needed that explicitly link individual, team, and organization outcomes with the enhanced capacity provided by IT for improving learning and performance. We recommend taking a cross-disciplinary approach to obtain the needed breadth for these research efforts.

Our insights and paradoxes also have implications for practice. As the capabilities of humans and technologies increasingly become intertwined, systematic thinking is needed to identify the moral issues, and hard decision making is needed to address them.

Conclusion

Our safari is over. As we unpack, put away supplies, and relive the high points, we invite you to view our adventure as the beginning of your adventure. We hope that you build on our experience and insights. We hope that you continue the dialogue. We challenge you to identify additional research and further implications for action. There is plenty of opportunity to add meaning to the conversation and to hone the thinking.

We've so benefited from our safari that we encourage you to plan a similar journey and invite us along. In the words of Dr. Seuss,

Today is your day!
Your mountain is waiting.
So...*get on your way!*

References

Cummings, T. G. & Feyerherm, A. E. (1995). Interventions in Large Systems. In W. J. Rothwell, R. Sullivan, & G. N. McLean (eds.), *Practicing organization development: A guide for consultants*. San Francisco: Jossey-Bass.

Dean, P. J. (1999). Designing better organizations with human performance technology and organization development. In H. D. Stolovitch & E. J. Keeps (eds.), *Handbook of human performance technology*. (2nd ed.). San Francisco: Jossey-Bass.

Dr. Seuss (1990). *Oh, the places you'll go!* New York: Random House.

DePree, M. (1998). What *is* Leadership? In H. R. Hickman (ed.). *Leading organizations: Perspectives for a new era*. Thousand Oaks: Sage.

Gilbert, T. (1975). *Human competence: Engineering worthy performance*. New York: McGraw-Hill.

Kaufman, R. (1997). A strategic-planning framework: Mega planning. In R. Kaufman, S. Thiagarajan, & P. MacGillis (eds.). *The guidebook for performance improvement: Working with individuals and organizations*.

Mager, R.M., & Pipe, P. (1984). *Analyzing performance problems*. Belmont, CA: Pitman Learning.

Nadler, D. A., & Tushman, M. L. (1997). *Competing by design: The power of organizational architecture*. New York: Oxford University Press.

Rosenberg, M. C. (1999). Part two: The general process of Human Performance Technology. In H. D. Stolovitch & E. J. Keeps (eds.), *Handbook of human performance technology*. (2nd ed.). San Francisco: Jossey-Bass.

Rossett, A. (1999). Analysis for Human Performance Technology. In H. D. Stolovitch & E. J. Keeps (eds.), *Handbook of human performance technology*. (2nd ed.). San Francisco: Jossey-Bass.

Swanson, R. A., & Gradous, D. B. (1988). *Forecasting financial benefits of human resource development*. San Francisco: Jossey-Bass.

Swanson, R.& Holton, E. F. III (1999). Results: How to assess performance, learning and perceptions in organizations. Berrett-Koehler: San Francisco.

Thiagarajan, S. (1999). Team activities for learning and performance. In H. D. Stolovitch & E. J. Keeps (eds.), *Handbook of human performance technology* (2nd ed.). San Francisco: Jossey-Bass.

Author Biographies

Alexander Ardichvili

Assistant Professor, Department of Human Resource Education, University of Illinois at Urbana/Champaign and Research Fellow at the National Center for Supercomputing Applications

As an assistant professor, Dr. Ardichvili teaches graduate HRD courses, advises Ph.D. students, develops and teaches courses for the on-line Global HRD graduate program. He is presently developing a graduate course for engineering students. He works as a Research Fellow at the National Center for Supercomputing Applications, where he conducts research in knowledge management and e-learning. In 1999-2000, as an AT&T Technology Fellow, Dr. Ardichvili researched interactive on-line delivery methods and technologies. In Fall-Summer 2000, as a recipient of a grant from the Center for International Business Education and Research, he developed an on-line graduate course in international HRD. In 1994-1997, as a director and senior director of training for the Midwest Energy Association and the Energy Training Network, he managed multimedia training and simulation software development projects and conducted research and evaluation of training management software, on-line training delivery systems, and courseware development software. In 1980-1988, as a research fellow at the Management Development Institute of Tbilisi, Georgia, and a Ph.D. student at the University of Moscow, Dr. Ardichvili developed computer-based business games, simulations, and programmed learning exercises and researched computer-supported active learning.

Mike Christie

eHR Strategy Consultant, Hewitt Inc.

Mike Christie is an e-HR Strategy Consultant and a member of Hewitt's Human Resource Effectiveness Practice in Lincolnshire, Illinois. He supports Hewitt's clients around the world in developing and executing HR operational transformation efforts. These efforts range from broad e-HR strategies to employee self-service tools, Websites, and portals. Christie is a frequent presenter at human resource conferences and is often quoted in industry publications. Organizations he has recently worked with include Siemens Corporation, Honeywell International, Verizon, Dell Computer, and Sears Roebuck and Co.

Gary J. Conti
Professor of Adult Education, Oklahoma State University

Dr. Conti has served as editor of *Adult Literacy and Basic Education* and as chair of the steering committee for the Adult Education Research Conference. He has worked extensively to conduct research and deliver educational programs in Hispanic and Native American communities. With a grant from the W. K. Kellogg Foundation, he was able to establish a Visiting Native American Scholars program at Oklahoma State University (OSU). He has received several awards for research and service and is the most recent recipient of the teaching excellence award at OSU-Tulsa. His ties to the tribal community led to co-chairing the 2001 Academy of Human Resource Development Globalization Pre-Conference. He has developed instruments for measuring teaching style and learning strategies and for identifying learning strategy preferences.

Roger L. Cude
Vice President, Human Resources, McLeodUSA

Cude is Vice President of Human Resources for McLeodUSA, a leading telecommunications provider. He has more than 15 years experience in human resources, training, and organization development. He has managed projects with a number of companies that focused on human resources strategy, international HR, customer service performance, technical training, leadership, and teambuilding. Prior to joining McLeod in 2001, Cude served as Vice President, Human Resources Strategy, for Williams, where he managed a staff of human resource professionals who provided performance and organizational improvement solutions to Williams employees. In addition, Cude was a professor on the faculty of the University of Tulsa.

Cude serves on the Boards of Directors for the National Alliance of Business, the National Employee Leadership Council, and the Center for Non-profit Management. He received a B.A. in Communications from Southern Utah University, an M.A. in Organizational Communication from Pepperdine University, and completed doctoral work in Organizational Communication at the University of Texas-Austin.

Tori Egherman
Consulting Partner, 36 Partners

Egherman is a consulting partner in a firm that focuses on the human-centered design of software and technology. Her background as Director of education for both the Transit Museum in Brooklyn and the Children's Discovery Museum of San Jose provided the basis for her understanding of program development and program evaluation. 36 Partners focuses on the human-centered design of software and technology. Her work integrates research, evaluation, and design. Her most recent article, "Extracting Meaning from Research," was published in InCA's spring 2001 issue *Design Research* (available on line in pdf format at http://www.idsa-sf.org/03inca/2001.issue1/inca.2001.issue1.pdf) She lives in Amsterdam and uses the Web and the telephone for long-distance communication.

Anne A. Ghost Bear
President, Ashby School Development, Inc.

Dr. Ghost Bear is president of Ashby School Development, Inc., a corporation that specializes in designing and facilitating learning events for adults in a variety of settings. She is also an adjunct professor of Adult Education at Oklahoma State University. Ghost Bear received her Ed.D. degree in Adult Education from Oklahoma State University.

Kathleen Hurson
Independent Contractor

Hurson is an independent contractor working on the development of various Web-based training programs. She was formerly the Vice President for Research and Development at AchieveGlobal. In that role, she was principal author of three award-winning AchieveGlobal leadership training programs: FrontLine Leadership, TeamLeadership, and Leadership 2000. These programs have been translated into 14 languages and are used by thousands of organizations around the world. She is a frequent speaker on leadership for such groups as the American Society for Training and Development, the American Society for Quality Control, and the Human Resource Executive. Her most recent books include *Everyone a Leader: A Grassroots Model for the New Workplace* (published by John Wiley and Sons) and *Leading Teams: Mastering the New Role* (published by Business One Irwin).

Ruth Pangilinan
Independent Contractor

Ruth Pangilinan is currently working as an independent contractor in the field of measurement and evaluation in the area of e-learning. Ruth has conducted research in the areas of sales performance and leadership and customer service performance. Previously Ruth had a successful career as a Sales Manager and Customer Service Manager.

Ruth C. King
Assistant Professor of Business Administration, University of Illinois at Urbana-Champaign

Dr. King teaches and conducts research in information technologies, the management of information technology, and information technology professional development. Her published work can be found in *Information Systems Research, Decision Science, Journal of Management Information Systems, Journal of Organizational Computing*, and *Electronic Commerce, and Information and Management*. She has written a chapter for the upcoming book *Emerging Information Technologies*. Dr. King earned her doctorate at the University of Texas, Austin.

Linda K. Lawson
Vice President, Human Resource Operations (Retired), Williams Companies

Lawson, employed by Williams for over twenty years, held both line and staff positions. Most recently, as VP of HR Operations, she was responsible for bringing a customer-service focus and operational excellence to the organization, which served 24,000 personnel prior to the spin off of its telecommunications business in 2000. She was responsible for implementing Williams' e-HR strategy and collaborated on Williams' recent consolidation of its HR Websites.

Other positions held by Lawson include COO for four start-up telecommunications businesses; investor relations officer for Williams, the publicly held company that traded on the New York Stock Exchange; financial controller for a refined petroleum pipeline subsidiary of Williams; and managerial accounting positions within the corporation.

She served on the boards of the Tulsa Literacy Coalition, Tulsa Youth Services, the Tulsa Sales Tax Overview Task Force, and was a member of Leadership Tulsa and Leadership Oklahoma. She received her B.A. in Accounting from the University of Denver and is a CPA, licensed in Oklahoma.

Joyce A. Lucca

Ph.D. Candidate and Center Associate, OSU Center for Research in Information Technology and Telecommunications (CRITT), Oklahoma State University

Lucca is a Ph.D. student in Management Information Systems at Oklahoma State University (OSU). Her research interests include knowledge management, telecommunications management, and computer-supported collaborative learning. A recent work by Ms. Lucca was awarded best student paper at the Academia Industry Working Conference on Research Challenges 2000. Lucca received an MS in Telecommunications Management (MSTM) from OSU. While in the MSTM program, she was awarded a Presidential Fellowship and worked as a teaching assistant in the telecommunications laboratory.

Hans Meeder

Senior Vice President of Workforce Development, National Alliance of Business (NAB).

Prior to joining NAB, Meeder served as Executive Director of the 21st Century Workforce Commission, an independent federal commission that reported on strategies to address the skill shortages in information technology fields. Meeder also operated Horizon Consulting Services, worked in the U.S. House of Representatives on staff with the Committee on Education and the Workforce, and served in the U.S. Department of Education under Presidents Reagan, Bush, and Clinton. Meeder received a B.A. from the University of Maryland College Park and is currently pursuing an MBA at the University of Maryland.

Nicholas C. Romano, Jr.

Assistant Professor of Management Information Systems, University of Tulsa

Dr. Romano teaches courses in systems analysis and design, database, and strategic information systems. His research interests are collaborative computing, Web-based application design and development, technology-supported learning, group support system interface design, knowledge creation and management, and electronic commerce customer relations management. Dr. Romano's work experience includes technical consulting for GroupSystems.com and work for the International Business Machines Corporation as a systems programmer. Dr. Romano founded and co-chaired minitracks on Electronic Commerce Customer Relations Management (ECCRM) for the America's Conference on Information Systems and the Hawaii International Conference on Systems Sciences. His published work can be found in the *Journal of Management Information Systems*, the *Journal of the American Society for Information Science*, the *Journal of Education for Management Information Systems*, and the *IBM AS/400 Systems Management Journal* and in the proceedings of the Hawaii International Conference on Systems Sciences, the Conference of the Association of Management, and the America's Conference on Information Systems. Dr. Romano received a Ph.D. in Management Information Systems from the University of Arizona.

Allison Rossett
Professor of Educational Technology, San Diego State University

Dr. Rossett is the Year 2000 inductee into the *TRAINING* magazine HRD Hall of Fame. She just published a new book, *Beyond the Podium: Delivering Training and Performance to a Digital World*. In 1999 she published *First Things Fast: A Handbook for Performance Analysis* and the Website, www.josseybass.com/rossett.html. The book and Website won the International Society for Performance Improvement's Instructional Communications Award for 1999. Rossett is the editor of the forthcoming (December, 2001) *ASTD E-Learning Handbook: Best Practices, Strategies, and Case Studies for an Emerging Field* (to be published by McGraw Hill). Dr. Rossett has published dozens of articles, edited journals, offered seminars, coached and advised business and government leaders, evaluated programs, and managed corporate contracts and federal and state grants. She received the Association for Educational Communications and Technology, Division of Instructional Development Book of the Year Award in 1989 for *Training Needs Assessment* (published by Educational Technology Publications in Englewood Cliffs, New Jersey). Her book, *A Handbook of Job Aids* (published by Jossey-Bass) won the International Society for Performance and Instruction 1991 top book award and the Association for Educational Technology, Division of Instructional Development Instructional Design Tool of the Year Award.

Darlene Russ-Eft,
Director of Research Services, AchieveGlobal, Inc.

Dr. Russ-Eft currently directs Research Services at AchieveGlobal, Inc., the world's leading resource for results-through-performance skills training and consulting. She has authored numerous books and articles about research and evaluation. Her most recent books include *Everyone a Leader: A Grassroots Model for the New Workplace* (published by John Wiley and Sons) and *Evaluation in Organizations: A Systematic Approach to Enhancing Learning Performance, and Change* (published by Perseus Press). She is a past chair of the Research Committee of the American Society for Training & Development (ASTD) and a past member of the Board of the American Evaluation Association. She received the 2000 Outstanding Scholar Award from the Academy of Human Resource Development and is the Editor of *Human Resource Development Quarterly.* She has been involved in software design and translation for educational games and simulations and in the evaluation of a variety of technologies, including CBT, interactive videodisc, and CD-ROM. Her M.A. and Ph.D. are in cognitive psychology from the University of Michigan.

George Scheets
Associate Professor, Electrical and Computer Engineering, Oklahoma State University

Dr. Scheets teaches courses in Modern Communications Theory, Telecommunications Systems, and Data Communications. He is a key player in the inter-disciplinary Telecommunications Management program. His research interests include telecommunications network analysis and design and signal processing for intercept receivers. Dr. Scheets has over 25 years of experience in the communications field, including 5 years as a U.S. Army Signal Corps officer, 4 years as a TV studio technician at Kansas State University, and over 14 years on the faculty at OSU, where he has engaged in numerous and ongoing applied research contracts with such companies as Williams Network, Raytheon Systems, MCI Worldcom, and SBC.

Dr. Scheets has a special interest in distance-learning techniques. He has taught classes at a distance via inter-active videoconferencing almost every semester for the last 13 years. He has been named a National Technological University Outstanding Instructor for the last eight school years. In 1999 he received OSU's Advancia Award for Excellence in Distance Education and was named a Regents Distinguished Teacher for his work with Distance Learning and with the Master of Science in Telecommunications Management program. His many publications in the field of signal processing and telecommunications include articles in *IEEE (Institute for Electrical and Electronic Engineering) Transactions*, conference presentations, technical reports to industry, and a recent chapter in a book on switched network carrying capacities.

Ramesh Sharda

Conoco Chair of Management of Technology and Regents Professor of Management Science and Information Systems, College of Business Administration, Oklahoma State University.

Dr. Sharda has developed and taught courses in information systems, the telecommunications industry, neural networks, and e-commerce technology. He started Oklahoma State University's MS in Telecommunications Management program and served as the interim director. He co-founded iTradefair.com, a company that produces virtual trade shows. Dr. Sharda is the author or co-author of over 90 papers in refereed journals, proceedings, and books. He is the founding editor of *Interactive Transactions of ORMS(ITORMS)*.

Catherine M. Sleezer

Associate Professor, Human Resource Development/Adult Education, Oklahoma State University

Dr. Sleezer conducts research and teaches human resource development (HRD) courses in the areas of needs analysis, technology and HRD, and instructional systems design. Her published works and presentations focus on using HRD research and theory to improve workplace learning and performance. She has edited and co-edited several books and has co-authored a course for the American Society for Training and Development titled, "Measuring Training and Performance" that has been offered at various universities in the U.S.

Sleezer has consulted with organizations to address learning and performance needs. Her projects include needs assessments, retraining the training department, leading culture change, implementing performance improvement systems, developing managers, and evaluating the learning and financial benefits of HRD activities.

Clifton L. Taulbert

President, Building Community Institute

Taulbert is an internationally acclaimed author and lecturer. He founded the Building Community Institute to extend the reach of the timeless and universal ideals he encountered while growing up in the Mississippi Delta. The Institute is based upon the principles outlined in his book, *The Eight Habits of the Heart,* which was chosen by USA TODAY as their 1997 year-end book to enrich our minds and lives. The international acceptance of

Taulbert's thoughts on the topic of "Building Community, a set of emotionally satisfying relationships" has partnered him with such respected business thought leaders as Tom Peters, Ken Blanchard and Larraine Segil, all part of the Ninth House Network, the only broadband e-learning environment for corporate development.

Taulbert has delivered his message on the role of Community for the 21st Century throughout the United States and around the world and has shared his views with audiences from the United States Supreme Court, The Library of Congress, Harvard University, Lockheed Martin, Williams, The FDIC, and State Farm Insurance. He often claims that "quality of life is determined by the quality of the community surrounding you at home, at work, in any place you spend time." Taulbert serves on the boards of the Oklahoma Investment Forum, the Oklahoma Public Television Trust, and The University of Tulsa Board of Trustees. His awards include a 1996 Image Award from the N.A.A.C.P. for outstanding contribution to literature and the Arthritis Foundation Volunteer of the Year. He was named to the United States Air Force Enlisted Airmen Hall of Fame. Taulbert and his wife Barbara live in Tulsa, Oklahoma, where they share the joy of their college age son, Marshall Danzy.

Mark E. Van Buren

Director of Research, The American Society for Training and Development.

Dr. Van Buren oversees ASTD's primary research initiatives in workplace learning and performance involving worldwide industry trends, training for low-skill and low-wage workers, and the development of standards of measurement. His current research includes studies on learner receptivity to technology-based training and metrics for e-learning. Prior to joining ASTD, he conducted research on new technologies and new forms of work at the University of North Carolina-Chapel Hill. In addition to a B.A., a Masters Degree, and a Ph.D. in Sociology, Van Buren has a B.S. in Computer Science. His work experience includes two years as a computer programmer.

Consuelo Waight

Ph.D. candidate and Fulbright Scholar, Human Resource Education, University of Illinois at Urbana-Champaign.

Waight is a research associate with the Knowledge and Learning Systems Group (KLSG) at the National Center for Supercomputing Applications (NCSA). She participates in the investigation of enterprise e-learning and knowledge management processes and practices and in the human, system and organizational issues common to business and industry. She also participates in the research and development of an integrative e-learning and knowledge management system. She has co-delivered on-line courses on e-learning, strategic planning and evaluation. Waight's dissertation examines the role of human resource development professionals in mergers and acquisitions.

Waight has consulted internationally in training and development and organization development in Central America, the Caribbean, Asia, and Africa. She is co-author of several articles on the relationship between human resource development and school-to-work. She received several awards, including the Rupert Evans Leadership Award for Excellence in Scholarship, Research, and Service, while engaged in advanced graduate study in Human Resource Development.

Minjuan Wang

Assistant Professor of Educational Technology, San Diego State University.

Dr. Wang teaches technologies for teaching, educational research, and instructional design. She earned her Ph.D. in the School of Information Science and Learning Technologies, University of Missouri-Columbia. Before coming to San Diego, she worked as a research coordinator for the Center for Technology Innovations in Education at the University of Missouri. She also collaborated with Motorola University in conducting research and evaluation on the Internet-based Expeditions program.

She has published articles in the *International Journal of Educational Technology*. A chapter by Dr. Wang on intergenerational and intercultural diversity in the technology-based classroom will appear in *Addressing Diversity in Our Classrooms* (to be published by Lawrence Erlbaum Associates, Inc.). In addition, she has several articles in refereed conference proceedings: *Computer Support for Collaborative Learning 1999*; the *Fourth International Conference of the Learning Sciences 2001*; and the *International Society for Performance Improvement 2001*.

Paul Wangemann

Manager, Learning Excellence, Motorola University, Motorola, Inc.

As Manager of Learning Excellence, Dr. Wangemann is responsible for the design and development of educational programs and services for Motorola's Education Systems Alliance Group. He has created problem-based learning programs for youth and teachers, which have been delivered in the United States, Europe, the Middle East, and Asia. Current projects include the use of the Internet as a vehicle for engaging youth in learning opportunities and connecting learning communities worldwide.

Prior to his current position,. Wangemann was Manager of Education for the Motorola Museum of Electronics. His responsibilities included the development, design, and management of museum exhibits, computer interactives, educational programs and tours, tour-guide training, and educational partnerships. Before joining Motorola, Wangemann did research for the Brigham Young University Elementary Education Department and participated in a number of roles within the university-public school partnership that was part of the National Network for Educational Renewal.

He holds a B.S. in Business Management and a Ph. D in Curriculum and Instructional Science from Brigham Young University. Wangemann also holds an Elementary Education Certificate and has taught in the public schools.

Mark Weiser

Director of the Master of Science in Telecommunications Management Program and Fleming Professor of Technology Management, Oklahoma State University

Dr. Weiser teaches Telecommunications Systems and the hands-on Telecommunications and Networking laboratory class. He has a deep interest in technology supported group work, education, and training. This interest includes the active use of technology to teach courses and a program of empirical research on the impact of technology in the workplace and in the classroom. He has published many papers about the impacts of technology on learning.

Dr. Weiser brings his passion for technology into the classroom and has been recognized at various levels for his work. He received the first Advancia Award for Excellence in Distance Education, the Amoco Innovation in Teaching award, and the Williams/Regents Faculty Innovator award. He pioneered the video streaming logistics techniques used at OSU to bring the full class content to the student, and he integrated support tools to increase student interaction with other students and faculty, regardless of location.

Tim L. Wentling

Professor of Education in the Department of Human Resource Education and Senior Research Scientist in the National Center for Supercomputing Applications (NCSA), University of Illinois at Urbana-Champaign.

Professor Wentling holds a PhD in Education, an MBA from the University of Illinois, and an MS in Educational Psychology from the University of Wisconsin. He is the leader of the Knowledge and Learning Systems Group at NCSA, where he heads a team of cross-disciplinary faculty, post docs, and graduate students. His current work is focused on the integration of e-learning and knowledge management systems. He recently directed research efforts that focused on the status of e-learning in major corporations and in higher education. He co-directed the design, development, and implementation of an on-line masters degree program for Human Resource Development professionals. He has also been involved in e-learning projects with World Bank, Asian Institute of Technology, University of Sao Paulo, and other universities.